SMART SAGE

Hacking your own shadow self for high-resolution lifestyle

Prashant Panigrahi

STARDOM BOOKS

www.StardomBooks.com

STARDOM BOOKS
112, Bordeaux Ct,
Coppell, TX 75019

Copyright © 2023 by Prashant Panigrahi

This book is copyright under the Berne Convention.
No reproduction without permission.
All rights reserved.

FIRST EDITION MAY 2023

STARDOM BOOKS

A Division of Stardom Alliance
112, Bordeaux Ct,
Coppell, TX 75019

www.stardombooks.com

Stardom Books, United States
Stardom Books, India

The authors and publishers have made all reasonable efforts to contact copyright-holders for permission, and apologize for any omissions or errors in the form of credits given. Corrections may be made to future editions.

SMART
SAGE

Prashant Panigrahi

p. 286
cm. 13.5 X 21.5

Category:
Self-Help: Personal Growth – Success
Body, Mind & Spirit: New Thought

ISBN: 978-1-957456-23-2

DEDICATION

This book is dedicated to my grandmother; Late Mrs. Rekha Panigrahi, who was one of the Smart-Sage I am inspired by.

And to all, who wish to move from:

Crazy to Easy;
Self to Source;
Desire to Quest
Impure to Pure;
Misery to Meaning;
Have-To to Want-To;
Hopeless to Hopeful;
Fragile to Antifragile;
Ignorance to Wisdom;
Fight & Flight to Creative;
Past & Future to Present;
Attachment to Equanimity;
Viscousness to Playfulness
Arrogance to Glory-With-Grace;
Entanglement to Involvement;
Compulsiveness to Consciousness;
Regret & Remorse to Joy & Peace;
Rat-Race to Success-With-Meaning & Purpose.

ENDORSEMENTS

"In the age of complexity and rapid change, Smartness alone will not be enough to live a vibrant life of success with purpose, whether it is personal or professional. Hence, there is a need for a conscious and powerful response to each stimulus in our life.

In his book Smart-Sage, Prashant Panigrahi has put forward a simple yet profound PEARL technique to reorient our response for high-resolution life. This technique leverages the power of our own causal muscles and empowers us to live with Smartness as well as Sage-ness. I strongly believe Smart-Sage is the way to go."

Dr. Ritu Anand
Former Executive and HR Leader, Tata Consultancy Services
https://www.linkedin.com/in/dr-ritu-anand-9343065/

"Our planet is billions of years old, and thousands of human generations have lived on this planet, but still, many people make a mess out of their life; we are still learning how to live!

In this modern, fast-changing, technology-driven world full of challenges and changes, *we as conscious energy beings need to know and manage our energies, internal and external, to live successfully with purpose.* The Smart Sage by Prashant Panigrahi provides you with the required rationales, tools, and techniques to hack yourself, manage energies and create a perfect balance between inner as well as outer well-being so that you can get the best from both your personal and professional life. Do read."

Prof. Chetan Singh Solanki, IIT Bombay.
Founder of Energy Swaraj Foundation, Solar Man of India
https://www.linkedin.com/in/chetan-singh-solanki-915bb7112/

CONTENTS

FOREWORD	I
ACKNOWLEDGMENTS	III
INTRODUCTION	1

PART I: PERSPECTIVE

1.	CURRENT AFFAIR OF SELF	7
2.	ANATOMY & PURPOSE OF SELF	21
3.	LEVELS OF SELF	47

PART II: POTENTIAL

4.	INTELLIGENCE	85
5.	EXPERIENCE	105
6.	EXISTENCE & EXPRESSION	123

PART III: PROBLEM

7.	IGNORANCE	145

8. Karma & Freewill — 169

Part IV: Persuasion

9. Muscles For Sage-Ness — 199

10. Techniques To Be Smart Sage — 223

11. Journey To Smart Sage — 243

Conclusion — 267

About The Author — 271

FOREWORD

Dear Reader,

   Driving desire to death delivering deal of sage-ness for smartness is the key of this book. Ignorance, I-ness, attractions, repulsions, obsessions dominate to create infinite to finiteness. For the very survival of creation. From this emerges Smartness. Sageness is forgotten. Leading to limited ness, confinement, and pettiness in us showing itself as the supreme value in life. As frog in the well.
   Expansion is life, contraction is death. To turn pettiness to sublimity by expansion leading to expression of Real Self. Sure, it also unlocks the door to smartness. So nicely brought out in this book. Slowness with awareness leading to cognitive excellence without losing expansive stretch of awareness manifests sageness in action to smartness. Speed emerges as an outcome of calmness. Running riot with workaholic tendency turns into creative intelligence of smartness. Often confused, silence, slowness and calmness are kept outdoors. Loosing Sage-ness component consciously.
   Truth of Bliss as Silence and peace unrecognized can lead to smartness without Sage-ness. Tranquility, harmony, peace, real joy of life become far off cry. Stress as imbalance turn to diseases if not pain and misery. Ending up with a life of dis-satisfaction and regret. SOPs for realization are in abundance, but a smart one fits the smart of modern age. From complicated ones to simpler ones. Sage-ness is

Childlike not childish. Simple yet sublime and fulfilling. *Kaizen* is the path ahead in everyone's life. To find newer paths of greater relevance for continuous growth. Perfection has no end. As TQM sets continuous growth goals. Evolving better more effective, easier, simpler tools of growth. To transcend the mundane to sublime, from smartness to sage-ness. Sage-ness to Saint-ness. To transcendental fullness of infinite smartness of the creator.

I congratulate, Mr. Prashant Panigrahi for bringing out the idea of Smart-Sage by harmonizing the power of ancient essence of experiential science and modern essence of experimental science. He could establish the relational clarity in dual purpose of human life (i.e., inner and outer).

In other words, he clarifies; *"while the outer purpose of human life is to express Smartness (i.e., manifest and experience abundance) the inner purpose is to express Sage-ness (i.e., getting awake and transcending to our true-self). In simple, we must achieve Smartness through Sage-ness."*

This book seeks your deeper intellectual involvement and ensures elite-entertainment for life-time. I wish you all the best in your journey from Street-Smart to become a Smart-Sage.

Dr. HR Nagendra, Padma Shri Awardee
Founder vice chancellor of Swami Vivekananda Yoga Anusandhana Samsthana (S-VYASA), Bengaluru
Founder Chairman of Vivekananda Yoga University (VaYU) in Los Angeles
https://en.wikipedia.org/wiki/H._R._Nagendra

ACKNOWLEDGEMENTS

I am extremely thankful to Dr. Anurag Satpathy and those wonderful people who encouraged me to bring out the idea of Smart Sage in form of a book.

I extend my deepest gratitude to Dr. Ritu Anand, and Prof. Chetan Singh Solanki for their early review of the manuscript and helpful feedback.

My humble devotion to **Guruji, Dr. HR Nagendra (Padma Shri awardee)** for his graceful guidance, blessing, and awakening message.

Also, I would like to express my love and gratitude to my life partner Mrs. Abha Panda and daughter Diya Panigrahi, for giving me the space to be, the space to write and sparing their self to make my shadow self (Vito) involved.

Finally, I will remain indebted to my parents, without whom this book would not have come in to existence.

INTRODUCTION

More than 90% of people end up dying, holding on to several regrets and remorse. The number one regret people have on their deathbeds is that they wished to live a life that was true to themselves and not the life others expected of them. Most people don't know "who they truly are beyond body and mind". Due to this fundamental ignorance throughout their life, they disturb the disposition of their body and mind away from their true self. In other words, despite all effective and efficient efforts in their life, they do not experience life to their fullest, even if they have material abundance in hand.

We have never met before, but I will read your mind now!

You feel that something meaningful and fulfilling is missing in your life, even if you've invested much time, money, and energy into your career, degree, and family-building assets effectively and efficiently. If this is true, are you OK to live the rest of your life in the same meaningless and purposeless way, or are you willing to adopt a different way to transform the disposition of your body and mind in line with your true self, which will allow you to live your life to your fullest?

If you are willing, then you are chosen by destiny to hold the right book in your hand. Also, know that you have now woken up from the slumber you're in, don't go back to sleep. Have you ever felt that you have to work to cover a glorious living in compliance with the status of your friends and society? Given an option, what will you opt out for?

This book will help you to repurpose "have to" to "want to," i.e., the compulsion to consciousness. In other words, you can even walk into hell with joy if the situation demands it. Also, there will be perfect harmony between life situations and life, enabling you to actualize; work with fun, credibility with character, relationship with love and trust, wisdom with humility, confidence with clarity, and abundance with inner well-being.

This book will let you know who you are in all possible ways, including on a quantitative scale. You will get clarity into your existential purpose in life. You will discover the potentialities and essence of your "own self" or life and how they vary with respect to different life situations. You will also learn what is locking and blocking your fundamental potential to get repurposed and expressed in this world with playfulness, joy, flow, freedom, meaning, and fulfillment. Finally, you will be lucky to know the secret master key to dissolve the blockers and unlock your real potential. Hence, you will transform the disposition of your body and mind to experience life to its fullest. In other words, you will live your life without hurt, residual regret, or remorse. Also, you will get visibility into the art of possibility in human potential and inner-wellbeing. In simple; you will master the art of becoming unshakably smarter as a professional and joyful sage; i.e., becoming Smart Sage, where smartness is the phenomenon of body-mind and sage-ness is the phenomenon beyond body-mind. This book will also burst your myth and bring you the discovery that Smartness and Sageness can co-exist in you.

The COVID-19 pandemic has put tremendous pressure on humanity. During this challenging period, I received many calls for counseling from people who were distressed and anxious about existential dilemmas on the meaning and purpose of life. Most were millennials and Gen-Y, at the peak of their career and societal responsibilities. My counseling experience in those two years validated my observation that people live with emptiness without meaning and fulfillment.

Thanks to the opportunity of two decades of dedicated research and experimental practice in balancing inner and outer well-being of life with the secret from meditation techniques like Vipassana, life-energy regulation techniques like pranayama, and reasoning on the existential meaning of life from Vedanta and science. Also, the same secret has been very beneficial for others in finding meaning and fulfillment in their life.

Based upon the request from beneficiaries, I have designed a simple and easily adaptable technique, which can be used in every life situation by people busy running rat race of the VUCA world (volatile, uncertain, complex, and ambiguous). While the idea and technique are straightforward, however the research behind it was complicated, hence the ramifications are profound. This tool inherits the critical secret and rationale from experimental and experiential science, including the Quantum physics, Dr. David Hawkins' the conscious map, self-actualization concept from Abraham Maslow, and many more.

This book will change your life.

But fair warning; considering the journey you are about to embark on is an inner adventure of self-discovery, you might not enjoy the process and the go out of course initially due to the new age lifestyle (i.e., distraction and low attention-span). I know I didn't either. But now, that I have been through this journey, I am eternally grateful.

Hence, I humbly suggest you treat this book like a scientific discovery to master the secret key for the perfect disposition of your true self beyond body-mind. Once you grasp this key, no one can stop you from living a life of success, joy: purpose, and meaning.

Happy reading!

PART I: PERSPECTIVE

1

CURRENT AFFAIR OF THE SELF
Ambiguities, Authenticity & Meaning

"More important than the quest for certainty is the quest for clarity."
—*Francois Gautier.*

Confidence or Clarity?

Confidence is the building block of success. It helps us socially and makes us believe in ourselves and our decision-making. We depend on the world, resources, and goals. Thus, confidence is essential, but it can no magic on its own.

What is clarity? Mental clarity refers to a state of mind where you are concentrated and your perspective is clear. We often forget the significance of clarity in our lives. An individual with poor eyesight can only walk on a busy street with the knowledge and description of what is in front of them. Vital attributes like confidence are only enough with clarity. Through this, we can understand what surrounds us and how we can use it to the best of our ability for our benefit. So, my readers, the issue frequently arises in our minds is how we can get clarity in our lives.

You can identify, analyze, and arrange your thoughts with mental clarity. Let's examine why mental clarity is crucial for your transformation and well-being and how to become more present in every moment.

Mental Clarity

Everyone wants to be in control, but no one wants to feel controlled by their circumstances.

Mental clarity, which, when it remains obscured, leads us to vaguely put forward our perspective of a situation. Recently, one of my colleagues narrated an incident. He used to offer rides to people who stayed near his house or worked in the same tech park as him. One day, he was gave a ride to two of his colleagues, and he decided to small talk with them. One of them was very enthusiastic while discussing work-life balance; however, the other guy was very gloomy and introverted. My colleague decided to speak to the gloomy person first out of curiosity. When asked about his life and career, he talked about feeling insecure in his present job and is uncertain about being laid off very soon. He was worried and depressed about his future and blamed the pandemic for creating this insecurity in his life and career. Moreover, he was worried about dying young, following news reports that the pandemic had claimed the lives of many celebrities in their prime. He said that, in contrast to the 2008 recession, which only affected professionals explicitly working in the IT field, the present pandemic had succeeded in creating havoc for the entire world by taking the lives of many.

On the other hand, the other guy was much more optimistic when asked the same question. This person believed everything would return to normal once we got over the pandemic. He said, "This too will pass." After narrating this incident, my colleague asked me about what made them think differently about the pandemic. When I listened to the question, I smiled a little, that people's differing opinions are based on their different levels of clarity on reality and consciousness, or, a different level of self.

However, from what my colleague had mentioned, I realized that the first person was acting from his mental clarity of lower self. I have encountered several professionals who react from their lower or higher selves. When asked about his take on the inevitable work-from-home situation during the pandemic, one of my colleagues at the office conveyed how good it felt to work from his home environment and how he managed the work-life balance in a very productive manner. He also expressed relief in not having to negotiate the heavy traffic for two to three hours daily. Yet, when I asked one of my friends the same question, he told me about his inability to be as productive as usual while working from home; he also missed socializing with others. He could sense a better work-life balance when he worked from the office. These conversations made me contemplate the differences experienced when people act from their lower or higher selves. Some questions disturbed me when I reflected on these incidents—why do certain people experience a work-life imbalance? Why are some people productive with joy and the rest non-productive with grief??

While I have narrated a few specific and real-life incidents on how professionals are dealing with the challenges with different levels of mental clarity, let's look in to challenge patterns of the 21st century and their impact on their inner well-being.

Self Is Constantly Disturbed In The World Of VUCA.

We often feel nostalgic about the simpler times they had lived in. Life in the 21st century has undoubtedly changed significantly. You may have also noticed that inner-wellbeing is becoming increasingly prevalent. Due to technological improvements, we live in a much more connected world where change is continuous. While the external world is changing rapidly, the inner world (collective consciousness) is yet to evolve proportionately to cope up with this continuous change. This disproportionate evolution of the intensity of external stimuli and our inner world's ability to respond is disastrously affecting inner well-being. It has reached a stage where the World Health Organization has dedicated the month of May to raising awareness around mental and behavioral health.

We witness chaos around us, whether it's personal or professional life, social or electronic media. To deal with this phenomenon; the management world of today has introduced an acronym – **VUCA**; which stands for *Volatility, Uncertainty, Complexity, and Ambiguity*. Each of these words articulates the characteristics of the daily stimulus, whether personal, professional, or social. It's also certain that the trend of VUCA in the outer world will further be intensified in the coming decades. Hence, it is very critical for us to understand how it impacts our inner well-being.

Let's start with **Volatility**. We all know that change is the only constant. Rapid changes in the external world are happening in the form of climate change, globalization, financial crisis, and geopolitical conflicts. However, the change is happening at a speed that the inner world is unprepared to deal with. Hence, it is often volatile. All these changes are coming to human beings as stimuli to which we must respond.

At a higher level, some examples of volatility would be terrorist attacks on India, the sudden slowdown in the world economy, U.K.'s Brexit vote, and the geopolitical tension between Ukraine and Russia. These high levels of volatility translate to low-level volatility in the form of a decrease in sales and an increase in prices, impacting the mental and inner well-being of people in personal and professional life in the form of stress and psychosomatic illness.

Uncertainty in VUCA denotes a world in which it is difficult to make predictions. We must navigate a world filled with unknowns. The world is changing at a breakneck pace, and we have no idea what the future holds for human civilization. While advancing technology like artificial intelligence and automation is easing predictability, it can create a cascading and negative impact on the job market. Furthermore, we must prepare to live in a world of robots and technology. Technological advancements are inevitable; however, we must be ready to embrace the changes. The evolving world of technology determines the external well-being of the world, leaving our inner worlds in turmoil because of ignorance.

This system addresses the rising **Complexity** of the world, which indicates the amount of information we are exposed to and the number of factors we are influenced by. We live in a world where we go online to select what to eat, where to travel, etc. So much information overload drains our energy and leads to decision fatigue.

Finally, **Ambiguity** refers to an absence of clarity. The COVID-19 pandemic was a visible example of the VUCA world and how we live in an uncertain world. The impact of this pandemic on our inner well-being and mental health was enormous.

Along with these disturbances in the VUCA world, professionals are also under psychological imprisonment due to social structure being are easily hack-able by technology.

Self Is Under Psychological Imprisonment

The expression, *"Boss is always right"* is often overused. The corporate cliché that the boss is always right is one of the most frequent among working people, and it is unlikely that anybody has not heard or overheard it. Whether the boss is always correct or occasionally correct depends on various things.

Working under a boss is believed to have two rules to follow. The first rule is that the boss is always correct. If the boss is mistaken, the second rule stipulates that you should resort to the first rule. The reality is that a boss may not always be correct, and what is right is that he stays a boss with proper respect, and this connection has long been regarded as one of the most exciting phases in our professional life. Doing this becomes extremely tiring for the self, and it remains locked up in the lower self.

Self Is Hack-Able By Technology

With the advancement of information technology; corporations and governments are collecting enormous amounts of data about our preferences; i.e., where we go, what we eat, when we eat, what we wear, what we read, what we search online, what we buy, etc. By leveraging this information and with the help of artificial intelligence, they can predict our emotions, intentions, and preferences with reasonably high accuracy. We often do not realize that anger or pride influences our decisions, but the data owner is aware. With this information, they can exploit our emotions and manipulate our behaviors.

Yuval Noah Harari, the Israeli historian, and author, explored in his book 'Homo Deus'- how a big watershed movement will arrive once they can start monitoring and surveying what is happening inside our bodies and brains. By leveraging bioinformatics, they can hack human beings; we're very close to this possibility. Even now, many people use Fitbit fitness trackers that constantly measure their heart rate and blood pressure. The device can access what one buys, search online, or read or watch on television. You watch a movie, and at the same time, Netflix knows what is happening with your heart rate or brain.

Everything has its positives and negatives. The smartness lies in how to take advantage of the positives without being impacted by the negatives. For example; while we take the above trend for predictive and preventive healthcare as a conscious response; can we prevent our inner temptations, exploited and provoked by manipulative stimulus attacks from the data or intelligence owners? Yes, it is possible to hack into ourselves with our consciousness.

Self Is In a Dilemma of Perspectives

The story of a person who approaches three quarry workers. Each of them was asked what he was up to. "What do I appear to be doing?" questioned the first man.

Then he angrily said, "I'm just shattering rocks."

The second man said that he was constructing a wall.

"I'm constructing a church," the third man explained with joy and playfulness.

All of these assertions are correct, yet they are not the same.

The first man was just concerned with the work at hand and the heat of the moment. He had a job to complete, and he was doing his job until it was time to go home. Every day was the same, hour after hour, day after day. Rocks were being broken.

The second man had a different perspective on the situation. He was able to support his family by breaking rocks. This was his personal goal, and he was serious about achieving it. It was crucial to him for their existence, but he had no purpose other than to make a decent life.

The third man claimed to be constructing a cathedral. That's a different viewpoint. He was smashing enormous boulders into smaller ones for a living, just like the other two guys, but he had a loftier ambition than simply doing a job and making a living.

The disparities in their responses indicate that their lifestyles are likewise disparate. Their phrases quantify the distance between the unthinking and the reflective, between the mundane and the magnificent, a gradual march from crushing rocks to constructing cathedrals, a narrative of change, a story of self-transcendence.

This story tells readers that the gateway to clarity can be achieved with a broader perspective. A higher perspective can enable us to have clarity on what our real and final purpose in life will be. This purpose shall provide us with higher experiences and joy and allow us to express ourselves fully. Joy in his efforts and passion in his work signifies higher expression. Making sense of the world, intelligible and cohesive, is frequently related to finding meaning in life. This is the cognitive component of meaning in life, which involves making sense of one's life events.

However, professionals are always in a dilemma; they need help making choices in their perspective when dealing with life situations. For example, in a business conclave on a working day, they believe the perspectives from their leaders that "One should have burning hunger and desire to grow." And on a non-working day, they live in the perspective of lifestyle-coach that "Desire is the root cause of all sufferings." Hence when a challenge is faced alone, they live in dilemma and paradox.

If one faces competition at work, one's perspective would require us to do better and kill our enemies, whereas the other would encourage fruitful collaboration between our peers and us. A scientific perspective encourages us to see first and then believe, whereas a philosophical outlook tells us that only if we believe shall we be able to see what is in front of us. Our ability to discern is affected by how willing we are to see and believe things. As a result, we sometimes want to believe ignorance is bliss, or we could also realize that ignorance is a kind of suffering. A scientific outlook towards life encourages ambition and enables us to believe that good results can give us life satisfaction. On the other hand, a philosophical outlook reminds us that greed can cause suffering and that no matter how successful we are, we will not be able to deliver positive results without internal satisfaction.

Dilemma Is Killing Authenticity of Self

The number one regret of people on their deathbed is that they wish they lived a life that was true to themselves and not the life that others expected of them. Whether we are authentic in our lives depends on whether we have clarity or dilemma in perspectives throughout our life. A scientific outlook would want us to believe that living in rational and experimental evidence in the external world is the most authentic. In contrast, a philosophical approach to life is to express our existence through self-intelligence and experience by taking the external world into cognizance.

You are less authentic if you see yourself as always trying to put up a strong face, running away from vulnerability, and indulging in us v/s them thinking. This will cause you to not depend upon anyone else, forcing you to be very independent. Here, your daily routine will be guided by demands, challenges, and duties – with little to no time for pleasure. On the other hand, a more authentic life will enable you to see yourself as an expression of universal values that can reach beyond your everyday existence.

You will seek agreement, conciliation, and cooperation through an authentic outlook. You shall be able to find a solution for all the ailments of your life. An authentic approach will not require you to indulge in an 'us v/s them' thinking as it will encourage you to find common ground with others. You shall be able to be patient and develop self-worth, aligning yourself with love, self-awareness, creativity, and wisdom.

To evaluate this, one must pay adequate attention to the authenticity of life. In today's environment, authenticity may be considered. Your polished online persona may appear more significant than your actual life. Like those around you and those who came before you, you join a shared goal of a profession, vehicle, house, and marriage. As this voyage progresses, it becomes clear that everything you've been given is owing to life, but that life has taken away a bit of what it is to be you. Authenticity reclaims its attraction in this alienated time.

You may believe that you must act a specific way around your employer or say certain things to your co-workers to be accepted. Instead of being yourself, you're pretending to be someone else to fit in or impress others. Most of us have been through similar experiences. Instead of acting authentically, we tell others what we believe they want to hear and act in ways that are contrary to our true character. In summary, we are leading an unauthentic life. Living and working this way, operating in an imbalanced self is unconsciously tiring, dispiriting, and confining. Here you are building and amplifying your outer self at the cost of life or self. Most professionals in the current world are in this state of self.

Authenticity is jeopardized when someone does not trust their inner understanding and instead relies on others and the outside world to define who they should be. The loss of authenticity can begin subtly, such as being taught that our true expression isn't acceptable or valid. Intuition about our needs to be more proper and recognized since we are children who don't know any better. Unfortunately, not understanding oneself in a deeper, intuitive, and self-loving sense can lead to a lifetime battle. Knowing yourself, understanding, embracing, expressing your feelings, and trusting your capacity to make the best decisions for yourself and your life is an essential part of life's journey.

Living honestly may have a big beneficial influence on your health and well-being.

According to studies, people who live more authentically have higher levels of psychological well-being. Greater mental health is usually accompanied by improved physical health. Stress is frequently caused in our thoughts and bodies when we cannot live from this actual place of authenticity. This stress may be unconscious initially, but it builds over time, causing mental and physical imbalances that manifest as anxiety, sadness, persistent rage, weariness, and chronic inner sickness.

You believe that you must constantly be powerful or hide or turn away from any show of weakness and vulnerability, attending to the demands of the ego and putting a lot of energy into status, money, possessions, and power to acquire the external trappings of success. Furthermore, by engaging in "us versus them" thinking, you protect yourself from feeling lonely and isolated, yet deep down, you are isolated. You rely on yourself more than anyone else instead of being open to different perspectives. Dilemmas remain deeply rooted within you and push you into ambiguous living without authenticity.

Self Is Missing the Meaning and Purpose of Life

Once, I came across a TEDx message from Adam Leipzig explaining his batch reunion (alums from Yale University). He explained how an informal survey was conducted during the annual alum meet. It was observed that all of them had abundance and affluence in their material life; however, nearly 80% were unhappy, miserable, and left without any meaning in life.

In another similar article from New York Times, they released a special magazine feature on The Future of Work. One of the articles within the feature was titled 'America's Professional Elite: Wealthy, Successful, and Miserable' by Charles Duhigg. He describes attending his Harvard Business School reunion fifteen years after graduating and encountering his former classmates, many of whom are highly successful and acclaimed. They are, with few exceptions, deeply unhappy.

He shares the example of a man who makes $1.2 million a year in a job that he hates, finds incredibly stressful and meaningless, and can't figure out how to escape.

Here is an excerpt from an article on Steve Jobs about his last words:

"In other eyes, my life is the essence of success, but aside from work, I have little joy. And in the end, wealth is just a fact of life to which I am accustomed"

"At this moment, lying on the bed, sick and remembering all my life, I realize that all my recognition and wealth is meaningless in the face of imminent death," it says. *"You can hire someone to drive a car, make money for you — but you cannot rent someone to carry the disease. One can find material things, but one thing cannot be found when it is lost — life.*

"Your true inner happiness does not come from the material things of this world. Whether you're flying first class or economy class — if the plane crashes, you crash with it."

While there are controversies about his last words, there is much evidence of a crisis of meaning in most people's lives despite their material abundance and affluence. Many people die without knowing what their life's purpose is. At least, that's how it seems to an outsider. Life's meaning is intimately and predominantly linked to eudemonia, where the sense of self is derived from the intrinsic dimension or inner self. Furthermore, importance as a dimension of life meaning is linked to the Japanese concept of *Ikigai*, which has no direct English equivalent but has been described as "That which makes one's life seem worth living."

"Life is never rendered unpleasant by circumstances, but only by a lack of meaning and purpose,"

- Viktor E. Frankl.

Frankl was a survivor of the most heinous conditions, having spent time in a Nazi concentration camp. His existence hinged on his ability to sustain this feeling of purpose in many respects. We must all search for our specific sense of purpose to find ourselves. This entails distinguishing our viewpoints from others' expectations of us. It involves asking oneself what our values are, what matters to us, and acting on those ideals. According to studies, the happiest people seek purpose rather than pleasure and are often excited when they have goals more significant than themselves. As a result, discovering yourself and your happiness is intrinsically related to finding the meaning and purpose of life. In summary, you need to discover your "self" to know your meaning and purpose in life.

According to Michael F. Steger, an eminent authority on this topic, meaning in life study looks up the hierarchical ladder of abstraction to conceptions of cosmic meaning, self-transcendence, spirituality, and universality. By assisting the field of meaning in life, research in descending the ladder a little and focusing on questions about how the brain creates, detects, defends, and repairs meaning. It offers a promising perspective on reviving our scientific quest to understand how people collect myriad streams of experience into the catch basin of consciousness. In summary, the meaning of life lies in what kind of experience we generate in life-situation.

Michael Steger arrived after psychological research that; people with higher meaning have 57% less hazardous to health and death. Discovering who we truly are is our biggest and most essential life adventure. Yet, many of us go through life either not knowing or listening to a nasty inner critic who tells us all the wrong things about ourselves. We confuse self-awareness with self-indulgence and go on without addressing the most crucial question we'll ever ask: Who am I? "What do you propose to do with your one wild and beautiful life?"

Also, Mary Oliver said, *"Finding yourself may appear to be a purely selfish objective, but a selfless process underpins everything we do."* To be the most important person in the world, the finest spouse, parent, and so on, we must first understand who we are, what we value, and, ultimately, what we have to offer. This is a personal journey that any person may benefit from. It's a process of removing layers that don't serve or reflect who we truly are. However, it also entails a massive act of development —

understanding who we want to be and pursuing our destiny – whatever that may be – with zeal. It's about acknowledging our strengths while remaining open and vulnerable to our experiences. It's not something to be afraid of or avoid at all costs, berating ourselves along the way, but something to seek out with the same interest and care we'd have for a fascinating new acquaintance.

Although self-awareness—knowing who we are and how we are perceived—is critical for job performance, career success, and leadership effectiveness, it is in limited supply in today's workplace. Researchers at Harvard discovered that whereas 95% of people believe they are self-aware, only 10% to 15% are. Unaware co-workers aren't just annoying; they may also reduce a team's odds of success by half and cause more stress, lower motivation, and higher attrition. Self-awareness is the ability to be present at the moment while observing it. It entails devoting a tiny percentage of your consciousness to observing yourself and others in encounters and taking in the big picture of an engagement rather than being only concerned with attaining your goal.

The meaning of life lies predominantly in our intrinsic experience and sense-of-self we collect while exploring and expressing in life-situation, which makes one's life seem worth living. In other words, it is the sense of self-derived from holistic well-being, i.e., inner and outer or smartness and sage-ness. Hence it depends on how much we know about our "self" in depth to harmonize our inner and outer well-being by transmuting or re-purposing the lower affair of self.

While we live in a very advanced, comfortable, and more convenient world than any other generation in history without taking the higher affair of self into cognizance, in other words, with insufficient mental clarity about the self, humanity suffers without inner well-being despite abundance in outer-wellbeing. This means we can derive our sense of self only from the external world and deprive ourselves of the same from our inner-self; i.e., we have access to only partial and limited meaning of life. Hence, it is important in this life to embark on the self. Understanding the self is the gateway to abundance, authenticity, and freedom. Let's dwell on the understanding of anatomy and the purpose of self. Once you grip it, you can hack it consciously above the conscience to harmonize your inner and outer disposition by transmuting or re-purposing the lower affair of self to move towards becoming Smart-Sage.

2

ANATOMY & PURPOSE OF SELF
Physical, Metaphysical, and Psychological

"True clarity and purpose emerge when we see ourselves -as we truly are."
— Eleesha Heart.

Inner and Outer Self

In the last chapter, we saw the educated human is in a rat race where we consider making progress as outer abundance, affluence, and sophistication. However, we struggle with inner well-being, meaning, and purpose. Any profound achievement in outer purpose without inner purpose is meaningless. For an analogy, let's take the number trillion (1,000,000,000,000) as your life's purpose. If the zero(s) represents the outer purpose, digit one represents the inner purpose. If we consider their existence separately, each of them has its significance; however, if we consider their fact holistically, "0" zero(s) have no significance without the digit "1". Hence it is essential and relevant in the current time to have a clarity of holistic self and purpose. Without this clarity, you will be sitting on the tail side (i.e., outer side) of the branch and enjoying the process of making cuts at the head side (i.e., outer side) of the branch of a tree till you realize that the real extent of your failure when you succeed in cutting the trunk in totality; i.e., at the time of death.

We, as human beings, have two dimensions of our life and the world; outer and inner life. There is a reasonable consensus that while science significantly contributes to the outer dimension, philosophy tremendously impacts the inner dimension. Hence to look holistically at life, we must embrace insight from both the self and our purpose dimensions.

As per scientific development around **The Unified Field** (a branch of quantum science), i.e., consciousness is the fundamental basis of all diverse laws of reality and nature governing the universe.

John Samuel Hagelin, an eminent quantum physicist and a leader of the Transcendental Meditation movement, states; *"Let me first emphasize that the discovery of the unified field is not a philosophical development. It is a scientific development of the foremost order—a rigorous mathematical development based upon the Lagrangian of the unified field. This highly compact mathematical formula describes the self-interacting dynamics of unity at the basis of all the diverse laws of nature governing the universe. Consciousness exists both in un-manifested and manifested forms."*

With this evidence, we can say in the conviction that our self is also derived from consciousness. We exist in manifested form (outer dimension) and un-manifested form of consciousness. Also, while the outer form or outer self exists in time-space till death, the inner self continues to exist even after death. The inner self continues its journey until it reaches its absolute state or level of consciousness.

In the philosophical world, this un-manifested self is called the soul or spirit. The scientific community as well subscribes to this idea of soul and spirit.

"Everyone who is seriously involved in the pursuit of science becomes convinced that some spirit is manifest in the laws of the universe, one that is vastly superior to that of man," said Albert Einstein.

> "On the philosophical level, both Buddhism and modern science share a deep suspicion of any notion of absolutes, whether conceptualized as a transcendent being, as an eternal, unchanging principle such as the soul or as a fundamental substratum of reality."
>
> - Dalai Lama.

If we continue investing in the structure of self with two fundamental criteria, i.e., the self should have a spectrum from un-manifested to manifest.

While the self has its roots in the un-manifested inner dimension of spirit, source, super-consciousness, or **The Field**, it expresses or manifests itself into higher density self as an outer dimension in the form of mind (i.e., psychological self) and body (i.e., physical self). This concept has been beautifully captured as an integrated framework of the self in yoga philosophy (an arm of Vedanta philosophy, which is 8000 years old) called *"Pancha-Kosha,"* or **Five-Sheaths of Consciousness Self**, just like the layers of an onion.

Self as Five Sheaths: A Continuum from Self to Source.

- **The Food Sheath** - This is the first and outermost level of the integrated system. The Sanskrit word *'Annamaya Kosha'* stands for the food sheath. This layer represents the physical or physiological self, nurtured or empowered by the right food intake. The content of this layer is our body, including DNA, cells, tissues, organs, bones, etc.

- **Energy Sheath** – This layer is the second layer from the outside, and in Sanskrit, it is called *Pranamaya Kosha*. The content of this layer is our life force, comprising energy fields including metaphysical elements like aura (the bio-magnetic field), nerves (*Nadis*), and the wheel (*Chakras*). This sheath is nurtured or empowered through mindful-breathing patterns.

- **Mental Sheath** - This layer is the third layer from the outside, and in Sanskrit, it is known as *Manomaya Kosha*. This sheath refers to our psychological body, composed of emotions, likes, dislikes, fears, and phobias. The right thought empowers this sheath. Those who understand and control the mental body are no longer afflicted by suffering.

- **Intellectual Sheath** - This layer is the fourth layer from the outside, and in Sanskrit, it is called *Vignanamaya Kosha*. This sheath is also known as the sheath of knowledge or wisdom. This sheath is empowered by the right intelligence, discriminative abilities or faculty (*Buddhi*), and the leverage of our five cognitive senses. As this sheath is refined, our intellect expands to reflect the objective instinct of consciousness beyond the subjective instinct of conscience. It becomes the "witness mind" or "innocence mind" when it is no longer entangled with the sheath outer to it, i.e., the sheath of mind, energy, and food; therefore, it can witness all illusion and perceive objective closure to the truth.

- **Bliss Sheath** – This is the innermost layer of the integrated system, and in Sanskrit, it is called the *Anandamaya Kosha*. This is also known as the causal body, as it is the cause for all four outer sheaths. This sheath is empowered by all intrinsic and non-perceptual experiences, i.e., an experience beyond memory and imagination. This sheath represents our innermost self, the absolute self, the soul, which is connected to the source or the field.

Swami Vivekananda once said, *"When you think you are only a body and mind, you are apart from the universe; when you think, you are a soul, you are a spark from the great Eternal."*

Therefore, when you say "I," and you get a reference to body and mind, you are not in your true self or higher self. As we can see, the sheaths are arranged outwards in order of their degree of density and manifestation, i.e., from subtlest to gross and from inner to outer. Also, each of these sheaths vibrates or operates at different levels of vibrational or conscious energy; i.e., the inner sheath operates at higher conscious energy than its outer sheath. We will discuss the same in the next chapter.

Three Bodies Encompass Five Sheaths.

The five sheaths we discussed are again described in a framework of three bodies for simplicity, ease of perception, and wider reference. The Food sheath belongs to the gross body, the Energy. Mental and Intellectual sheath leads to the astral body, and the Bliss sheath maps to the causal body. Each body is an energetic field of different densities that can vibrate at different frequencies. So, both sheath and body are part of the anatomy of the self. While the gross and astral bodies operate locally (i.e., only within time and space), the causal body can operate beyond the local dimension (i.e., non-local). In other words, causal body is intrinsic in nature and not disturbed by external dimension. More is the density of the self (i.e., sheath or body), less is the lifespan; i.e., for the sake of comprehension; if the lifespan of the gross body is around 100 years; the same for the causal body is "n" time 100; where n depends on rate the at which the vibrational-conscious-energy level of "self" is getting transcended to reach its absolute-self.

Gross body or physical self – This is the densest body and consists of the five sense organs, the five organs of action; i.e., it's the physiological body, which interacts with gross elements of the external world and is responsible for being the agency between the gross world and astral world.

Subtle Body or psychological self – This body vibrates at a much higher frequency than the gross body and is beyond the perception of our ordinary physical senses. It interacts with cosmic elements of the external world (i.e., thought, emotion, intelligence, imagination, ideas, reasoning, dreams, subconscious projections, perceptual experience, etc.). It acts as a gateway between the gross or outer world on one side and the causal or inner world on the other.

Causal body or causal self - It is the innermost body of the self and has the subtlest vibration within the creation of the human being. This contains all potentialities for astral and gross-body. It resembles seed energy, which sprouts the subtle and physical body as it germinates. It reflects its tendencies on astral and gross layers. Hence gross and astral layers do not have their tendencies.

Therefore, it is said that the world doesn't exist without the body, the body never exists without the mind, the mind never exists without the causal body, and the causal body never exists without consciousness or reality. This body is also called the Karmic body, the residual causal energy from the past. It interacts with the causal layer of the universe, i.e., with feeling, impression, temptation, and karma. All our feelings and experiences happen and operate at this level of the body. Also, it is through this body that we experience our deepest connection to that which is our innermost core or true self. In other words, the causal body links individual consciousness with the collective and cosmic consciousness, higher intelligence, or the source field or great causal body. Bringing the analogy with fruit to self, if the gross and astral body is the peel, the causal body is the pulp, and the source is the seed. The way peel is meaningless and useless without pulp and seed; similarly, the gross and astral body is useless without a causal body and source. Hence the meaning of life has to connect or touch to causal self and source. We can touch this space during deep sleep and meditation. Very importantly, all karmic transmutation (or repurposing) and reconciliation happen at this level when we embrace the lower emotions, essence, feeling, and sensation. As this body contains all potentialities or essence for the astral and gross body, it is time to know what these potentialities or essence of self that gets sprouted in the astral and gross body are.

While the gross body (physical self) and astral body (psychological self) are dominated by the four-fundamental elements - earth, water, air, and fire, the causal body is dominated by ether or space. Ether is the fundamental energy of the quantum field. In the language of spirituality, it can be equated with spirit. This causal self or spirit exists as un-manifested at a metaphysical level, which can only be experienced and not directly experimented on.

Sri Krishna says in Bhagavat Gita (10.20) that *"I am seated in the heart of all living entities. I am the beginning, middle, and end of all beings."*

Here the causal, astral, and gross body represents the beginning, middle, and end, respectively. The causal body or causal-self stores the potentialities for true transformation in self. Hence, Vedic science focuses on the health of the causal body in addition to the gross (i.e., physical) and shuttle (psychological) body, whereas modern science limits its focus to gross and shuttle levels. Hence hacking our deeper self is possible only when we know our "self" at a causal level.

The body and mind (i.e., physical, and psychological self) is just a shadow of the causal self, which is the source of life and light for the former two selves. So, the causal self has higher intelligence and knows what will happen before the former two through telepathy, intuition, etc. Accordingly, the former two selves influence only a limited aspect of our lives and situations. Only when one touches the causal self, which can govern the former two selves, does life-situation transformation happen with limitless possibilities.

Another important point is that once you are connected to your causal self, your time becomes me-time, even if your body-mind is involved with other people or situations. However, most people suffer as they are trapped with aversion and cravings of body and mind without touching the causal self. In other words, they do not know 'Who they truly are' beyond body and mind. This is solely because they are distracted at the body and mind levels. They are deprived of attention to their causal-self.

As Nobel Prize winner Herbert Simon said in the 1970s: *"In an information-rich world, the wealth of information means a dearth of something else: a scarcity of whatever it is that information consumes. What information consumes is rather obvious: it consumes the attention of its recipients. Hence a wealth of information creates a poverty of attention and a need to allocate that attention efficiently among the overabundance of information sources that might consume it."*

However, if we can pay enough attention to anything, some of its aspects can snowball into something profound in our life. The same rule can be applied to paying attention to the causal self.

In the later part of this book, we will discuss how to hack, pay attention, and develop a few causal muscles in the later part of this book for vibrant living and high-resolution life.

Who are you beyond Body & Mind? Three Essences of the Self

As per *Vedanta* philosophy, 'self' (i.e., sheath, body, or vibrational-conscious-energy) is flavored with three cosmic essences or potentialities: **Sat, Chit,** and **Ananda**. Hence self is also called the trinity self with a single word, **"Satchidananda,"** or **Sat-Chit-Ananda**.

SAT means absolute existence essence, being or timeless essence of self, or the absolute un-manifested existence of self is expressed as the manifested world. Hence the un-manifested *Sat* is the "existence" of self, and manifested *Sat* is the "expression" of self. This essence holds the continuum from absolute to derivatives, un-manifested to manifested, and temporary to permanence. Put simply, *Sat* is your existential quality and its expression into this world.

CHIT means consciousness or intelligence essence to comprehend reality. It is the knowledge of the true nature of the self, *Sat-Chit-Ananda*. This essence holds from ignorance to wisdom, misperception to ultimate perception, or illusion to mental clarity. *Chit* reflects how the "self" or you perceive the world, which decides your resolution of experience of the world and expression into the world.

ANANDA means experience essence. It is the rupture or the bliss of self. This essence holds the continuum from transient or temporary happiness of life-situation to continuous & permanent happiness of life, which exists even after death. While the former happiness is based on the perception of the mind and senses, the latter is beyond the same. The permanent happiness or bliss (in Sanskrit called *Ananda*) is derived directly from the source or life in every situation. Sat reflects how the "self" or you experience the world. This essence of self, shares the name with the innermost layer of the sheath (i.e., *Anandamaya Kosha* or bliss sheath), which maps to the causal body in an integrated yogic framework of self.

This causal body in-house all three essences in their subtlest form (*Sat-Chit-Ananda*) and is the cause of other bodies or self (i.e., mind and body) as the projection of the source or the field. These essences are crude potentialities and manifest in other bodies of self (astral and gross) as a reflection of the source.

Hence *Sat-Chit-Ananda* or trinity-self indicates a state of the ever-conscious-blissful state. Interestingly, the other two will arise automatically if one essence is developed. And hence, the three essences (or potentialities) are interrelated like the three sides of the **Trinity Self**. This state represents the ultimate neural pattern in the human brain having potentialities for peak existence, intelligence, experience, and expression. Specifically, these three essences (or potentialities) are the same and are one "Sachidananda."

That is why famous people primarily connect deeply to one of the three routes of "Sachidananda." For example, Eckhart connected to SAT; he talks about this in his magnum opus – 'Power of Now.' On the other hand, CHIT is deeply connected by Swami Vivekananda, who enhances the concept of consciousness to super-consciousness. Likewise, ANANDA is ruthlessly connected by Buddha, who stressed the importance of attaining a blissful or Nirvana state in life.

Also, Joseph Campbell, one of the great psychologists, once mentioned, *"Now I came to this idea of bliss because, in Sanskrit, which is the great spiritual language of the world, there are three terms that represent the brink, the jumping-off place to the ocean of transcendence: Sat-Chit-Ananda. Sat means* being, *'Chit'* means consciousness, and *'Ananda'* means bliss or rapture. I thought, *'I don't know whether my consciousness is proper consciousness or not; I don't know whether what I know of my being is my proper being, but I do know where my rapture is. So let me hang on to rapture, which will bring me both my consciousness and my being, and it worked."*

Once you were called a baby. Then you grew into a young boy or girl. Then you were a teenager, a student. In the future, you become a boyfriend, a girlfriend, and a spouse. You obtained several new roles. A husband becomes a father, then a grandfather, then a great-grandfather, then an older man, and, ultimately, he becomes a dead body. These are all changes that happen in the gross and astral levels - as an expression of your causal body, which is the sheath of *Sat-Chit-Ananda*, the personal experience of the ever-changing reality. After knowing the structure, and essence of self, it is time to understand how to identify the level of consciousness.

Are you Entangled or Involved?

Butter is entangled within milk before it gets churned out. Objectification negates the identification process, and involvement negates the entanglement process. If you are identified with something, you become the same. For example, when you watch a movie in a cinema hall, you completely forget the external world; i.e., you get identified or entangled with the cinema until the screen projection ends. Many people cry or cheer-up depending on what happens to their favorite character. A similar thing also happens in our dream; till we wake up from it. Hence, here objectification process activates the **"seer"** to see or observe the **"seen"** and also get dis-identified from the "seen." The "seen," i.e., the stage of "seer," expands with an increase in the level of consciousness (LOC) of self, where the "seer" observer witnesses the "seen" or worldly drama on the stage. This "seer" is real you above your ego-self. Hence, once you activate your "seer" within, it can act as your guide or Guru for your inner purpose, and you do not need your worldly Guru.

The people or "self" are those who can't objectify their gross body;

i.e., they get identified or entangled with it and become seriously concerned about their physical appearance or look. Hence if they have a gorgeous or handsome look, they become proud; if not, they become jealous of the same of others. These people are unconsciously operating from the gross body and all other outer-self.

In the same way, suppose now you are identified with your mind; i.e., you cannot objectify and get dis-identified or untangled from it. It means while you are angry, at that time, you are not able to know or realize that you are in anger. In other words, you are entangled with anger and are tempted to behave and act as per the conscious level of anger. So, you will be dancing to the tune of grief, fear, desire, anger, pride, etc. In other words, you will derive your sense of self from these emotions and also defend the same at cost. You are unconsciously operating from your mental sheath. You can transmute (or re-purpose) your lower vibrational conscious energy and transcend towards its peak; only when you can objectify and get dis-identified from it by activating your "seer" within.

Until you are identified with your gross body (physiological) and astral body (psychological) before you are transcending, you must operate from the causal body to transcend your gross and astral body. The litmus test for operating at the causal-body level is that; you can objectify and get misidentified from the astral body (psychological self) and gross body (physiological self) in real-time. Once you activate your "seer" within, you will feel the impact of temptation and the sensation of your causal body at astral and gross-body real-time. In other words, you can create a space or distance between your causal-self and your ego-self, identity, or identified self (combination of astral and gross-body).

It is extremely magical, miraculous, and blissful to live in this world with an identity-self; as a son, father, daughter, mother, teacher, doctor, professional, Indian, and so on becomes the "seen" by your true-self as the seer; where there is no entanglement between both-self. This is where; the identity-self operates as "seen" in the presence of a higher-self "seer." Also, this "seer" dissolves the entanglement and mental conflict due to different levels of intelligence, i.e., consciousness and conscience. Where consciousness is the objective intelligence of the misidentified self and conscience is the subjective intelligence of the identified self. This clarity in life enables; involvement without entanglement, credibility with character, relationship with love and trust, wisdom with humility, innovation with creative intelligence, confidence with clarity, abundance with authenticity, outer wellbeing with inner wellbeing, entertainment with enlightenment, growth & transformation with transcendence, outer-purpose with inner-purpose and so on. It will allow you to live as a real actor on the world's stage with the co-existence of "seer" and "seen" without entanglement. We are discussing so many details on entanglement because it creates friction and experience of hurt, pain, and unpleasantness. Also, it gets carried forward as regret and remorse in his life, whereas involvement responds to life-situation with detachment. Hence, it creates frictionless flow, freedom, meaning, and fulfillment.

Co-Existence of "Seer" and "Seen"

Can the "seer" and "seen" co-exist with involvement and without entanglement, i.e., can you see your thoughts and emotion in real time?

The answer is – **YES!**

Deepak Chopra also ascertains the same in his book 'Meta-Human.' He says, *"To end the whole sorry mess involves shifting from human to metahuman. Both states exist here and now. There is nowhere to go to reach meta-reality. Like the two birds in the tree, you are feasting on life and looking on. But the looking-on part is being ignored, suppressed, overlooked, and undervalued. The transformation that makes you metahuman is known in the world's spiritual traditions as 'waking up.' Once someone rises to the state of metahuman, it seems like the old everyday self was a sleepwalker, barely conscious of life's infinite possibilities".*

To achieve the state of self where there is a co-existence of meaning and making, abundance and authenticity, life and life-situation or self and outer world, we must live, i.e., operate from a level of causal self by objectifying our ego or identified-self (i.e., gross and astral self). Once we operate from this state, there is a reconciliation between life and life situation, meaning and making, abundance and authenticity, inner and outer self, and inner and outer world, which is the true purpose of life (or self). All these reconciliations happen at the level of conscious energy or consciousness. Initially, the "seer" may pop up momentarily as a spark of the soul. However, with practice, it can be sustained.

What is your Primary Purpose in Life?

Suppose you are a business owner, and you are still identified and entangled with this role. So, in this situation, what are your inner and outer purpose?

According to the microcosm–macrocosm analogy hypothesis, the human being (i.e., the little order or miniature universe) and the cosmos macrocosm (i.e., the universe as a whole) has structural similarities. In other words, truths regarding the nature of the cosmos as a whole may be drawn from facts about human nature and vice versa, using this basic parallel. It is said; once, during deep meditation, Swami Vivekananda experienced the macrocosm within the microcosm.

Eckhart Tolle says, *"If you look within rather than only without, however, you discover that you have an inner and an outer purpose, and since you are a microcosmic reflection of the macrocosm, it follows that the universe too has an inner and outer-purpose inseparable from yours. The outer purpose of the universe is to create form and experience the interaction of forms—the play, the dream, the drama, or whatever you choose to call it. Its inner purpose is to awaken to its formless essence. Then comes the reconciliation of outer and inner purpose: to bring that essence—consciousness—into the world of form and thereby transform the world. The ultimate purpose of that transformation goes far beyond anything the human mind can imagine or comprehend. And yet, on this planet, that transformation is the task allotted to us. That is the reconciliation of outer and inner purpose."*

Suppose a human being (microcosm) must follow the universe (macrocosm). In that case, it also has two purposes, outer and inner, and there must be reconciliation between both through the common essence of *Sat-Chit-Ananda*. In other words, the outer purpose is to express un-manifested and formless essence—*Sat-Chit-Ananda*—into the world of manifested form. Then the inner purpose is achieving the outer-purpose through awakening, ascending, or transcending to the absolute self, *Sat-Chit-Ananda*.

The outer purpose is the transformation of life-situation; which is to achieve the goal we have set in the outer world; i.e., abundance, prosperity, pleasure, comfort, position, recognition, etc. However, the inner purpose is the inner transformation of life (or self) or transcendence towards absolute self; *Sat-Chit-Ananda*. For example, if you are a business owner, your outer purpose (i.e., Smartness) is making profitable growth to satisfy your stakeholder; however, your inner purpose is getting dis-identified from your identity-self (business owner) by activating your "seer" within.

The outer purpose is to express Smartness, and the inner purpose is to express Sage-ness. Here Smartness deals with life situations, and Sage-ness deals with life (or self, *Sat-Chit-Ananda*). Also, life (or self) enters a state of involvement only when there is reconciliation between Smartness and Sage-ness; otherwise, there is residual hurt, regret, or remorse from life-situation. When there is a reconciliation between inner purpose (i.e., Sage-ness) and outer purpose (i.e., Smartness), life has authenticity, meaning, and purpose.

Life and life situations are not the same; both are two aspects of the "self" or consciousness, i.e., like two sides of the same coin. While life is the inner essence of self to be experienced, life situation is the outer ambiance of self to be expressed or perceived by senses. In other words, life-situation is a three-dimensional immersive movie as a projection of life. Hence, what you think and tell of others in a life situation doesn't define others; rather, it defines you.

Let's consider two life situations. One, where a patient died while the doctor was operating with good intention, love, and utmost diligence, i.e., embracing all constraints to make it successful. After he failed, he moved to the next case. Another situation was where the victim survived while a murderer attempted to kill him. After this incident, he was in constant fear of getting caught. Here, while both doctor and murderer failed in outer purpose (i.e., Smartness), only the doctor succeeded in inner purpose (i.e., Sage-ness) as he was not entangled with process or result. In other words, there was no residual hurt, regret, or remorse from his life situation. While the inner purpose (Sage-ness) is the purpose of life (or self), the outer purpose (i.e., Smartness) is the purpose of life-situation. Hence, both purpose is necessary in this world to be truly successful.

Now, which purpose matters the most, or what can be called our primary purpose?

Let's consider a life situation where you have to open your bank locker, and to open the same two keys are required. However, first, you must go to the bank with your key and then request the banker to bring his key, which is the primary condition. You are not responsible for the banker's key. Hence your key becomes the primary key.

Similarly, the inner purpose (Sage-ness) is innate, existential, and fundamental to you. Hence it is your primary purpose. As peel is meaningless and useless without pulp and seed, in the same way, the outer purpose (i.e., Smartness) is meaningless and pointless without inner purpose (Sage-ness); i.e., entangled life is meaningless and useless without involvement in life. Also, as a response to a similar question, Mr. Eckhart Tolle says, *"Outer will matter to you if you haven't realized your inner purpose,"* (Sage-ness).

After that, the outer purpose (i.e., Smartness) is just a game you may continue playing simply because you enjoy it. It is also possible to fail in your outer purpose (i.e., Smartness) and simultaneously succeed in your inner purpose (Sage-ness). Or the other way around, which is more common: outer riches and inner poverty, or to *"Gain the world and lose your soul,"* as Jesus puts it. Ultimately, of course, every outer purpose (i.e., Smartness) is doomed to "fail" sooner or later because it is subject to the law of impermanence of all things. The sooner you realize that your outer purpose (i.e., Smartness) cannot give you lasting fulfillment, the better".

Also, according to ancient Greek philosophers — especially Socrates, Plato, and Aristotle one's existential aim or purpose of life is *eudaemonia*, which is an ancient Greek word. Eudaemonia means the inner peace, happiness, or contentment that comes beyond external world; i.e., purely intrinsic (Sage-ness)

We search for happiness, purpose and meaning, because we lack those. As we cannot just go outside and pluck happiness from a tree or buy it off the shelf of a super market, we resort to all sorts of proxies to deliver us happiness. So, we work on our bodies, we chase promotions, position, power, money, and success, we seek appreciations, recognition, pleasure, and convenience; we try to make others love and follow us, and so on. We do all these things with Smartness - sometimes for years or decades - in the hope that they will eventually give us what we most want. We do this as we are cent percent convinced that happiness is the product of external conditions. But, we are in illusion. Real happiness, purpose and meaning is entirely an inside job and intrinsic; which is beyond body-mind phenomenon (Sage-ness)

"Seen" (i.e., Smartness) alone cannot make life meaningful.

A stressed-out businessman once relaxed on the beach in a little Brazilian community. After catching several large fish, he sat and watched a Brazilian fisherman paddle a small boat towards the shore. "How long does it take to catch so many fish?" the merchant asked the fisherman.

"Oh, just a little time," the fisherman said.

"Why don't you remain at sea longer and capture even more?" The businessman was taken aback.

"This will feed my entire family," the fisherman stated.

"So, what do you do for the remainder of the day?" the businessman said.

"Well, I normally get up early in the morning, go out to sea, catch a few fish, then come home and play with my kids," the fisherman explained. "Afternoons are spent with my wife napping, and evenings are spent with my mates in the village for a drink — we play the guitar, sing, and dance all night."

The businessman gave the fisherman some advice. "I have a doctorate in business administration." I could assist you in becoming a more successful individual. You should spend more time at sea, attempting to capture as many fish as possible. You may purchase a larger boat and catch even more fish when you have enough savings. Soon, you'll be able to afford to acquire more boats and establish your own business, a canning facility, and a distribution network. By then, you'll have relocated out of this area and into Sao Paulo, where you may establish a headquarters to handle your other branches."

"And then what?" the fisherman continues.

"After that," the businessman exclaims, "you can live like a king in your own house, and when the time comes, you can go public and float your shares on the Stock Exchange, and you'll be rich."

"And then what?" the fisherman inquires.

"After that, you can finally retire," the businessman says. "You can move to a house near the fishing village, wake up early, catch a few fish, then return home to play with your kids. You may take a nice afternoon nap with your wife, and when evening comes, you can join your buddies for a drink, play the guitar, sing, and dance all night!"

The fisherman smiled with inner richness. His smile has transcended the consciousness of the outer-rich and stressed-out businessman to a higher level. Also, it changed his priorities and lifestyle for good. In summary, the inner purpose (Sage-ness) has surpassed the outer purpose (i.e., Smartness).

Hence when the inner purpose (i.e., Sage-ness) becomes our primary purpose, we get a holistic, true purpose in life. So, to live with true purpose, we must go beyond the outer or secondary purpose. The conventional definition of success in the world is tuned predominantly towards an outer purpose (i.e., Smartness) and outer well-being, which is a narrower view. However, if you have a little inclination towards the subjective and inner-wellbeing along with outer well-being; you have to go back to the basic of self and move beyond conventional; which has promisingly offered success in tune with a dual purpose; outer and inner subjective and objective, transformation, and transcendence. Make an analogy in the manufacturing industry; if the primary product represents the primary purpose, the by-product represents the secondary purpose. Hence, it is essential to note that while pursuing your primary product of meaning and existential purpose in life, no one will take away your by-product of material success in life situations to enjoy (i.e., wealth, position, power, name, fame). All will be available as a mandatory offering by the law of nature. In simple, your Smartness can be an automatic by-product of Sage-ness. The only point is to retain the purity of Sage-ness. You should be careful is, not to derive your sense of self from these by-products (i.e., detached from Smartness). If you can do these little things, this will emerge as a creative process within you, and you will be able live as Smart-Sage.

Self-Actualization is the Highest Human Need

Abraham Harold Maslow, the well-known American psychologist, developed the hierarchy of needs, later named after him and showed the highest level of psychological development. It also highlights how personal potential is fully realized when the body's basic needs are fulfilled. The need for transcendence arises only after basic needs are fulfilled. He classified the initial four levels of need as basic needs-

The first level of needs is gross or physiological: food, water, sleep, and sexual reproduction.

Once the individual acquires these needs, one can move on to **the second level of needs: psychological** safety and security. This includes the need for a secure condition to keep oneself safe from unnatural events, natural calamities, animal attacks, and emotional safety. This also includes the need for financial security and health insurance. The different actions undertaken by individuals for fulfilling these needs are finding a job, getting enrolled for an insurance claim, discovering a safe neighborhood for settling down, etc., which would also come under this category.

The third level of need is the social need, also known as the need for love and belongingness. Once the individuals have fulfilled their psychological and safety requirements, they seek acceptance and validation from society, which is often felt in love, belongingness, etc. Emotions are experienced during this stage to a condition where they realize that they need to develop an intimate relationship with others. The love and belongingness experienced among friends, the compassions felt in family relations, the intimate relations that individuals develop with their partners, and the feeling of belongingness experienced in social groups come under this category.

After social validation comes to the need for esteem at the **fourth level**; at this level, the individual slowly develops the need to be recognized in society. Being recognized can be a condition when they are recognized through their success in outer purpose (i.e., Smartness) or where the individual develops self-respect in society. This, again, is connected to the need to have self-esteem. This phase of life signifies growth and individuation. In fact, until this level of needs, individuals strive predominantly for an outer purpose (i.e., Smartness), which is the secondary purpose.

The final, fifth, or highest level of needs in Maslow's hierarchy is the need for self-actualization and transcendence. Individuals reach this level when they realize their full potential, i.e., Smartness and Sageness. At this level, their true potential emerges from peak potentialities of self, *Sat-Chit-Ananda*. While self-actualization is often thought of as a purely individualistic or self-centered pursuit, Maslow believed that to fully realize potential requires a merging between self and the world. He has recognized the need for the inner purpose (i.e., Sage-ness) of transcendence for self-actualization. He says without inner purpose (i.e., Sage-ness) there is no peak existence, expression, intelligence, and expression.

Vedanta philosophy classifies the outer purpose (i.e., Smartness) into **Artha** and **Kama**, i.e., wealth creation and enjoyment. And it classifies the inner purpose (i.e., Sage-ness) **Dharma** & **Moksha**, i.e., service beyond self and enlightenment.

Today there is unimaginable progress and advancement in all

dimensions of self-centric outer purpose (i.e., Smartness) but not much focus to-wards inner-purpose (i.e., Sage-ness). Hence people are stuck within the first four levels of needs - please accept me, please like me, love me, and please respect me. Due to this low consciousness, they are missing the bus for "transcendence" and self-actualization, i.e., the actualization of peak existence, expression, intelligence, and peak expression.

Most people think inner purpose (i.e., Sage-ness) is a post-retirement phenomenon. Also, people with this mindset park their joy till the weekend after spending workdays in jail. This is making both work and joy entangled. However, you will discover in subsequent chapters that inner purpose (i.e., Sage-ness) can be achieved and is to be achieved in parallel with an outer purpose (i.e., Smartness) in life situations between a stimulus and response, which will help you to move toward living like a Smart-Sage.

Actualized-self and Three Essences

A self-actualized person is closer to the ultimate neural pattern for peak existence, intelligence, expression, and expression (i.e., *Sat-Chit-Ananda*). Maslow also studied individuals he believed to be self-actualized, including Abraham Lincoln, Thomas Jefferson, Albert Einstein, and others, to derive the common characteristics of the self-actualized person. He articulated all important characteristics in his book Motivation and Personality. Assuming you will also be self-actualized one day, let's visualize your peak experience, intelligence, and expression characteristics.

Your Peak Experience

When you have a "peak experience," – you will enjoy the journey and not just the destination; i.e., you will focus on finding self and the meaning behind every task instead of chasing results. Even when working in an intense situation, you will experience the peak in both perceptual and non-perceptual experiences. You will be able to enjoy every moment of your journey with courage and in a meditative way. You will be comfortable with solitude as you will have inner happiness and bliss independent of life-situation. Hence you will tend to have a smaller friend circle with genuine and authentic relationships. In other words, you will enjoy life's meaning and purpose along with life situations and live with the flow and meditative experience.

Your Peak Intelligence

With a higher perspective of reality, you will have clarity of life and life situations. The ability to embrace the unknown and the ambiguous. At the same time, you need no validation or acceptance of your conviction from a larger group. You have "seer" as your intimate Guru. You will be inherently unconventional; however, you will not seek to shock or disturb anyone. You will not be troubled by small things as you tend to have a larger perspective. Also, with a sense of oneness, you will show indifference to the religions and enculturation. You will possess a very democratic view of the world and have high self-acceptance. You will listen to, leverage, and depend on spiritual and intuitive intelligence compared to ego-based intelligence. While you recognize the illusion and ignorance in the world, you can get involved in life-situation with relevance and pragmatism.

Your Peak Expression

You can form a deep connection with every creation in nature and the human race. Hence, you can participate in life-situation with a feeling of inter-connectedness. You will understand that not everything in their life can be credited to free will; some things result from destiny. You will possess an excellent command of solving problems and can look at problems with ease and playfulness. Hence you will not be hostile toward humor. Your effort, energy, and actions will be motivated by quest and passion rather than desire and obsession. In other words, your thoughts, words, and actions (outer Karma) will not have any residual aversion and craving (inner Karma, or Karmic energy).

Meaning and Self-actualization at Work

The days are gone when, if you can see your employees working, they're productive. If you pay them more, they'll work harder. The new trend is "Meaning Is the New Money." After the recent pandemic (covid-19), there is an increasing quest for meaning compared to money. I recently read an article from Harvard Business Review (HBR) titled "9 Out of 10 People Are Willing to Earn Less Money to Do More-Meaningful Work". In other words, people of the twenty-first century VUCA world are intuitively hungry to derive their sense of self from a primary product of meaning and existential purpose of life instead of by-products of life situations (wealth, power, positions, name, and fame). Hence it is time for all enterprises and corporates to start thinking about what is meaningful for their employee and how it can amplify value for all by pursuing a purpose-driven workplace.

Mr. Satya Nadella, the CEO of Microsoft, advocates focusing on meaning while working by saying, *"I want to work in a place where everybody gets more meaning out of their work on an everyday basis." Life in the workplace is full of paradoxes. For many of you, the competing and interwoven demands are a source of conflict. The meaning will emerge only when you can have an answer."*

1. **How can you create abundance in core business with empathy and authenticity?**
2. **How do you balance work and life?**
3. **How can you express your peak existence with peak intelligence and experience?**

The need for meaning at work resonates with the topmost level of need in Maslow's hierarchy, which is also very closely associated with meaning and the inner purpose (i.e., Sage-ness) of life.

Inner-purpose (i.e., Sage-ness) of life lies in the quality of inner place and causal body, which are experiential. This is what we learned in this chapter qualitatively from the experience of an ancient scientist. However, around 78% of the world's population lives primarily with logical and rational values. Hence, to develop an ability to improve and operate from an inner place or causal body, you need a perceivable and measurable framework, without which your persuasion for meaning and purpose will be surficial and dogmatic.

Call to Action

As per Viktor Frankl, the meaning of life isn't prescribed. It's created. Each person's life has its own unique, context-specific meaning. We can discover this meaning in life in three different ways:

1. **By creating a work or doing a deed;**

2. **By experiencing something**

3. **By consciously choosing right response towards challenging life-situations & suffering.**

Now, try to mix & match above ways (1,2, 3) with dimensions of self (a, b, c) as below:

(a) Expression *(Sat)*

(b) Intelligence *(Chit)*

(c) Experience *(Ananda)*

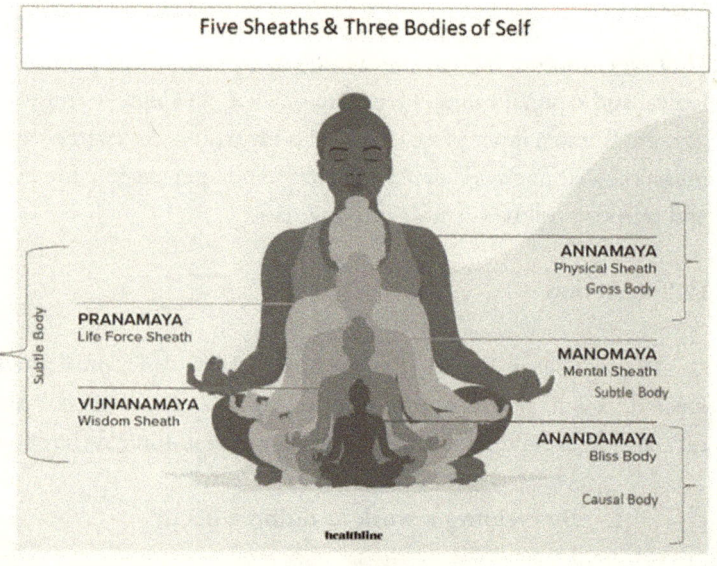

Five Sheaths & Three Bodies of Self

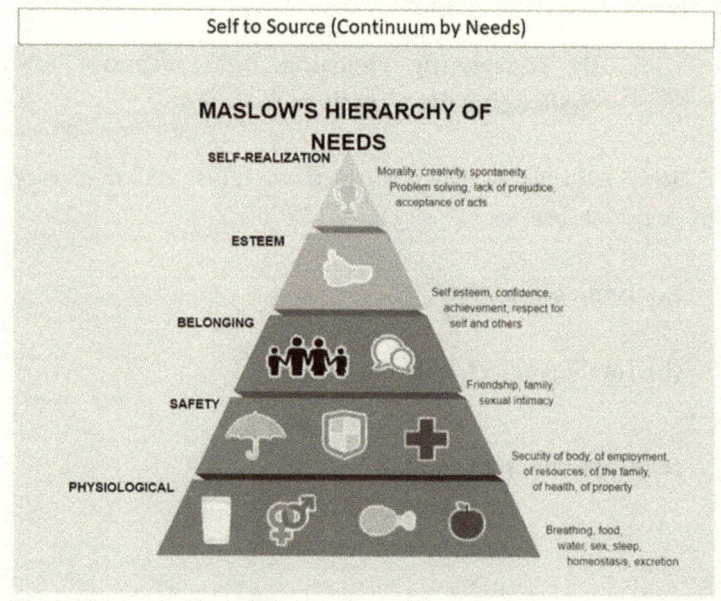

Self to Source (Continuum by Needs)

Self to Source (Continuum by Density)

Source / Field
The Absolute

Great-Causal Body
(body of Knowledge; the God state; Awareness-Love-Light)

Causal Body
(body of ignorance, nothingness or space)

Subtle Body
(mental body)

Gross Body
(physical body)

3

LEVELS OF SELF
Self as Levels of Conscious Energy

"If you don't know who you truly are, you'll never know what you really want."

— Roy T. Bennett.

Anything Not Measurable, Is Not-manageable

I have two friends in the healthcare industry; one runs a health diagnosis and pathology test services business, and the other is a renowned medicine specialist. As a part of practicing and pursuing their primary purpose, they go to remote villages for free services, where people do not have access to hospitals; but both go on different days; i.e., the medicine specialist goes after a few days of diagnosis and pathology services. One day the medicine specialist went to a village to distribute free medicine based on the report from the diagnosis and pathology services report. To his surprise; out of a few hundred patients in the queue, he was able to help only a dozen of them with free medicine as others did not have their reports due to various reasons; i.e., either they had not got earlier, they lost it, forgot it and so on. The story's moral is to measure the root cause to get an accurate solution.

> Yogananda Paramahansa says, *"Millions of people never analyze themselves. Mentally, they are mechanical products of their environment, preoccupied with breakfast, lunch, and dinner, working and sleeping, and going here and there to be entertained. They don't know what or why they seek, nor why they never realize complete happiness. By evading self-analysis, people become robots, conditioned by their environment. True self-analysis is the greatest art of progress."*

Knowing who we truly are and from which inner space we operate implies that we need a plan to live meaningfully and purposefully. To know what we want; we need to measure all possible dimensions qualitatively and quantitatively; i.e., experientially, and experimentally. In ancient times, this measurement was done by observation, sensory perception, and experience. For example, in contemporary times, we refer to the "bio-clock" as the experiential measures of an ideal time to wake up, rest, have meals, and much more. With the arrival of advanced science and technology, there is increased experimental scrutiny on time and how to optimize it. So measuring is always essential to continuously align with purpose, whether experiential or experimental.

Now the world has become goal-oriented, which is possible through data. We are obsessed with data and measurement. You cannot get justice without a traceable system as data evidence; we no longer trust people. Also, we know that not measuring and monitoring vital health parameters, including inner well-being, can make us vulnerable in life. If you intend to provide a quality service to your customer, it is important to monitor their complaints and interact with them to find solutions. One needs to invest resources in a profitable area or pull resources from an area that is performing poorly.

There are negative consequences of not measuring the performance of any process or system. Specifically, if we do not measure the performance, we do no better than guessing. Hence, we need to find out if our actions are profitable. Furthermore, we shall propagate mediocrity as we won't be able to anticipate, prevent or mitigate problems. If we can't agree on what success looks like, we can't objectively prioritize, and thus we suffer due to uncertainty and lack of self-efficacy.

For our meaning and holistic progress, measurement is not only required in the space of outer progress (Smartness); it is imperative to measure our inner progress (i.e., Sage-ness); till we transcend the need for goals and analysis. Knowing yourself allows you to establish your ideals, maintain personal boundaries, identify your strengths and shortcomings, and make realistic and wise judgments while being calm and empathic toward your peers. While awareness is knowing something, consciousness is being aware of the inner space from which the awareness is emerging. So, the intensity of awareness depends on the degree of consciousness or quality of the inner place. Humans are aware of our emotions, sensory patterns, and feelings.

Moreover, we are self-aware concerning our voluntary actions, as voluntary action happens consciously. In addition to these behaviors, we are also capable of involuntary behaviors that we are unaware of. So, measuring our consciousness will let us know who we truly are or from which inner space we are operating while responding to external stimuli and situations. This inner state of consciousness is nothing but a level of energy in vibration. Everything in life is vibration, as per Albert Einstein.

> Mr. Nikola Tesla said, *"If you want to find the secrets of the Universe, think in terms of energy, frequency, and vibration."*

In a study on human consciousness by Dr. David R. Hawkins, the measured levels of self (or being) are represented as the "conscious map." This model is in complete alignment and resonance with the structural model of self (the gross, astral, and causal) and essences or potentialities of self (*Sat*: existence, *Chit*: Intelligence, *Ananda*: experience).

Conscious Map: The Measure of your Inner-Space

Dr. Hawkins' most significant contribution to humanity was the development of Applied Kinesiology, a muscle-testing technique that can assess the degree of awareness of individuals. With the help of a unique muscle-testing technique, Dr. Hawkins conducted more than 250,000 calibrations over 20 years. His research was focused on defining a range of values, attitudes, and emotions that can help us comprehend the various levels of consciousness. Today, this range of values is known as the logarithmic scale that measures up to 1000 levels of consciousness - known as the **Map of Consciousness**. For the first time, he introduced this idea in his seminal work, **Power vs. Force**.

His research discovered that man's kinesiological response to a stimulus conveyed a capacity to differentiate positive from negative stimuli and the truth from falsity. According to him, the greatest weakness in humans is their inability to distinguish between truth and deception. He documented the non-linear spiritual realm on a level of consciousness (LOC) map. Although the statistics from his research are arbitrary, the map is scaled from 1 to 1000, something that our linear, left-brained thinking can understand. Because the scale is logarithmic, 200 is not twice the power of 100. Instead, each number is the tenth power. So, the number on the scale represents algorithmic calibration (measurable vibratory frequencies on a scale that increases in 10th power). This means that even a slight change in the scale can greatly impact the person and the group. Each **level of consciousness (LOC)** corresponds to observable human emotion, perspectives, or views on self or Life. Each level symbolizes a corresponding attractor field of diverse strengths that can exist beyond our three-dimensional world.

For example, if a man is operating or vibrating at 125 (desirous being) has the quality of the inner space as 'disappointing and enslavement,' i.e., the desirous being operates with a disappointed and enslaved mindset. Hence, they perceive their life situation and stimulus as 'denying.' Their primary emotion, behavior, or response is 'craving.' Here inner space is part of the causal body, perception is part of the astral body, and response is either the gross or astral body. If you heard someone is sick, there would be two kinds of response. If you just shared "get well soon," the response is astral. However, if you do a thoughtful action, the response will be part of the gross body. This is in complete alignment with the principle of *"Yat pinde tat brahmande"*; i.e., that is outside you is within you. Low-consciousness cultures and high-consciousness societies work in distinct ways. Higher awareness civilizations have less crime, homelessness, greater freedom, and more creative expression.

The levels of this scale go from 0 to 1000 for humans, and for non-physical beings, it can go beyond 1000. Humans do not exceed 1000 because the nervous system cannot handle that power level. As one's thoughts focus on higher ideals, these new ideas create strong, energetic fields, which Hawkins calls attractor fields. This is where the Law of Attraction is powerfully in action. Old thought forms and beliefs driven by force are transformed as new belief systems based on higher expanded consciousness. As more and more people focus their thoughts on higher levels of consciousness, larger and larger energetic fields are created, hence the higher manifestations.

This measurement method of **"Level of Consciousness" (LOC)** is not only applicable to human beings; hence it can be applied to ideas, life situations, philosophies, places, religions…

Once you master this measurement through experience, you can determine how much truth something has within it. For example, *"Hatha Yoga"* is calibrated at 250, *"Kundalini Yoga"* is calibrated at 500, and *"Karma Yoga"* is calibrated at 700. Considering the applicability of "level of consciousness" (LOC) for life situations as well, the practitioners of "laws of attraction" attempt to create a LOC for themself, resonating with the LOC for the life situation. For example, "qualifying in an interview" is a life situation that has a level of LOC, and someone to qualify the same need to elevate their LOC to that of "qualifying in an interview."

"Self" as Level of Consciousness (LOC)

The original work by Dr. Hawkins segmented the map into two, i.e., **linear** (up to reason, 400) and **nonlinear** (beyond reason, >400). This is based upon the Newtonian Paradigm worldview based on the principle of causality. Also, there is further segmentation of **ego-self** (LOC below courage, i.e., <200) and beyond ego or true-self (LOC of courage and above, with LOC 200 to 1000). Considering his segmentation, for the context of our discussion on levels of self, I have segmented the total LOC continuum into four by superimposing segmentation based on courage (200) and reason (400).

The ego-self (0-199 or <200) is further sub-segmented into **lowest-self** (0-100) and **lower self** (101-199). And the **real, true, or pure self** (401-1000) is further sub-segmented as **higher-self** (200-400) and **highest-self** (401-100). In this chapter, we will discuss the framework of four self(s), i.e., **lowest (L-), lower (L), higher (H), and highest (H+)**. In the subsequent chapter, we will discuss how the essences or potentialities of "self" (i.e., *Sat-Chit-Ananda*) evolve and function along four segments.

Any hacking action is always conscious and intense; however, it reveals the life-changing secret and creative intelligence behind an illusion. While hacking the outer world involves **logical and emotional intelligence (IQ & EQ)**, hacking the inner world needs **spiritual intelligence (SQ, i.e., knowing our existential self)**. Also, as we know, IQ & EQ are dominant in the ego-self, whereas SQ is dominant in the higher self. Hence you need to understand the quality of four levels of self and seventeen LOC or elements. Please invest your quality time (if required, in multiple slots) to have a grip on it. I assure you; it will make your reading experience of the remaining chapters thrilling and adventurous. You may also use the chart in this book to create your mental map.

Ego-Self (0-199) vs. True-Self (200-1000)

The false, virtual, or ego-self thrives on the emotions of survival. It pursues comfort and certainty either by avoiding pain or pursuing pleasure. In other words, it pursues Smartness by any means. These beings are identified and entangled by their aversion and craving. They are dominated by it (with vibrational-conscious energy, below courage 200) and consider outer purpose (i.e., Smartness) as the primary purpose in life. From this perspective, they see their life situation and others as objects as a means to personal survival and gain. They perceive life-situation as more powerful than their own life or self (i.e., level of consciousness of self), or they live with a fragile mindset. In this zone, the individual processes things first through the amygdala of the brain, which produces an emotional, visceral response before conscious cognitive processes. Stimulation of the amygdala causes intense emotion, such as anxiety, aggression, fear, anger, or pride. In other words, the ego-self is pathological.

As per Dr. Hawkins, around 78% of the world's population is below courage (200), i.e., ego self. Hence, one of this book's prime intentions is to move you to the vibrational frequency of courage (200) and beyond, i.e., toward your true self.

At the level of courage (200), a huge transition occurs in human consciousness where right-brain dominance reveals the rise in influence of spiritual energy, and a shift occurs where the person now relies on Power then Force. In other words, they feel more empowered by nature than by struggling alone. In this range, input goes directly to the prefrontal cortex and the emotional center rather than the amygdala. This influence creates progressive awareness and opens us to the energy of love. These levels also increasingly align with truth and reality. People at this level can objectify as "seers" and get misidentified or un-entangled from "seen"; their aversion and cravings in real-time. In other words, they are equanimous. Einstein, Freud, Newton, and Aristotle are the most famous geniuses of all time - all calibrated around 499. This level corresponds to the energy and vibration of the causal body; hence, people look for causal needs and satisfaction as per

Maslow's hierarchy, i.e., self-actualization. Hence, they thrive on an intrinsic sense of self rather than survival and pursue comfort and certainty by any means. Hence, they pursue to realize their potentialities or essences of self, Sat-Chit-Ananda (i.e., existence, Intelligence, experience). They perceive their life (or self) as more powerful than their life situation. In simple, these people consider inner purpose (i.e., Sage-ness) as the primary purpose in life. Also, they live in an antifragile and playful mindset.

To have a deeper comprehension of self, which is at the core of meaning and purpose, let's delve a bit deeper into every four sub-segments; (L-), (L), (H), and (H+). Here each LOC corresponds to a predominant attribute of self, which we refer to as an element. For example, the element of courage corresponds to a LOC of 200. Courage encompasses 200-degree *Sat-Chit-Ananda*. Each LOC has a different quality or disposition of inner space, perception towards self, and perception towards the world, including the other self. Accordingly, there is a variation in their intelligence, expression (i.e., behavior), and experience.

Hence, our true intentional behaviors (i.e., not managed or manipulated by the media) reflect or define our true selves. For example, if you aspire to be a loving being, give love, respect, trust, and so on. Also, what you think and tell of others doesn't define others; rather, it reflects or defines you, i.e., your "self." Hence each relationship we have with people represents different mirrors to show us our true selves.

Elements of Lowest Self (L-, 0 -100)

This sub-segment of self has five elements or attributes; shame, guilt, apathy, grief, and fear in increasing order of LOC. At these levels, people experience an emotional state that can drive them to resist or avoid the pain, which we call an aversive being. This level corresponds to the energy and vibration of the **gross body**. In other words, the self is identified with the **physical-self.** Hence, people look for a gross or physiological need and satisfaction per Maslow's first layer of hierarchy, i.e., down, food, physical safety, etc.

Shame (20): The quality or disposition of the inner space at this level is "**hateful and eliminative**"; i.e., a shameful being operates with hatefulness and an eliminative mindset. Hence, it perceives its life situation and stimulus as "**despising**." The primary emotion, behavior, or response is "**humiliation**." According to David Hawkins, shame is one step above death. Being so close to death, this is where most thoughts of suicide are found. Those who have experienced sexual abuse are often at this level. People operating at this level for long periods can become serial killers, rapists, and even moral extremists.

Guilt (30): The quality or disposition of the inner space at this level is "**evil and destructive**," i.e., a guilty being operates with an evil and destructive mindset. Hence, it perceives its life situation and stimulus as "**vindictive**." Its primary emotion, behavior, or response is "**blaming**." When one is stuck on this level, feelings of worthlessness and an inability to forgive oneself are common. This level cultivates destruction.

Apathy (50): The quality or disposition of the inner space at this level is "**hopelessness and abduction**." Hence, an apathetic being perceives life-situation and stimulus as "**condemning**," and its primary emotion, behavior, or response to life-situation is "**despair**." This is a common kind of consciousness found among people who are homeless, aged, diseased, or living in poverty. At this level, one has become resigned to their current situation and feels numb to life.

Grief (75): The quality or disposition of the inner space at this level is "**tragic & despondency**," i.e., a grieved being operates with tragic and a sad mindset. Hence, it perceives its life-situation and stimulus as "uncaring." Its primary emotion, behavior, or response is "regret." Many of us have felt this at moments of loss in our lives. Grief during the last pandemic (covid-19) was intense. Like any other state and emotion, some life situations may bring grief; however, having this as your primary level of consciousness will propel you to experience constant regret and remorse. This is where you feel you have missed all your opportunities. You ultimately feel you are a failure without a future.

Fear (100): The quality or disposition of the inner space at this level is "frightening and anxiety," i.e., a fearful being operates with a frightful and anxious mindset. Hence, it perceives its life situation and stimulus as "punitive, dangerous, and threatening," and its primary emotion, behavior, or response is "fear." People living under a dictatorship or with a previous history in an abusive relationship are at this level. Common fear at play in the professional world today is fear of rejection, fear of failure, fear of uncertainty, fear of challenges, and fear of loss, which disturbs mental health and inner well-being.

On this level of consciousness, people are constantly hyper-aroused and frequently remain there for extended periods. Pathological manifestations of fear include anxiety disorders, phobias, PTSD, social withdrawal, and even drug addiction. The physiological and emotional sensation of fear is unpleasant. Ironically, fear itself is frequently the thing we are most afraid of.

Elements of Lower Self (L, 101-199)

This sub-segment of self has three elements or attributes; desire, anger, and pride in increasing order of LOC. At these levels, people experience an emotional state that can drive them to crave more pleasure. This level corresponds to the energy and vibration of the **astral body**; i.e., this self or being is identified with the psychological self. Hence, people at this level are identified or attached to their **psychological-self** and hence look for astral needs and satisfaction as per Maslow's second layer of hierarchy, i.e., psychological safety, love, self-esteem, etc.

Desire (125): The quality or disposition of the inner space at this level is **"disappointing and enslavement,"** i.e., a desire minded being operates with a disappointed and enslaved mindset. Hence, it perceives its life situation and stimulus as **"denying"**. Also, the primary emotion, behavior, or response of the self or being is **"craving."** One begins to have desires as one moves out of apathy, fear, and grief. Much of our society is motivated by desire. Although desire can be a motivator for change, it can also lead to the enslavement of one's appetite. This is the level of addiction to things such as money, growth, prestige, power, and addictive substances. Hence this level of desire is always self-centric instead of eco-system-centric. In other words, desire is the imagination, visualization with expectation, attachment and entanglement with the outcome. Hence this kind of desire is insatiable. On the level of desire, we assume that the source of happiness and satisfaction solely depends on the certainty of extrinsic outcome or Smartness. Also, we hope a new car, property, or relationship will make us complete. And when we realize that one thing is not the answer to our fears, we go after another thing. Desire frequently causes pain because it breeds resentment, envy, and jealousy. The truth is that instead of desire, we can achieve our goals through Quest and willingness (300) to embrace the life situation, where an exception is without attachment.

Anger (150): The quality or disposition of the inner space at this level is **"antagonism and aggression,"** i.e., an angry being operates with an antagonistic and aggressive mindset. Hence, it perceives its life situation and stimulus as **"vengeful."** Its primary emotion, behavior, or response are **"hatred and revenge."** If desire (125) or expectation is left unfulfilled, it leads to frustration, leading to anger. For example, if you are desiring but not getting a promotion this year, you may get angry with your boss, depending on the level of your being. Also, you may go back to a level of grief (75) if your society starts commenting on you for not getting a promotion. An angry being tends to harbor resentment and is often irritable and oversensitive. Anger can then result in rage, temper problems, and intense dislike, which easily degrades the quality of a person's life. Occasionally, anger can manifest as harmful behavior and physical assault. In our relationships, this may be expressed as domestic abuse. A person harboring so much anger tries to get everything done with intimidation and dominant behavior. Behavior propelled by anger helps us lose sight of a problem and prevent the possibility of resolving them.

Pride (175): The quality or disposition of the inner space at this level is **"demand and inflation,"** i.e., a proud being operates with a demanding & inflated mindset." Hence, it perceives the life situation and stimulus as **"indifferent,"** and its primary emotion, behavior or response are **"scorning and arrogance."** For example, suppose you are desiring (125) and getting a promotion this year. In that case, you may become proud (175) of your performance, depending on the level of your being, and become arrogant towards non-performers. According to David Hawkins, this is the level that most people aspire to because most people are below this point. Compared to shame and guilt, one begins to feel positive here; however, it's a false positive, i.e., the good feeling comes from an inflated ego perspective, being better than someone else and looking down on others. It has an attachment to Smartness, i.e., to external conditions such as money, status, or power. It is often also the cause of racism, nationalism, self-righteousness and religious fanaticism, and war. People take pride in their material possessions and external conditions.

It is vulnerable because such conditions are transient and temporary. A person with a false self-esteem of pride is vulnerable and can be brought to the level of shame (20). Pride is divisive and can foster me versus you or us versus them mentality. Hence, they cannot embrace inclusion. You strongly identify with your beliefs and world perspective at this level. You take every criticism personally and consider an attack on your beliefs an attack on yourself. Hence, it is said that being with Pride (175) cannot stay as non-judgmental or neutral (250). It is a matter of fact that social media is running by serving pride to people, where people are glorifying their lower selves in all possible ways.

Ego-Self is the "Shadow or Robotic Self"

If you are attached to your gross and astral self (i.e., body and mind) means you have not touched your causal-body or causal-self. If you are not able to touch your causal-self, you are living as your ego-self (LOC<200). However, once you cross LOC > 200, another self, parallel to your ego-self emerges; which is called true-self. This true-self has the ability to objectify, observe and watch your own ego-self on a real time basis. Hence in the presence of true-self; the ego-self becomes a parallel shadow self (i.e., shadow Sat-Chit-Ananda). This means till LOC <200, your true-self does not exist and hence you exist only as your shadow self. If you exist only as shadow self (<200); your body and mind will get compulsively driven by a software with improper disposition; i.e., by bipolar impulses of aversion and craving. Hence, you become a robotic-self, which is not being driven or represented by your true-self. You live in fallacy or virtual-reality without having an existential meaning of life. In summary the shadow or robotic self has two sub-self; i.e., lowest or aversive shadow self (0-100) and lower or craving shadow self (101-199); which is incapable of holding intrinsic essence; i.e., true equanimity, love, joy, peace, bliss and meaning of life.

To be very frank, we have been cowardly (<200) to own our shadow self and transmute or repurpose its disposition to hold equanimity, love, joy, and peace. Once you hack and own it, you will realize no one or situation in this plant is pure evil except this shadow self. Everyone behaves badly because of improper disposition of their shadow self; which is under insecurities, uncertainty, and ambiguity. Hence this shadow self with pettiness deserves our ownership with compassion. This shadow is not just a source of darkness but also the source of power, creativity and personal growth and transformation; if it is hacked, embraced, transmuted, or repurposed. This can enable us to unleash our true potential; i.e., true Sat-Chit-Ananda. But the big question is how do we hack and deal with our shadow self?

When you are alone and do not have any work to do— just notice your mind's doing. Don't disturb it, don't prevent it, don't repress it;

don't judge it, don't do anything at all on your part. During this period there might be some unpleasant sensation, inconvenience, irritation, itching on your body (on surface or inside). Just be the watcher to the same as well. The miracle of this watching is meditation. As you watch, slowly the mind becomes empty of thoughts, body is with neutral sensation; but you are not falling asleep, you are becoming more alert, more aware. You have become your true self beyond the entanglement of body-mind and with the ability to objectify, hack and watch your shadow self.

Elements of Higher Self (H, 200- 400):

Higher-self is identified with our **causal-body** and has five elements or attributes; courage, neutrality, willingness, acceptance, and reason in increasing order of LOC. Hence it is called as unanimous true self.

Courage (200): The quality or disposition of the inner space at this level is **"feasibility and empowerment,"** i.e., a courageous being operates with a feasible and empowered mindset. Hence, it perceives its life situation and stimulus as permitting, and its primary emotion, behavior, or response is affirmative. It is where our biggest shift happens. Also known as the stage of integrity, 200 is where we start discerning truth from falsehood, essence from ego. You dare to renounce your, and your growth is not dependent on pain, pleasure, and desire. Courage is the doorway to your higher self, where you may not be free of negative emotions but has the tools to deal with them healthily. This is the first level in which you are not compulsively absorbing life energy from cowardice or situations around you; rather, you are emitting life energy towards cowardice being life-situation and transforming it towards growth, glory, and grace. Hence courage is the realization that you do not need to be emotionally reactive to your external circumstances.

This empowerment teaches you that you are solely responsible for your growth and success. Realizing that there is a gap between stimulus and response and that you can choose how to respond makes you inherently human. The tipping point is the line between force and real power. The life view is feasible, and anything is manageable since the person can harness the power to deal with situations in life. You are confident in your ability to overcome obstacles. Challenges that would have defeated you at lower levels are stimulating at higher levels. On the individual level, courage is characterized by brevity, and on the social level, by standing out.

Unlike physical courage or brevity, here courage refers to courage of morality and beyond; where one stands assertively and confidently for truth and welfare beyond-self. For example, the courage demonstrated by Mr. Sam Manekshaw; the chief of the Army Staff of the Indian Army during the Indo-Pakistani War of 1971. He was the man who stood against the rest of the cabinet; who were very powerful and compulsive, to stop the Indo-Pak war in April 1971 for the unpreparedness of the Indian army at that moment and hence its anticipated higher impact on the economy of the country. Good thing is he finally convinced the then prime-minister Ms. Indira Gandhi assertively and confidently. Then all precautions and preparations happened before the war. This type of courage is the doorway to become Smart-Sage and live a vibrant and high-resolution life.

Neutrality (250): The quality or disposition of the inner space at this level is **"satisfaction and release,"** i.e., a neutral being operates with a satisfactory mindset. Hence, it perceives its life situation and stimulus as enabling, and its primary emotion, behavior, or response is trust. Neutrality is the level of flexibility. To be neutral, you are primarily unattached to outcomes (125) and pride (175). At this level, the emotion is trust and safety. People here are non-judgmental, objective, and able to see things for what they truly are. They aren't attached to things, situations, or outcomes and can roll with the punches in life. They are equally content with settling for something else if they cannot obtain something. On the individual level, neutrality is characterized by unanimous, unbiased, and integrity; at the level of society, it is characterized by justice.

Willingness (310): The quality or disposition of the inner space at this level is **"feasibility, empowerment and curiosity,"** i.e., a willingly being operates with a feasible, probable, possible, empowered, and curious mindset. Here, curiosity refers to curiosity about possibilities in cause-and-effect equations in nature within reality. Hence, it perceives its life situation and stimulus as permitting, and its primary emotion, behavior, or response is affirmative. This is the state of mind of perpetual optimists who see life as a strong possibility rather than conclusive certainty. Unlike desire (125), this state leads to a quest, which is imagination without attachment or entanglement. Here one no longer remains stagnant with complacency and is willing to embrace any challenge or risk with containment.

At willingness, the individual is open to doing anything and everything, which we call will-power. They are not constrained by the opinions of others or by limitations. At this level, one is committed to participating in life, tasks become playful, and effort becomes effortless. They are willing to fight inner issues, tend to become self-correcting, and learn from others. At this level, you have people who have willpower and perform exceptionally well in their careers in corporations and start-ups. On the individual level, willingness is characterized by emotional agility and playfulness, and on the social level, inclusiveness, or equality.

Acceptance (350): The quality or disposition of the inner space at this level is **"harmony, inclusivity,"** i.e., a harmonious or inclusive being operates with a harmonious and transcending mindset. Hence, it perceives its life situation and stimulus as merciful, and its primary emotion, behavior, or response is forgiveness. Here is where you become the creator of your life's experiences consciously. At this level, you begin to accept complete responsibility for your life. You recognize that you are the source and creator of your life experience. Here, you reclaim your power and realize that happiness and love are created within yourself and not obtained from outside sources; you can distinguish between your inner and outer purpose (i.e., Sage-ness and Smartness) to prioritize the response and live a meaningful life. Your perception is less distorted from reality, and you begin to see the bigger picture. Only at this level do people start enthusiastically accepting and embracing their KARMA (stimulus and life situation). As embracing dissolves entanglement and bring-up involvement, there is no friction, hurt, regret, or remorse. In other words, it brings flow, freedom, meaning, and fulfillment in life. Hence, on the individual level, acceptance is characterized by emotional calm and mastery, and on the social level, by inclusion. Hence all philosophy advocates acceptance as a pre-requisite for inner-wellbeing (Sage-ness).

Reason (400): The quality or disposition of the inner space at this level is "meaning and abstraction," i.e., a rational being operates with a meaningful and abstract mindset. Hence, it perceives their life situation and stimulus as an agency of wisdom, and their primary emotion, behavior, or response is understanding and rationality, even beyond conscience. The real search for meaning starts at the level of courage; the meaning is discovered here. Newton perceived the incident of an apple falling as a source of wisdom. Hence, he could discover the principle of gravity and the meaning of life. This is the level of science, medicine, philosophy, and a quest for knowledge. You don't waste time on activities that aren't intellectually stimulating. You start categorizing life's experiences as proofs, postulates, and theories. Before reaching conclusions, one gathers vast amounts of data and analyses it in minute detail. Over-intellectualization of reason leads to the process of abstraction or preoccupation with data. At this level, one uses their abilities and talents to make meaningful contributions to the world. On the individual level, the reason is characterized by intelligence and emotional transcendence, and on the social level, by rationalism.

Before moving to our discussion on highest- self (H+); let's observe the instance of higher being emanating from Mr. Ratan Tata; a business leader, philanthropist, and the winner of two civilian awards in India- Padma Bhushan and Padma Vibhushan. His contribution to business and humanity is immense. Under his leadership, Tata Motors launched India's first fully designed and built indigenous car, the Tata Indica, in 1998. However, sales were poor, and Tata was forced to sell the car manufacturing unit. In 1999, they decided to negotiate a deal with the American automaker Ford. Ratan Tata and his team flew to the United States and met with Bill Ford, the then-chairman of Ford. Bill Ford made derogatory remarks such as, "Why did Tata get into manufacturing without knowing anything about car production?" Ford stated that if he purchases a Tata car unit, he will do Tata a favor; they still need to reach an agreement. Mr. Ratan Tata accepted (350) his life situation as it came. Then it's only his courage (200) to embrace the mortifying experience lead situation with greater focus, emotional calmness, and playfulness. He demonstrated the Sage-ness in him. He made the decision not to sell the production unit. What happened next is one of the best failure-turned-success stories in business history. After nine years, the United States experienced a recession, and Ford went bankrupt.

Tata stepped in and offered to purchase Jaguar and Land Rover (JLR) for $2.3 billion cash. And Ford said that "Tata did a favor for Ford by buying JLR." It is definitely an act of neutrality from Mr. Ratan Tata against his mortifying experience; he requested Ford to buy Tata Motor at the time of its crisis. Under his leadership, Tata transformed JLR into one of the industry's most profitable automakers. Tata stepped into the global motor industry from there and has since become a world player in the automotive industry, thanks to his leadership, willingness, and optimism. The joint ventures with Brazil's Marco Polo buses, South Korea's Daewoo trucks, Fiat Chrysler, Hitachi Heavy Machinery, and an aerospace and defense division. His Smartness continued till today.

He showed the world how human attributes like courage, neutrality, willingness, acceptance, and reason could turn a challenge into outer success with inner satisfaction and bring abundance with authenticity. Now he is playful his busy making meaningful contributions to the world with his resources, talent, and grace. His reason behind the meaning of life is "making a difference," not only at the level of Smartness but also at the level of Sage-ness. Hats off to the Smart-Sage.

Elements of Highest Self (H+, 401-1000):

Highest-self is identified with our **great-causal-body** and has four elements or attributes; love, joy, peace, and enlightenment in increasing order of LOC. For people at this level consider the outer-purpose (smartness) is the same as inner purpose (i.e., Sage-ness). Hence this self is also called oneness-true-self... Only 4 percent of the world's population can reach the level of 500, and 0.4 percent reach the level of 540.

Love (500): The quality or disposition of the inner space at this level is "**benign and revelation**," i.e., a loving operates with a benign and revelation mindset. Hence, it perceives its life situation and stimulus as loving, and its primary emotion, behavior, or response is reverence.

This is where you begin to apply what you learned in your reasoning and allow your heart to take over rather than your mind - you live by intuition. For example, non-violence was the reason behind the meaning of life for Gandhi, whereas selfless service was for Mother Theresa. This is the level of charity - selfless love with no desire other than the well-being of those around them. Love does not depend upon external factors and is forgiving, nurturing, and supportive. It does not come from the mind but instead radiates from the heart. This intuition opens the way to benevolence, mercy, and forgiveness. Hawkins claims only 0.4% of the population (1 in every 250 people) ever reach this level. One person at this level counterbalances 750,000 people below 200.

Once in the 1970s, Ratan Tata traveled to Nashik in a car with his team of Managers. The car had a flat tire halfway through the journey, and as the driver pulled up, the occupants -including Mr. Tata - got out for a small break, leaving the driver to replace the tire. Some managers were happy to have a small break because it gave them a much-needed opportunity to smoke. Some took advantage of the opportunity to stretch, smile, and crack a joke. Then one of them noticed that Mr. Tata was nowhere to be found and wondered aloud where Ratan Tata had gone. Was he hiding behind a bush? Had he gone into the roadside Dhaba for a quick cup of tea? Or was he conversing with passers-by and listening to their stories? The answer was none; Ratan Tata was busy helping the driver with love (500) to change tires while his colleagues were taking a break. With his sleeves rolled up, tie swatted away over the shoulder, hands expertly working the jack and spanner, bouncing the spare tire to ensure proper pressure. Droplets of sweat on the brow and a smile on the face. Hats off to his merciful love (500) for another self and benevolence. His love (500) and compassion are not limited to human beings. Once, he decided not to receive the lifetime achievement award personally in London, organized by Prince Charles, as one of his pet dogs (Tango and Titto) was sick. Salute to his authentic love. Many people think authenticity restricts abundance. However, his life continuously disapproves of the same. Hats off to Smart-Sage.

Joy (540): The quality or disposition of the inner space at this level is **"complete,"** i.e., the self, at this level, operates with a completeness mindset. Hence, they perceive their life situation and stimulus as oneness, and their primary emotion, behavior, or response is serenity. As love becomes more unconditional, true happiness becomes a constant companion. No personal tragedy or global event could ever shake someone at this level of awareness. They appear to inspire and uplift all who come into contact with them. Your life is completely in sync with the will of Divinity, and the fruits of that sync manifest in your joy as synchronicity and miracle. Nothing disturbs the inner joy (540) of Mr. Ratan Tata. You might know how calm and courageous he was when Hotel Taj in Mumbai was under a terrorist attack. Also, he is always humble, even when he receives awards of the highest order. While he speaks very less, his inner joy inspires all genres. He is truly a corporate sage.

Peace (600): The quality or disposition of the inner space at this level is **"perfection and illumination,"** i.e., a peaceful being operates with a perfect and illuminated mindset. Hence, it perceives its life situation and stimulus as divine, and its primary emotion, behavior, or response is bliss. Peace comes after a life of total surrender to the creator. It is the point at which you have transcended everything and entered what Hawkins calls illumination. Here, mental stillness and silence are attained, allowing for constant revelation. Only one in every ten million people reaches this level. This level is associated with transcendence and self-realization. An individual at this level counterbalances the aversion and cravings of 10 million people below courage (200).

Enlightenment (700- 1000): The quality or disposition of the inner space at this level is **"purity,"** i.e., the self, at this level, operates with no mind. Hence, they perceive their life situation and stimulus as consciousness, and their primary emotion, behavior, or response is ineffable. This is the highest level of human consciousness, and here one has become like cosmic consciousness (divine). Many see this as Christ, Buddha, or Krishna. According to Hawkins, in 1995, when he wrote Power vs. Force, there were 31 sages on the planet calibrating at this level.

Only a True-Self Can Stay Untangled From a Shadow Self

It is important to observe when the consciousness, vibration, and energy of inner-space increases the ego or shadow reduces. In other words, when the LOC <200, only the shadow self exists with aversion and craving. When it moves to the LOC range of 200-400, both shadow and true self co-exist. Finally, when the LOC range becomes 401-1000, gradually shadow merges or becomes one with true-self.

Also, the consciousness, vibration, and energy of inner space vary with time and life situations; it is not constant at all points of time in life. Suppose you were expecting your promotion last week, but it got delayed, putting you in fear of failure, and then you became angry today with your boss as you did not get it. So, your inner space moved from desire (125) to fear (100) and then to anger (150) within a week. Suppose you plan to attend a motivational session tomorrow morning, then your inner space will move to courage (200) or willingness (310).

Additionally, suppose you know tomorrow evening that your daughter became a national topper in a talent hunt; your inner space will move to pride (175). While these variations cannot be avoided for low-level self, it is possible to get misidentified because of this at high-level consciousness. A higher element can objectify a lower element. We have discussed objectification, entanglement, and involvement in the previous chapter; by articulating how butter gets dis-identified from the subjectivity of milk through the objectification process. Also, we discussed that the astral body gets misidentified from the subjectivity of the gross body.

Similarly, the high-conscious element can objectify the low-conscious elements. For example, pride (175) can objectify fear (105), or pride can get misidentified from fear, while it can get involved with fear. Here the fear can be within one's own shadow self or that of another individual. To understand this further, let's visualize an auditorium with four levels of seats and call the uppermost level as "highest self,"; the lowermost level as "lowest self," and the other two as "higher self" and "lower self" in descending order. In this setup, the audience in the upper-most level can see the audience in the other three levels. To translate this concept into the context of self, a person operating from higher-self will be able to perceive the emotional content and possible response of a person operating below the higher self (i.e., lower self and lowest self). Again, here the person can be their self or other self. In other words, a higher self can get misidentified from their lower-level thought, emotion, cognition, imagination, feeling, sensation, stimuli, and responses; in real-time. In general, a high-conscious self is always misidentified or disentangled from lower consciousness; but there is involvement on a need basis. The highly conscious self can also objectify the lower conscious self. Hence, the higher conscious self is free from suffering related to lower consciousness. For example, a low-conscious doctor will find it difficult to operate on his child's body, and he is attached (<200) to his child.

Dimensions of Self in Summary

While the self is comprehended in various dimensions or paradigms, this book mainly deals with three. **Firstly,** the dimension, paradigm, or continuum of density, where the causal, astral (or shuttle), and gross (physiological) selves co-exist in layers from low to high density, respectively, i.e., from metaphysical to psychological to physical. All these three selves constantly change through the transmutation (or repurposing) of energy. The **second dimension** is a continuum of changeless to changing. The changeless self is also referred to as "seer" of shadow self and the changing self as "seen" as shadow self. "Seer" is the "observer" as a witness without any judgment, and "seen" is the "observed." While the "seer & seen" is the most spoken and generic reference for this dimension, there are also different referenced names for all three essences (or potentialities) of Self. To be specific, in the context of intelligence (Chit) and experience (Ananda), it is also referred to as "knower & known," and in the context of existence and expression (Sat), it is referred to as "un-manifested and manifested." Scientifically, this un-manifested is the quantum-field and manifested is all the forms and phenomena happening in time and space. While the "seer," "knower", "observer," and "un-manifested" represents true-self *(Sat chit Ananda)*, the "seen", "known", "observed" and "manifested" represents shadow self. Hence, it is also very important to note a difference shere that the "seer, "knower," "observer," and "un-manifested" derive their sense of self beyond body - mind, i.e., from an intrinsic and causal dimension.

When we engage ourselves in the world to move towards "seer" we call it an inner journey. However, if we engage yourself in the world to move away from "seer" is called an outer journey. Hence the **third dimension** is a continuum of inner to outer. In other words, the inner dimension deals with causal self, whereas the outer-dimension deals with gross and astral self. **Fourthly,** the dimension or paradigm of vibrational conscious energy or Level of Consciousness (LOC) decreases with increases in the density of self; i.e., the gross body vibrates at lesser LOC than an astral body. Per the consciousness map, the peak LOC in time-space is "1000". All dimensions or paradigms in time and space merge at LOC= 1000 or Buddha-self. This LOC represents an ultimate neural pattern and brain wave having potentialities for peak existence or expression, intelligence, and experience (*Sat-Chit-Ananda*). Hence, if you take any point or particle in any of the above dimensions in time-space, it always reverberates with three essences; existence and expression (*Sat*), intelligence (*Chit*), and experience (*Ananda*) in different degrees of vibrancy from 0 to 1000. That is why it is said, divinity is not derived from heaven but an evaluation of a being, e.g., a human being. It will be extremely important and helpful for you to comprehend these paradigms to hack and master your "shadow self."

Paradox of Desire and Quest at work

Comprehending self only in terms of body and mind is gross ignorance and limited perception. This creates a false sense of self, growth, transformation, and satisfaction. Hence, from the outside, most top performers look to be operating from a higher self; however, they operate from a lower self (<200) in their inner space. In other words, from the outside, these performers are high achievers, highly social, take the initiative proactively, are loyal beyond belief, have attention to detail, have relentless determination, pointed focus, and passion. However, from the inside, they are operating with problems sleeping, constant worry, overthinking, and people pleasing, negative and repeated self-talk, and fear of failure. They are in constant anxiety. This is because their desire in inner space drives achievement; instead of Quest and curiosity about possibilities in the cause-and-effect equation within reality. Let's consider an analogy to understand the paradox of desire and quest.

In two scenarios, foods are tasty. Firstly, when your stomach is empty, and you are hungry for food. In this case, you will not look for many options; even simple food will give you a sense of satisfaction. This scenario will not make you addicted; i.e., you will enjoy your meal with joy and grace. This generally happens to people who are not much worried about what is there in their next meal even if they have imagination of many options in their kitchen, i.e., people with monks-mindset. These categories of people are extremely open to new possibilities, antifragile and playful. Hence, whenever they encounter any sense-pleasing element in food (i.e., taste to the tongue, aroma or flavor for the nose, presentable to the eye); they are full of joyful gratitude, appreciation, and contentment with the present moment.

Secondly, foods are tasty when you are not so hungry, but the food is appealing or pleasant to the senses (i.e., taste to the tongue, aroma or flavor for the nose, presentable to the eye). Most of the food industry is running to fulfill the craving of these categories of people. When the sense-pleasing elements are not enough, people start to imagine adding alcohol and nicotine content. Also, they become attached to their imagination. This scenario makes you addicted. These categories of people are extremely choosy, judgmental, and not open to new possibilities. Hence, they live fragile and serious lives. Hence, even if they encounter any sense pleasing element, they demand the next demand for a more pleasing element and are not discontent with the present moment.

In both above cases, there is involvement of imagination, visualization, or fantasy and hence dopamine release happens to motivate you, drive you and make you happy. However, there is one finer difference that creates and solves the paradox of desire vs. quest. In one case, imagination, visualization, or fantasy is accompanied with expectation and attachment; i.e., there will be pride if the outcome is positive and anger if the outcome is negative. Also, there will be an element of fear of uncertainty throughout the endeavor. However, in other cases, imagination, visualization, or fantasy has no expectation and attachment but curiosity and enthusiasm on art of possibilities. In other words, in one case imagination and visualization are conscious, but in another case it is compulsive.

One makes you addicted and fragile, but the other makes you free and playful. The same is the case for desire vs. quest. While the dopamine of desire is based on addiction or attachment to results, a quest is based upon curiosity and enthusiasm for new possibilities like a child. In summary, desire is the imagination or fantasy with expectation and attachment, hence it binds you to anger, pride and suffering. However, the quest is imagination or fantasy without expectation, attachment and frees you with fearlessness, playfulness, and being antifragile. A quest is based on passion, and desire is based on obsession. The Japanese principle *Ikigai* also communicates the same very beautifully.

This is what Sri Krishna said to Arjun in Bhagvat Gita (2.47); "*कर्मण्येवाधिकारस्ते मा फलेषु कदाचन,*" which means; "*do your action without attachment to result of the action.*"

Buddha also said; "*desire is the cause of sorrow.*"

To prevent attachment and live on a quest, we must look carefully at whether our effort in every of our endeavor is motivated by real hunger for meaning and existential purpose in life or by a hunger for the sake of pleasing our mind, ego, and senses, i.e., wealth, position, power, comparison, name, fame and so on. It is also important to note that while you are pursuing your primary product of meaning and existential purpose in life, no one will take away your by-product of material success (i.e., wealth, position, power, name, fame). All will be available to you by the law of nature. The only point is you should not derive your sense of self from these by-products and focus only on the product.

Quantitatively, let's be aware that desire is the aspect of the lower self (<200), and hence it pulls them to the lowest self (fear and anxiety, <200). In contrast, quest, willingness, and curiosity are the aspects of the higher self (200 – 499). This top performer juggles around the energy level of 75 to 199 for their whole professional life, which can ruin their mental health and inner well-being. This phenomenon is called toxic positivity. If this describes you, it's time to shift to your higher self and operate with a quest, willingness, with curiosity. Showing true emotions (i.e., inner emotion) at work, especially the more complicated ones, still seems inconceivable for many professionals. Some fear losing face or authority, while others think they'll be perceived as soft or weak. This is simply show-up and just fake. For many of us, "toxic positivity" is still the default culture that outlines how we show up, manage and lead. This showing-up and faking will continue until we develop our intelligence, process it experientially, and express it (i.e., respond, manage, and lead). Our situation may look glorified, but our lives will be miserable.

Once, I was in a zoo near my house. I saw a grand tiger in a cage chased by a small cat outside the cell. At that moment, I realized that when trapped, even a mighty tiger with the potential to chase anyone away by its mere glance becomes helpless and overwhelmed by a tiny cat. While this tiger was in a metal cage, human beings often, if not always, stayed inside a mental - imaginary cage; built with grief, fears, self-doubt, lack of confidence, low self-esteem, guilt, overthinking, anger, pride, etc. Hence unless you know the potential of "self," the suffering will continue.

Before we explore the essences and potentialities of self, Sat-Chit-Ananda (existence to expression, intelligence, experience), you may like to assess the current state of your own self (or life) quantitatively in terms of your dominant LOC.

Assess Your LOC, With NETI Questionnaire

At your leisure, spend some time to know your dominant LOC. I recommend you repeat this every six to twelve months to measure your progress. Please specify how frequently the following events occur to you. Only one answer should be circled (note: scores are reversed for questions 4, 8, 14, and 16): While responding, try to be at your true inner space from where you operate daily without showing up, faking, or displaying positive toxicity. Per my practice and observation, the following is the rough assessment guideline. If you were always operating from the zone of highest self; you would score 100, and if you were never operating from the zone of highest self; you would score 20. Both are rare extreme cases. If you score around 40, you are operating in the lowest self, 60 in the lower self, 80 from the higher self.

1. Never
2. Rarely
3. Sometimes
4. Most of the time
5. All of the time

1. An inner contentment that is not dependent on circumstances, objects, or the actions of others.

1) Never
2) Rarely
3) Sometimes
4) Most of the time
5) All of the time

2. Accepting (rather than fighting) whatever sensation I am experiencing.

1) Never
2) Rarely
3) Sometimes
4) Most of the time
5) All of the time

3. Rather than feeling a certain way, an interest in clearly perceiving the reality or truth about myself, the world, and others.

1) Never
2) Rarely
3) Sometimes
4) Most of the time
5) All of the time

4. A notion that I am defending or defending a self-image or concept that I hold dear.

1) Never
2) Rarely
3) Sometimes
4) Most of the time
5) All of the time

5. Deep love and appreciation for everything I encounter.

1) Never
2) Rarely
3) Sometimes
4) Most of the time
5) All of the time

6. Recognizing that there is ultimately no distinction between what I term my "self" and the entirety of existence.

1) Never
2) Rarely
3) Sometimes
4) Most of the time
5) All of the time

7. I'm feeling completely at peace, no matter where I am or what circumstances I'm in.

1) Never
2) Rarely
3) Sometimes
4) Most of the time
5) All of the time

8. A feeling that my behaviors are motivated by fear or mistrust.

1) Never
2) Rarely
3) Sometimes
4) Most of the time
5) All of the time

9. Conscious realization of my intrinsic oneness with a transcendent reality, source, higher force, or God.

1) Never
2) Rarely
3) Sometimes
4) Most of the time
5) All of the time

10. Not having a personal stake in or attachment to my thoughts and concepts.

1) Never
2) Rarely
3) Sometimes
4) Most of the time
5) All of the time

11. Even in the midst of action and noise, an unwavering sense of stillness/quietness.

1) Never
2) Rarely
3) Sometimes
4) Most of the time
5) All of the time

12. Acting without assigning myself or others a role or identity.

1) Never
2) Rarely
3) Sometimes
4) Most of the time
5) All of the time

13. In my present experience, I have a sense of great freedom and opportunity.

1) Never
2) Rarely
3) Sometimes
4) Most of the time
5) All of the time

14. A desire for others to understand you.

1) Never
2) Rarely
3) Sometimes
4) Most of the time
5) All of the time

15. Concern or apprehension about your past or the future that is to come.

1) Never
2) Rarely
3) Sometimes
4) Most of the time
5) All of the time

16. Fear or worry that prevents me from taking decisions.

1) Never
2) Rarely
3) Sometimes
4) Most of the time
5) All of the time

17. A strong sense of aliveness and vigour.

1) Never
2) Rarely
3) Sometimes
4) Most of the time
5) All of the time

18. Acting with no intention of changing anyone or anything.

1) Never
2) Rarely
3) Sometimes
4) Most of the time
5) All of the time

19. Feelings of gratitude and open curiosity about all experiences.

1) Never
2) Rarely
3) Sometimes
4) Most of the time
5) All of the time

20. A sense of the flawlessness and beauty of everything and everyone, just as they are.

SMART SAGE

1) Never
2) Rarely
3) Sometimes
4) Most of the time.
5) All of the time

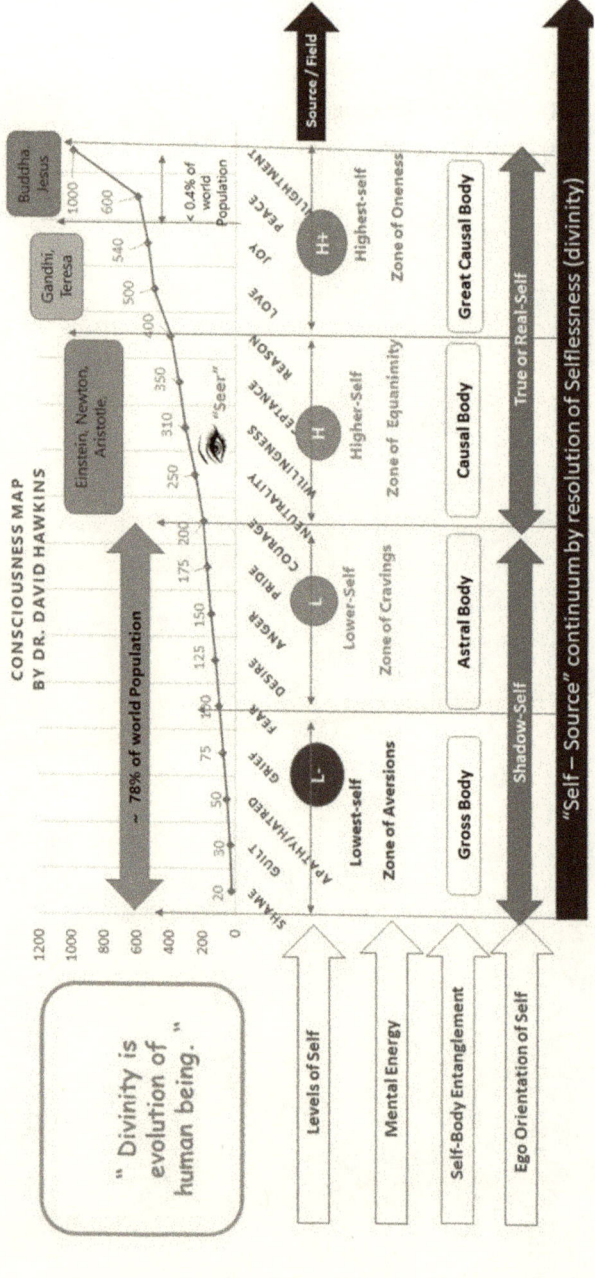

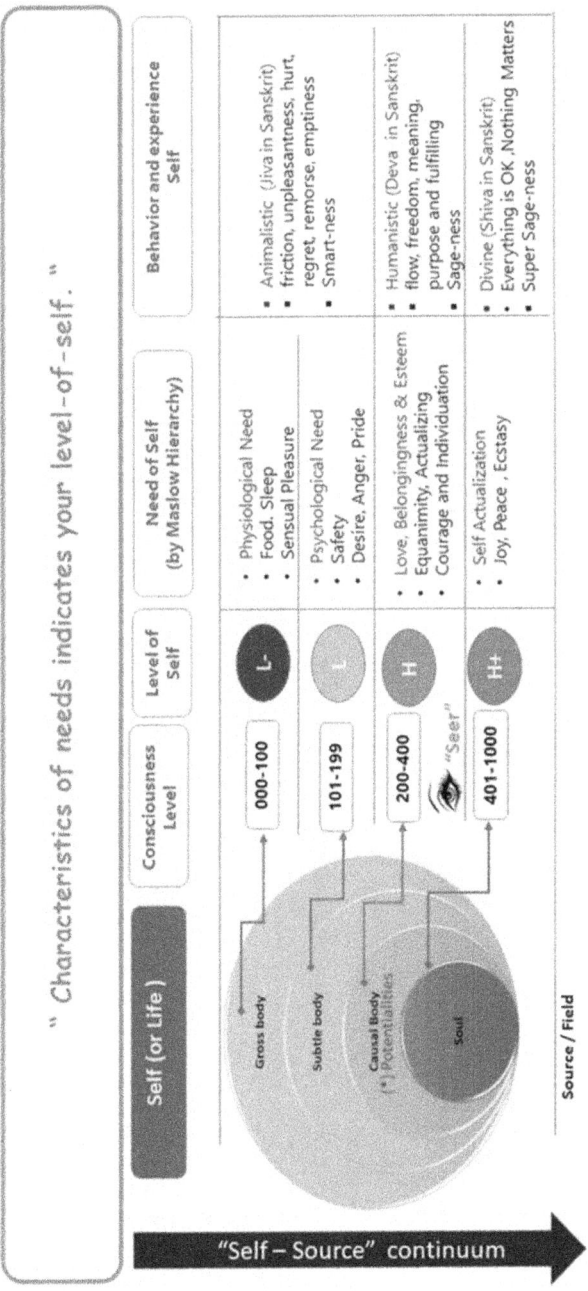

PART II: POTENTIAL

4

INTELLIGENCE
High-Resolution Intelligence Comes Beyond Courage

"The difference between intelligence and education is this- intelligence will make you a good living."
—Charles F. Kettering.

An elderly father and businessman desired to leave his whole estate to one among his three truly intelligent sons, but he was unsure which one. He handed each of them a few dollars and instructed them to go out and buy something to fill their living room. The first guy spent all and purchased straw, but they needed more to fill the chamber, and he was extremely anxious about the result. The second son also spent all the money and purchased several sticks, but they needed to be more adequate to fill the space. The third son bought a small candle and a pack of matches. The light from the candle illuminated the entire room. He leveraged the remaining for the welfare of all workers for their estate and was in his joy without much worrying about the result. After an assessment, the third son received the whole estate due to his true intelligence satisfying the logical condition of this father's instruction and inner intent. As Osho, an Indian philosopher, says, "*The intelligent person will go inward first. Before going anywhere else, you will go into your being. That is the first thing, and it should have the first preference. Only when you have known yourself can you go anywhere else? Then wherever you go, you will carry blissfulness around you, a peace, a silence, a celebration.*" Hence, we can also say that the third son could go inward and put the knowledge into the context of optimal value creation; i.e., his inner space touched the CHIT essence of self.

CHIT: The Awareness, Consciousness, and Intelligence

Let's take another analogy to comprehend the distinction between awareness and consciousness. During daytime, you can see all the objects in the room. Considering that there is a power cut at night; still, you can locate the object with some difficulties due to your awareness, but you will need more time to handle it. However, you can do it again efficiently if you put the torchlight on it. You will be able to handle efficiently those objects on which your touch light is focused. The way light helps you to handle objects efficiently in the material world, consciousness helps you to handle the self efficiently. You as "seer" will be able to objectify your "shadow self as seen" For example, an angry person (150) can only control his anger when his "self" or innermost space vibrates with higher consciousness than anger (>150). This can also be applied to your anger; i.e., when your "self" has higher consciousness than anger (>150), you will be able to recognize your inner stimulus of anger as a "seer" and handle it accordingly. In other words, your "self," or life, is not identified or not entangled with your anger. Here your innermost space is the "seer" and your anger is an object of observation (or "seen"). It's like the two birds in the tree, one is eating, and the other is observing.

When you as the "self" is not-entangled or not- identified with a piece of knowledge (as seen) and can handle the same consciously or voluntarily, you can call that knowledge in your consciousness as intelligence; else, it will be just in your awareness. All awareness within consciousness is intelligence; however, due to our accumulated ignorance, we can only realize intelligence as a subset of awareness. This is similar to; if there is a dark black spot on the transparent surface of touch light; it will again make a subset of the lighted area dark, and you lose your ability to handle it consciously or voluntarily. Ignorance is impure impressions in the outer self-accumulated from the past, which are also the nutrients for the shadow self. Hence when the intellect is in partnership with ego, the intelligence (*Chit*) is limited, and therefore the experience (*Ananda*) and expression (*Sat*) as well get limited. Hence ignorance differentiates intellectuals from intelligent. We will discuss in detail about ignorance in subsequent chapters.

Hence, while you know many things, you are conscious of only limited things. For example, while many people are aware that "love" is appreciative involvement in life-situation, they unconsciously pursue, act or respond to life-situation with possessive entanglement, which is limited to "like". In simple, while they are aware of love (500), they cannot vibrate at that energy and restrict themselves to "like" with possessiveness and desire (125). This happens because of our ignorance. Hence, if you can expand your consciousness, you can leverage all knowledge in your awareness as intelligence and handle more stuff consciously and voluntarily with involvement without entanglement, i.e., with flow, freedom, meaning, and fulfillment. In other words, your intellect can inspire your "mind" to leverage higher intelligence. Now let's try to understand how intellect operates across LOC, self(s), three bodies (gross, astral, and causal), and its preference towards life's purpose: the inner and outer.

Process of Judgement and Purpose of Life

As per Vedic science, there are four faculties of self in the judgment process or process of making a choice. They are **Manas, Chitta, Buddhi, and Ahankara**. Out of four, *Chitta* resides in the causal body, or inner self, and the rest reside in the astral body, which is part of the outer self, whereas *Manas* is the outer intelligence in the form of memory; *Chitta* is the inner or higher intelligence; which has a linkage to comic intelligence. The third element is *Buddhi*, the cognitive and judging faculty in the astral layer. The final and fourth element is *Ahankara*; which is composed of preferences and perception of the shadow self, which pulls the self to remain below courage (<200). Also, this prevents cognition from becoming meta-cognition.

To map these four elements into psychology, **Manas is the mind (conscious and subconscious mind); *Chitta* is the unconscious mind; *Buddhi* is the intellect; *Ahankara* is the ego**. The word unconscious is used differently in psychology, philosophy, and medicine. In psychology and philosophy, it refers to the memory and intelligence inaccessible to the conscious mind; due to ignorance or low vibrational energy of self. However, in the medical world, it refers to zero consciousness (i.e., coma). Let's understand how these four elements play together for a choice or judgment.

Manas: This is intelligence based on memory and imagination of a manifested world. Hence this intelligence is subjective intelligence and limited to cognition. *Manas* is the primary operating organ that creates visual, auditory, and gustatory perceptions leveraging the senses. For example, you would put a few grains of sugar on a sleeping man's tongue, it will not cause him to taste it because his *Manas* (mind) is disconnected from the tongue during sleeping. After creating perception, it imprints the memory bank of the subconscious and unconscious mind. *Manas* also is in charge of the sense and movement organs; i.e., it directs the senses to take action or respond to life-situation; after receiving the judgment is done by intellect (*Buddhi*).

Chitta: It is the objective intelligence of self, without memory and imagination of the identified self from the world. Hence this intelligence leads to meta-cognition with cosmic order. While the mind is off during sleep, *Chitta* is always on whether you are awake or asleep. All bodily functions leverage this intelligence. Only the "seer of shadow self" has access to this intelligence; i.e., the identified self or shadow self has no access to *Chitta*.

Buddhi: It is the faculty in charge of discriminating, judging, and deciding with the analytics, insights, and intelligence from *Manas* (memory and imagination), *Ahankara* or ego (personal preference including tendencies), and *Chitta* (cosmic order of intelligence). The objective intelligence of *Chitta* is available or accessible only when the "seer of shadow self" emerges. In other words, *Buddhi* chooses and directs *Manas* to respond based on cognition or meta-cognition. Hence our final response to a life situation depends on the quality of choice made by intellect (*Buddhi*). When intellect vibrates with low energy (<200), it strongly associates with ego and shadow self. Hence, it makes a judgment within the comfort zone of shadow self. Finally, the low-level impressions and tendencies manifest as craving and aversion in the astral body and pleasant and unpleasant sensations in the gross body. However, when intellect vibrates with higher energy (>199), i.e., the "seer" of shadow self (<200) emerges, it accesses and leverages the objective intelligence (meta-cognition) of *Chitta* and inspires the ego to cross its comfort-zone and self-centeredness consciously. Hence, it chooses to transmute or repurpose the low-level impression, tendencies, aversion, and cravings to equanimity (>200). Once this inspiration and transmutation (or repurposing) happens, the shadow essences (or Shadow *Sat-Chit-Ananda*) get repurposed into higher essences (*Sat-chit-Ananda*).

Ahankara: It is the ego, Identity, "I," and personal preferences of shadow self. It always likes to avoid crossing the comfort zone. It always wants to stay within its boundaries of aversion, craving, comfort, and self-glorification, i.e., below courage (<200). Hence, the ego will respond even in a dream or shallow sleep state. For example, you will not wake up if called by a different name. John will not wake up if he is called out as Jacob while shallowly sleeping. John must be summoned as John. The ego is so deeply linked with the name and form of self. Because of its aberration due to ignorance, it wants to operate only in the outer self; i.e., it doesn't prefer harmony with the other self. It wants to live with the duality of the opposite.

For most people, there is always a strong affiliation between Intellect (*Buddhi*) and Ego (*Ahankara*); which vibrates with energy below courage (<200). Hence the Karmic recollections recorded in the causal body get colored by the 'I' of the Ego (*Ahankara*) through the intellect. Finally, they operate in the comfort zone of outer purpose only (i.e., Smartness) and ignore the inner purpose (i.e., Sage-ness). While it is a struggle, intellect can objectify or get misidentified with this coloring only when convinced that inner purpose (i.e., Sage-ness) is the primary purpose. Once convinced, it can inspire the Ego (*Ahankara*) to embrace the craving and aversion in the astral body and pleasant and unpleasant sensations in the gross body. This embracing process transmutes (or repurposes) the aversion and craving of ego (*Ahankara*) to neutrality and allows access to higher intelligence. Hence depending on the intensity of embracing, intellect deals with four types of intelligence in life situations, namely physical or physiological intelligence (PI), logical Intelligence (LI), emotional intelligence (EI), spiritual intelligence (SI), and cosmic intelligence (CI). Just to map intelligence to three bodies, PI is dominant in the gross body, LI & EI are dominant in the astral body, and SI is dominant in the causal body. They are measured in terms of quotients, i.e., physical quotient (PQ), logical or intelligence quotient (IQ), emotional quotient (EQ), spiritual quotient (SQ), and cosmic quotient (CQ), respectively. In simple lower Qs (PQ, IQ, EQ) dominate shadow self and may be termed shadow intelligence of true or real Qs(SQ and CQ).

Physical Intelligence (PQ)

Our gross body has some intelligence for physical safety, survival, and living; i.e., it signals us to eat and drink in times of hunger and thirst; it closes our eyes when insects come before our eyes. These are at the primitive level. These bits of intelligence are available to everyone, even to the lowest self. As per the recent definition by Claire Dale and Patricia Peyton in their book Physical Intelligence;

"It is the ability to detect and actively manage the balance of chemicals in our brains so that we can achieve more, experience less stress and live more happily."

Physical intelligence is built on four pillars: strength, flexibility, resilience, and endurance. These physical characteristics help intellect (*Buddhi*) to inspire ego (*Ahankara*) to embrace aversion and craving and cross the comfort zone only at the gross level. The Physical Intelligence paradigm is based on neuroplasticity, the brain's ability to alter and adapt at the gross level. Hence, we may make targeted adjustments to our mental, emotional, and physiological architecture using our Physical Intelligence. As a result, we can automatically improve our talents and attributes while learning new ones. In other words, we can adjust our IQ, EQ, and SQ indirectly to some extent but not significantly, as they are under the direct control of the astral and causal body. It is capable primarily of handling life situations related to physiological and gross levels. In other words, PQ in silo (i.e., without IQ, EQ, SQ), it becomes fearful and vulnerable to aversion (<101) in challenging life situations. In such situations, it also operates with an inferiority complex. In other words, it is the primary and dominant intelligence of the lowest self (i.e., aversive shadow self). Hence, with this intelligence alone, the aversive shadow self has no courage (<200) and tolerance to crossing the comfort zone when life-situation needs IQ, EQ & SQ. Hence, the intellect (*Buddhi*) of self cannot inspire the ego (*Ahankara*) to embrace aversion, cross the comfort zone, and appreciate the inner purpose (i.e., Sage-ness) as the primary purpose. In summary, physical intelligence derives its sense of self from the physical or gross world.

Logical Intelligence (IQ)

Logical intelligence is the LI or IQ that arises from the left brain. When your left brain is active, your attention goes to only objective and gross aspects of reality, and hence the neural processing happens based on logical and rational thinking. Accordingly, people dominated by IQ frequently avoid working with subjective and experiential information in favor of precise facts and factual data from experiments using statistics, science, etc. In other words; they are good at maximizing outcomes from the material world with analytics and experiments only for themselves and are least concerned about others; i.e., self-centered

(<200). This happens because; IQ is in a silo; i.e., without consideration of the emotional aspect (EQ), it has a lower perception of reality and hence operates only for self-survival (<200). Thus the ego (*Ahankara*) influences the *Buddhi* in favor of aversion and craving. Hence getting what the ego wants by leveraging IQ becomes their top priority because it is the key to our pleasure and survival. Their sense of self is derived from the amount of money they earn, their belongings, their fame, their status, their appearance, the success of their family members, or a variety of other factors related to their ego needs. It becomes the most crucial incentive for our decisions.

To make matters worse, even when they get what they want, they still become unhappy and change their concentration to "gaining more" or "getting something different"; in other words, want becomes greed. When the desire (125) or greed is not fulfilled, they become angry (150), and when it gets fulfilled, they become proud. In other words, the lower self (or craving-shadow self) is the primary residence for LI or IQ. Hence, it derives its sense of self mostly from logic and lower emotions like desire, anger, arrogance, jealousy, and so on, with no consideration of the emotional needs of others.

Emotional Intelligence (EQ)

Emotional intelligence is the (EI) or EQ that arises from the right brain. When your right brain is active, your attention goes to only the subjective and astral aspects of reality. Hence, neural processing happens based on emotional thinking with subjective or emotional processing. Daniel Goleman's book on Emotional Intelligence rates emotional intelligence (EI or EQ) over the intelligence quotient (IQ) for any leadership and socially accountable citizen. Humans are driven by their emotions, so they need to be emotionally understood to influence results from them. Also, to influence, one has to resonate with their emotions. Unlike IQ, it derives its sense of self not only from logic but they are from the control of its lower emotions like desire, anger, arrogance, and jealousy, and also considerate of the emotional needs of others. Hence according to Daniel, five key components of

EQ are self-awareness, self-regulation, self-motivation, empathy, and social skills.

Emotional intelligence (EI) is becoming increasingly important in the digital world as technology such as artificial intelligence (AI) and automation partially or entirely replace human participation. A time will come when AI can reproduce digital Einstein and Leonardo Da Vinci. In such a digital future, humans will be valued only when they have distinct features and skills which AI cannot replicate. Otherwise, humanity will suffer from a huge inferiority complex (<100), which would be a great disaster. Hence, humanity urgently needs to enhance its intelligence beyond IQ.

We all have those moments when we react out of frustration, greed, anger, and pride. Then afterward, we say, that's not who I want to be. Emotional intelligence can help you to close this gap. An important point to note here is that EQ is in a silo; without support from other intelligence (PQ, IQ, and SQ), it is the primary intelligence of the lower self or craving-shadow self (101-199). The superiority complex side of ego drives it. Hence the ego (*Ahankara*) influences the *Buddhi* in favor of aversion and craving. When it works in a silo, it may work only for your outer purpose (i.e., Smartness), i.e., to manipulate or exploit other's emotions for personal benefit. However, when it works beyond ego, it will help you to promote your primary purpose; you will leverage your EI to empathize and embrace others. To understand this, let's compare honey bees and cows. Both produce substance for the service of humanity. However, though everyone loves to keep a cow at home, they keep them away from honey bees for their dunking nature without SQ. All three bits of intelligence (PI, LI, and EI); when working in a silo, work for ego, shadow self, and self-centeredness. Accordingly, they vibrate below the courage line (<200). Hence they ignore the inner purpose (i.e., Sage-ness) and pursue only outer-purpose (i.e., Smartness) by exploiting the muscular energy, nature, and emotions of others.

Spiritual Intelligence (SQ)

There is enough evidence from psychology, neuroscience, anthropology, and cognitive science to establish that there is another intelligence called Spiritual Intelligence (SI, SQ). SQ arises when both the left and right brain process objective and subjective information in parallel and with positive collaboration and coherence. Hence neural processing balances reason and emotion, considering the aspect of survival and transcendence in life situations. The resonance effect of collaboration; enhance the intensity of intelligence to objectify lower or shadow Qs (PQ, IQ & EQ) from total intelligence; i.e., SQ is the "seer" or "knower" of lower or shadow Qs. In other words, once you have SQ, you co-exist as a shadow and true self. At this point, the intellect (*Buddhi*) inspires the ego (*Ahankara*), which operates in silos of IQ and EQ. As Richard, a subject matter expert on consciousness and spiritual intelligence, says; this positive collaboration and coherence repurpose the other Q's (PQ, IQ, and EQ). It transmutes (or repurposes) the aversion and craving of shadow self (<200) within other Qs to neutrality and stability. Hence the same intelligence leverages metacognition and gets expressed courageously with acceptance by embracing life-situation. Hence SQ is the primary intelligence of the higher self and promotes inner purpose (i.e., Sage-ness). In other words, the shadow self (<200) entangled with the shadow-intelligence (PQ, IQ, and EQ) of the body-mind cannot access SQ and hence Sage-ness.

When positive coherence between both brains (left and right) matures, it also induces a resonance between the frequency of the total brain and heart. This resonance brings a shift in intelligence quality from mind-based to heart-based intelligence, i.e., from outer intelligence to inner intelligence called intuition. Intuition is the process of perceiving or knowing something without reasoning: knowledge of events such as an act of nature that has yet to happen. As per HeartMath Institute's research, the heart possesses a unique intelligence: the flow of awareness, understanding, and intuition we experience when the mind and emotions are brought into coherent alignment with the heart. Heart intelligence is the deep intuition that empowers the SQ with higher vibration leading to love. This intelligence and love are without memory and imagination. Finally, the intellect inspires the ego to embrace the best choice, even if it has to embrace the lower tendencies and impressions. As Gregg Braden, New York Times bestselling author of The Wisdom Codes: Ancient Words to Rewire Our Brains and Heal Our Hearts, says, "Heart Intelligence gives new meaning to the role of your heart—while awakening the deep intuition that can empower the best choices you will ever make." The heart's intelligence with deeper intuition acts as a transition from the higher self (200-400) to the highest self (401-1000). Also, this is the point where the neural pattern and brain waves start aligning towards peak potentialities of existence-expression, intelligence, and experience (i.e., *Sat-Chit-Ananda*).

Danah Zohar, An American-British author, and speaker on physics, philosophy, and management, has done extensive research on this topic to demystify the power of SQ in the current context. She mentioned in her book "Spiritual Intelligence: The Ultimate Intelligence" say; SQ is uniquely human. She also claims that the most fundamental intelligence, SQ, generates our quest for purpose, vision, and worth. It enables us to dream and strive. It underpins our beliefs and the role our beliefs and values play in the actions we perform and the way we create our lives. As per Donah Zohar, let's analyze the attributes of a spiritually intelligent being **(SIB)**. Their inner space reverberates with elements of the higher self, i.e., courage, neutrality, willingness, acceptance, reasoning, and love. Let's see how you will operate if you raise your vibration and consciousness to spiritual intelligence.

Courage (200) of SIB: At this level, you will be able to stand courageously against the crowd and have your humble convictions and expression; without being disturbed by acceptance or rejection of your conviction, i.e., you will become field independent in a compulsive life-situation.

Neutrality, willingness, and acceptance (250 - 350) of SIB: At this level, you will live in and become responsive to the life situation of the moment with spontaneity, irrespective of whether it is adversity or a boon. Additionally, you will be a playful actor in a larger drama without any aversion or craving.

Reasoning (400) of SIB: At this level, you will be able to stand back from a life situation to see the bigger and wider perspective and have a quest to mystify the significance of the life situation in context with your existential purpose.

Love (500) of SIB: At this level, you will feel a strong interconnectedness with other beings and be able to celebrate diversity; i.e., you will value and include other beings despite differences. Additionally, you will have a strong sense of compassion and vocation, i.e., an urge to serve humanity.

I vividly correlate the power of spiritual intelligence at one of the industry-level crisis scenarios. When the whole IT Industry globally was laying off its old staff due to rapid change in digital technology in 2018'.

However, Mr.N Chandrasekharan, the then chairman of Tata Consultancy Services, made his genius statement; *"We are retraining people. There are legacy technologies, not legacy people."*

What a higher perspective and courage (200) to stand outside the crowd, one of the key characteristics of SIP. With this, the company embraced the higher perspective with innovative re-skilling initiatives in the digital space. In the same year, the company had a quantum leap in market capitalization by around 25%, reaching more than 100 billion dollars and leaving behind the competition with a huge gap. When the inner purpose (i.e., Sage-ness) becomes your product, outer purpose (i.e., Smartness) becomes a by-product. This discussion disproves the misconception that people with high SQ devote all their attention, time, and effort to their inner purpose (i.e., Sage-ness) only. It also clarifies that embracing a higher perspective is to deal with the life situation or outer purpose (i.e., Smartness) playfully, with no residual hurt, regret, or remorse.

Consciousness Wins Conscience

Conscience is the subjective intelligence of the identified self; i.e., it is based upon the compulsive inner voice from memory and conditioning of society. However, consciousness is the objective intelligence of the misidentified self; i.e., it is independent of the compulsive inner voice from memory and conditioning of society. Consciousness is an inner voice when you conquer your shadow self (lowest and lower self). This is where; your compulsive shadow self operates as "seen" in the presence of your higher self as "seer." Also, this "seer" dissolves entanglement and mental conflict. Once you attain a LOC range of 600-800, you become permanently independent of conscience. Hence, people operating from their higher consciousness are always misunderstood by society. People like Mahatma Gandhi became victims of society when they went beyond their conscience.

Once, one of my friends got invited to a grand spiritual function planned by his close relatives for their son's outer-wellbeing (i.e., Smartness). And on the same day, he had one critical business meeting to atted and no backup. He was in a big dilemma. On the one hand, as per his social rule and conscience memory, he will be totally rejected by his family on the side of relatives if he does not join the family gathering. On the other hand, if he does not join the business meeting, it will be a big loss for his organization. It might impact multiple families' inner-wellbeing (i.e., Sage-ness), as there was no backup mechanism. The date and timing were the same and unchangeable on both sides. To resolve the dilemma, my friend asked me my opinion and asked, what could you have done in this situation? I suggested the former is a choice of conscience without any possibility of material impact. The latter is a choice of consciousness with some material impact.

Hence, I could have joined the family in advance and shared my blessing, wishes, and gift in advance, and I could have joined the business meeting on schedule to follow the principle of Smart-Sage. My friend also did the same. However, he was still rejected socially by the expected group. He was in grief for a few weeks but recovered in the spirit of Smart-Sage. After a few years, he was approached by rejecting his family, asking for a job recommendation for their son, as he had been unemployed for a long time. My friend did it with humility and grace. Then the rejecting family became their follower to him. Hence it is said that once you follow your higher consciousness, people limited with a conscience will first ignore you, then laugh at you, then attack you, but finally, you will win, and they will follow you.

Intelligence is Proportional to LOC

While we discussed each intelligence separately concerning LOC and different selves, you have to note that they influence each other significantly upward and downward. For example, PQ influences other Qs positively; however, it gets weakened in the absence of other Qs. For example, even if the PQ of an athlete is high, it gets weakened if he cannot handle the high expectation of his fans. As you go upward in the conscious map, you experience the repurposed influence of lower intelligence; i.e., a person operating from a higher self (200- 400) will have SQ, which is the repurposed lower or shadow Qs (PQ, IQ, and EQ). In simple, intelligence is proportional to consciousness. In the current state of humanity, IQ and EQ have been taken a higher priority. Hence, the outer purpose (i.e., Smartness) has grown disproportionately as compared to the inner purpose (i.e., Sage-ness). This imbalance has made humans hack-able beings through technology like Artificial Intelligence (AI). AI is capable of handling IQ better than humans. Also, time is pretty close; it can compete in the EI space. However, fortunately, it may not be able to process SQ, as it is purely intuitive and human. This way, higher consciousness can objectify lower conscious elements. Hence unless humanity pauses, relooks at the trend, and embraces some change to improve SQ, we are inviting disaster into our life.

In many cases, scientists with the highest level of IQ considered physical science as a subset of a higher science, i.e., spirituality. Scientists, such as astronomer Johannes Kepler (1571-1630), saw the scientific investigation as a spiritual discipline.

Einstein said, *"Everyone who is truly interested in the study of science becomes convinced that a spirit is manifest in-laws of the Universe - a spirit enormously bigger than that of man, one in the face of which we with our meager powers must feel humble."*

Recently, we have witnessed the convergence of Science and Spirituality in the life and Times of India's People's President - Dr.Abdul Kalam - mind igniter! The Father of India, Mahatma Gandhi, was a firm believer in Science and Scientists to the extent of their value to humankind's well-being, in keeping with his life of Spirituality. This gives us faith in science as the finest kind of Spirituality, and Spirituality is the highest form of science, with Truth being the ultimate pursuit of universal peace.

As per Swami Vivekananda, an Indian monk; who saw spirituality through the prism of science, spirituality is the science of the soul. He also says, *"I've encountered several scientists who were both scientifically and spiritually practical. There will come a moment when every person must be quite realistic in both."*

John D. Rockefeller, the founder of Standard Oil, the parent company of today's Exxon Mobil, was one of the important Americans whose mind Swami Ji had read. In the 1890s, Rockefeller met Swami Vivekananda. Rockefeller was in his mid-fifties and a very wealthy and successful person at his outer purpose (i.e., Smartness), while his inner intelligence was far from spiritual intelligence (SQ); i.e., he earned a vast fortune through unethical and monopolistic activities. However, his insatiable need to gain money at any cost came at a high price. Rockefeller's health deteriorated, and he eventually was so sick that he was on the verge of death. His digestive system had deteriorated, so he could only eat milk and crackers. He was also depressed and had lost his hair due to a medical ailment. According to legend, Rockefeller used to resemble a walking mummy. These multiple health issues likely prompted Rockefeller to seek out Swami Vivekananda, whose exceptional yogic skills he had heard about from his affluent acquaintances. Swami Vivekananda was most likely alluding to the fact that by following Swami Ji's spiritual instruction (SQ), Rockefeller had made a step toward changing destiny and therefore owed Swami Ji a debt of gratitude. Rockefeller raised his consciousness and SQ, evolving into a more spiritual being by not hoarding his money but using it to aid others with a sense of vocation and compassion, which is one of the characteristics of SIP. It's worth noting that several writers have speculated that Rockefeller's transformation from a greedy (IQ) and astute businessman to a philanthropist (SQ) occurred during the 1890s. As a result, Swamiji's instruction is likely to have brought about this development. Following this era, Rockefeller's compassionate contributions (SQ) to humanity continuously rose. He understood he wouldn't take his fortune with him upon death, so he invested in hospitals and colleges. This change from mind to heart-based intelligence aided him so much that his health gradually recovered, and he lived till 97.

Cosmic Intelligence.

The intelligence next to SI is cosmic intelligence (CI or CQ), the dominant intelligence of the highest self (500 to 100); intelligence is not only a function of willing intention and neural network but simply an intuition and synchronicity. In other words, the neural pattern and brain waves achieve their ultimate level having peak human potentialities of existence-expression, intelligence, and experience (i.e., Sat-Chit-Ananda). At this level, the cosmos and nature know the intention of the highest self and serve it with oneness; i.e., the "knower" gets merged with the known. The shadow self gets merged with the true self. Also, for the highest self, there is no difference between outer and inner purpose (i.e., Smartness and Sage-ness), and the purpose becomes singular.

Once we wake up to this level of consciousness, we can objectify all "known" from the knower at the source of expression in time and space. If the known are the expressions, the knower is our existence; if the known is the nature, the knower is the source; If the known are the potentials and knower is the potentialities; if the known are the quantum particles, the knower is the quantum wave or field, if the known are feeling-tones (positive, negative, and neutral), the knower is emptiness, if known are subjective, the knower is objective. If known are possessions, the knower is non-possessiveness; if known is effort, the knower is effortlessness. Also, if known is the time (past and future), the knower is timeless (now, forever, "*Sat*"); if known are sufferings, the knower is the non-suffering (bliss, "*Ananda*"). In simple, if known is ego, the knower is enlightening; if known is human experience, the knower is the observer of the experience (i.e., being). If known is the "seen," the knower is the "seer." In this state, we have the ultimate knowledge and simplest of all experiences because it requires no thought, only feeling with space, silence, and stillness; i.e., You know that you exist; that's all. When this knower experience remains for good like a constant stream of water from a faucet; you are at the peak of your experience; i.e., bliss (*Ananda*) and the peak of your existence (*Sat*); which is the true self with fulfillment.

> Rupert Spira says, *"All yearning for change finds its pinnacle at the level of the true self, for only here is 'I am' enough to provide absolute fulfillment."*

> Sadhguru, an Indian mystic, says, *"If you touch this dimension of your mind, which is the linking point to one's consciousness, you do not even have to wish for anything, you do not have to dream of anything – the best possible thing that can happen to you will anyway happen."*

> In Bhagvat Gita (7.10), Krishna also said, *"I am the original seed of all existences, the intelligence of the intelligent, and the prowess of all powerful men."*

We also discussed earlier that; *Sat-Chit-Ananda* (existence to expression, Intelligence, and experience) are three essences of our trinity-self; i.e., all essences are holographic. Our intelligence (*Chit*) is a true reflection of our being, i.e., existence (*Sat*) and experience (bliss, *Ananda*).

Call to Action

Let's say you are offered to experience one of the following three options of song performances happening simultaneously in three theaters of the same ambiance with a payment of $20:

Option-1: A song performance by a celebrity singer but recorded by the latest digital technology; with the highest audio and video quality.

In Option-1, you are deriving your sense of self by appreciating and celebrating the power of technology or physical law and hence driven by logical intelligence (IQ)

Option-2: A live song performance by a non-celebrity but a well-established singer with the same voice and singing quality.

In Option-2, you are deriving your sense of self by appreciating and celebrating your connection with another being in NOW and hence driven by emotional intelligence (EQ).

Option-3: A live song performance by a poor bagger with the same voice and singing quality.
If you choose:

In Option-3, you are deriving your sense of self not only by appreciating and celebrating your connection with another being in NOW but also by celebrating your sense of vocation in elevating a deprived being. Hence you are driven by spiritual intelligence (SQ).

SMART SAGE

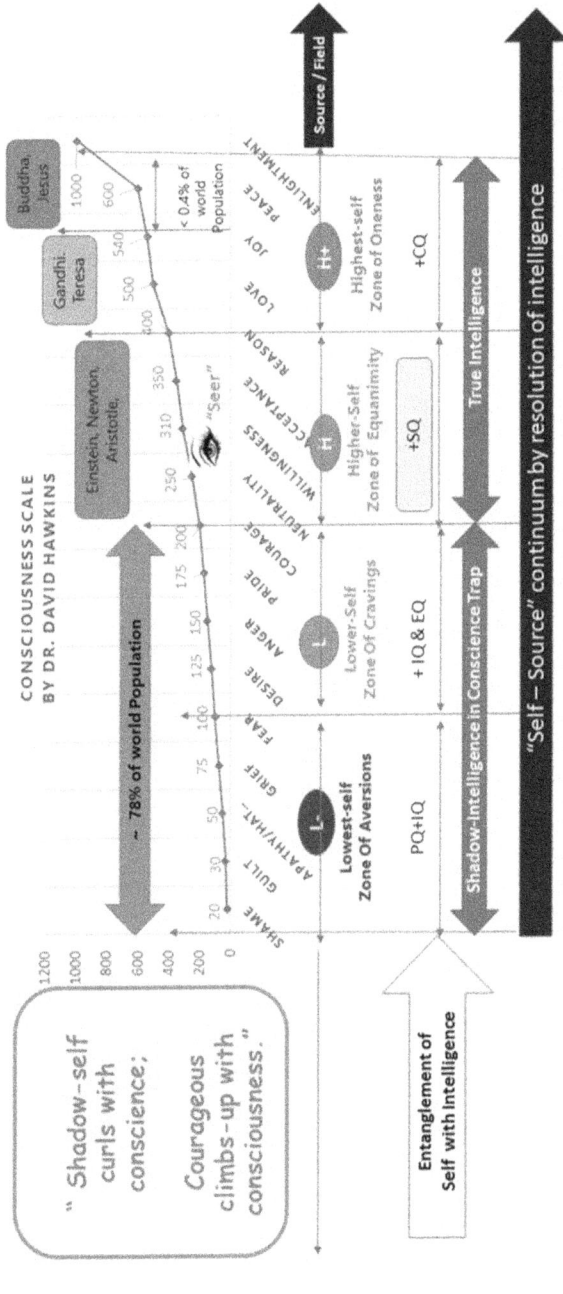

5

EXPERIENCE

High-Resolution Experience Comes Beyond Courage

> *"We are not human beings having a spiritual experience. We are spiritual beings having a human experience."*
>
> - Pierre Teilhard de Chardin

Meeting with My Shadow Self through Experience

Once, I had a serious gum health issue due to a calcium deposit and other severe infections. Due to negligence for a few days, the inflammation became very critical. When I visited the dentist, he advised surgical intervention of the entire gum. The setting and procedure started. Most of you might have had some experience of this kind, directly or indirectly. I started feeling some fear and then physical pain. Also, it took me to my psychological past and future and started creating thoughts around aversion, rejection, blame, regret, anxiety, and inferiority complex. At the same time, the mind was craving for a quick release from sitting. However, within a few minutes, I could observe, catch and objectify my experience of negative feeling-tone and pain in the body as separating me as "seen." Also, the inner intelligence or intuitive feeling of temporariness gave me the courage (200) and inspiration to sustain that state. This state was gradually neutralizing or dissolving the pain in the body and its associated mental narratives of my shadow self (i.e., aversions and cravings). While there was some minor tingling and irritation, I was able to remain in a state of calmness till the end of the sitting and procedure for around two hours. Thoughts were floating like clouds in the sky and had no roots in me. They came and went away. It was a joy to silently date with the painting body and its narratives without being judgmental or discriminative. I was involved with pain but not entangled with it; i.e., there was a pain in my outer self, but there was no pain in my inner self. In simple terms, I embraced and conquered the sense of touch between surgical instruments and my physical gum. Though I saw the infected blood in the wash basin while rinsing and cleaning my mouth, it was a compassionate farewell between my "inner-self" and outer self. It was an experience of self (i.e., beyond gross and perceptual experience), where there was pain without painfulness or suffering, an inferiority complex without being disappointed, farewell without missing, and involvement without entanglement. In simple, I was operating beyond shadow self. Then, I was released from procedural sitting and came to the doctor's consultation cabin to discuss post-treatment care. Before he started his advisory and recommendation, he asked me gently with curiosity, were you not feeling any pain during the session? I responded; the pain was there but without painfulness, pain without suffering. He said we generally do such critical procedures only under anesthesia, but today was a different experience. This situation made me realize that. "We are spiritual beings having a human experience."

Experiences are meant for Our Well-Being.

As Swami Vivekananda said, experience is the basis of all knowledge; not only do we need experience to exist, but also to learn and grow. How is experience associated with self or life? A man discovered a butterfly cocoon. A little hole developed in one day. He stayed for several hours, watching the butterfly try to squeeze its body through that tiny opening. Then it seemed to cease moving forward. It looked to have gone as far as it could and couldn't go any farther.

The man then decided to aid the butterfly by snipping off the cocoon's last portion with scissors. The butterfly then effortlessly emerged. Its torso was enlarged, and its wings were little and shriveled. The guy remained to observe the butterfly because he expected the wings to increase and extend to support the body, which would compress with time.

Neither occurred! In reality, the butterfly crawled around for the remainder of its life with a bloated body and withered wings. It was never able to take to the skies. In his goodwill and haste, this guy did not comprehend that the restrictive cocoon and the effort required for the butterfly to get out of the tiny aperture were nature's way of driving fluid from its body into its wings, preparing it for flight once free of the cocoon. Sometimes the experience of adversity is precisely designed by nature for our existence and experience of life. We would be crippled if nature permitted us to walk through our lives without hurdles. We would not have been as powerful and progressive as we could have been, and we'd never be able to fly.

Experience is an Existential Need.

Now to have more clarity on the type of experience, let's consider a life situation; one bright morning, you are fresh and energetic after breakfast. Then you are locked in a closed room for four hours without access to the outdoors and your belongings- including your books, watch, cell phone, etc. What will happen? First, you will look for any opportunity to engage your senses within or outside the room for the gross experience, i.e., watch, listen, smell, taste, and touch. Then the second possibility is you will enter into your psychological world; where you will have your thought and imagination go toward what you like or dislike in your life; i.e., "books are not right," "girlfriend is beautiful," "you will go to the Miami beach next summer" etc. In other words, you will either be in a state of mental aversion or craving an astral experience. If you are exhausted with all other options, you may try to sleep for the remaining time before freedom, which is an experience of the causal body unconsciously. If you know some techniques, you may also try meditation, an experience of the causal body that happens consciously. At a basic level, you exist to experience, whether the experience is gross, astral, causal, conscious, or unconscious. In other words, experience is also existential essence like intelligence.

Experience as a Function of Sensation and Perception

Gross experience is the experience through the senses. For example, consider the life event of you having a cup of coffee on a wet morning. Your five senses, vision, hearing (audition), smell (olfaction), taste (gustation), and touch (somatosensory), are in action now. Your lips are touching, sensing, and feeling the warmth of coffee and the texture of the foam, and your eye is seeing and feeling its color; the nose is smelling and feeling the aroma, the tongue is feeling the taste, and the ear is hearing the gentle sound of the coffee cup on the table. Call for Sensory receptors are neurons with particular functions that respond to certain inputs. Sensory reactions are detected by sensory receptors, which results in sensation. Light entering the eye, for example, causes chemical changes in the cells that line the back of the eye. These cells provide messages and information to the central nervous system through action potentials. Transforming sensory input energy into action potential is known as transduction. Our sensory preceptors collect the relevant information, like sensors, and send it to the brain. Finally, the brain creates electrochemical impulses. Depending on the quality of these electro-chemical impulses, we experience consciousness as a knowing of a conscious event and consciousness itself. Now the issue is, where is this consciousness? Though some scientists claim that it is produced in the brain, there is no region in the brain connected with consciousness, and there is no acceptable response to the question to following questions:

How can bio-electrochemical impulses produce color, sound, taste, smell, touch, and other sensory experiences?

How does a neuronal pattern cause a conscious event to occur? (i.e., thought, imagination, intention, perception, etc.)

Because of these unknowns, this domain in science is referred to as the "Hard Problem of Consciousness." While psycho-neuro-bio-electrochemical impulses occur in the brain (i.e., in time-space or local), consciousness and experience occur in a domain beyond time and space (i.e., non-local or causal-body), allowing humans to perceive spiritual essence in space and time.

There are two types of sensations; outer and inner. While outer sensation originates from sense objects, inner sensation originates from the causal body. These sensations deal with bio-chemical and electromagnetic impulses at the cellular or molecular level to produce the raw or un-distorted experience in the non-local or causal domain.

The factor that influences the quality and degree of our sensation is our sensory receptors' sensitivity. An absolute threshold can evaluate a sensory system's sensitivity to the relevant inputs. The absolute threshold is the amount of stimulus life energy that must be present 50% of the time for the stimulus to be recognized. In a way, how dim or quiet a light or sound may be and yet be detected. Sometimes, the sensitivity of our sensory receptors may be amazing. On a clear night, the sensory cells at the back of the eye are very sensitive. We can also receive signals that are conveyed below the level of our awareness, which are referred to as subliminal messages. When a stimulus is powerful enough to stimulate sensory receptors and transmit nerve impulses to the brain, it reaches a physiological threshold. This is an absolute threshold for the experience. A communication that falls below that threshold is called subliminal: we receive it but are unaware of it. Consequently, the message was received, but for whatever reason, it was not selected for processing by our brains. Human sensory receptors have a different absolute threshold sensitivity level than birds and animals. That is why before the giant waves of tsunami slammed into Sri Lanka and India's coastlines, coastal animals seemed to sense something was coming and fled to safer places a few days before the calamity. Apart from the difference in absolute threshold sensitivity between different species, the difference also exists within the human species. Hence one can test the wine and chocolate better than the other. This aspect creates a difference in experiencing the true reality or objective reality. In addition, there are perceptual factors and filters at the astral level that creates a different experience of true or objective reality among humans.

Before we experience the raw bio-electrochemical impulses in non-local space or causal self, another factor that distorts our experience is our perception, which acts as a filter. Perception is how the brain chooses, organizes, and interprets the information our sensory receptors receive about the physical world. In simple terms, Perception is a series of unconscious processes perceived through self-intelligence (PI, LI, EI, and SI) received as input from each sense we are exposed to. Then the mind combines these fragmented perceptions (from each sense) into a coherent vision in time and space. It also produces meaningful inferences or perceptions of life-situation or life-event, which influences the degree of experience by creating decisions of like and dislike. In other words, the quality of experience influences our intelligence, decision, and hence the choice of purpose in life. Because each person's brain interprets inputs differently based on their learning, memories, emotions, and expectations, perception of the same senses might change from person to person. Hence perception is purely personal. This is why the same life situation is not experienced in the same way by two different persons. Our perceptions of the world around us validate our prior assumptions about how the world works. If our assumptions are based on ignorance or illusion about reality, our perception and experience will be berated. This is how ignorance brings aberration in intelligence, decision, and hence in choosing life's purpose. In fact, it is already happening in this way for a large population today; i.e., we are living with illusory experience and purpose.

On an occasion to celebrate an achievement, I threw a party for my project team in a hotel called Royal Plaza. We made an elaborate plan to take care of the end-to-end experience of my team, including a seven-course delicious dinner, an entertaining musical and comedy show, a remembrance of recognition with a personal note from our CEO, and finally, the pick-up and drop service. All went in exceptionally well. It was a Friday dinner; the next two days were the weekend. On Monday morning, when I started collecting feedback, while I received a higher level of motivation from a few, I observed an overall low motivation compared to another large project team. It was very shocking for me. It took some time before I understood that the team scored low on social media compared to the previous Friday party at Royal Heritage, which I organized for another large team. Then I was curious to know the reason for the high social media scoring of Royal Heritage compared to Royal Plaza; even if they were alike in all arrangement parameters, the star status of the hotel, food, entertainment, and recognition was the same. Again, to my surprise, the root of the reason was that; Royal Heritage has a dedicated social media team to promote the same to their advantage. Here the gross experience of the team at Royal Plaza was influenced by their perceptual filters about social media and comparative expectations. In other words, the real objective experience is getting hijacked by personal perception. In this way, most people are deprived of gross or real experience, even if it is available.

Simply put, they are denied inner purpose (i.e., Sage-ness) due to their primary focus on outer purpose (i.e., Smartness). Numerous astral factors disturb the gross experience.

Another aspect is even if you do not have any gross experience in the present time, you can simulate the experience in your imagination. Objects are imagined consciously in this realm of imagination, i.e., a series of conscious events from which the mind constructs perception and experience.

Similarly, a dream is formed by the mind and brain from our memory when cut off from the body and the outside world.

Our perceptions influence the kind of activities we engage in, the amount of effort we put into those activities, and the likelihood that we will engage in those activities again. Hence the perception of self, world, and life situation alters our experience. In simple, like intelligence, experience is also proportional to vibrational-conscious-energy (i.e., LOC) of self. Let's explore how self-perception influences experience at different levels of self, i.e., shadow self (lowest, lower) and true self (higher and highest)

Experience of Shadow Self (<200) (L- & L, 0-199)

As we know from the consciousness map, the lowest self (0-100) is the aversive shadow self, perceiving itself as hopeless, helpless, and frightening. In contrast, the life situation is perceived as vindictive, condemning, uncaring and punitive. The inner space is full of aversion, rejection, blame, regret, anxiety, and an inferiority complex. For example, in professional space, they appear as fear of competition, loss of job, falling short of the target, and escalations. In summary, all these are kinds of perceptual filters to original sensation; in other words, they are far away from the true experience of life situations. All these filters distort the electromagnetic charge of sensation in a negative direction from the original or normal charge. In other words, it forms a field of negative energy in the outer self, hence a negative feeling tone in the causal body. We know it as an unpleasant experience or negative excitement. With this consciousness, people do not perceive the danger and gradually move towards suicidal or criminal attempts. In other words, this space is very similar to the apologue of the boiling frog, where a frog is being slowly boiled alive. It is unaware of the danger that it will be cooked to death. People in this space are far from perceiving the need for an inner purpose (i.e., Sage-ness). Moreover, they must focus more on their outer purpose (i.e., Smartness).

Similarly, the lower self (101-199) is the craving-shadow self, and it perceives itself as lacking, agnostic, and demanding, whereas the life situation is perceived as denying and vengeful. The inner space is full of craving, greed, pride, hatred, and a superiority complex. For example, in a professional space, it appears as controlling, commanding, demanding, criticizing, and hungry for power and position.

In summary, all these are kinds of perceptual filters to original sensation; in other words, they are far away from the true experience of life situations. All these filters distort the electromagnetic charge of sensation in a positive direction than the original or normal charge. In other words, it forms a field of positive energy in the outer self and a positive feeling tone in the causal body. We know it as a pleasant experience or positive excitement. We call this charge or feeling-tone positive or pleasant to represent the opposite of negative, just like the opposite poles of electric and magnetic fields. A system only survives in peace when there is neutrality. It means a negative energy to be in peace; it will invite a positive energy and vice versa. Also, lower feeling tones (i.e., positive and negative) are irrelevant; the external world triggers them in the present time or from the residual past stored in the causal body. However, the neutral feeling tone is intrinsic. Hence, if residual non-neutral energy, i.e., the residual, is not dissolved, d or re-purposed with higher consciousness, the bi-polarity nature continues in an infinite loop. Which is the main cause of human suffering.

However, in terms of experience, it is far below the normal experience of the self, i.e., meditative, joy, and bliss. Because of the low level of consciousness, perception, intelligence, and experience, the shadow self (<200) is not conscious of the inner purpose (i.e., Sage-ness) as the primary purpose, even if it is aware of it. Hence, it lives life with entanglement experience with the world and outer purpose (i.e., Smartness). With this inner space, people will be sitting on the tail side (i.e., outer side) of the branch and enjoying the process of cutting the head side (i.e., inner side) of the branch of a tree till they realize the real failure, i.e., only when they succeed in cutting the trunk in totality. In summary, due to the entanglement, people in this zone carry residual friction, unpleasantness, hurt, regret, and remorse from their life situation. While it may maintain coolness at the surface, a blast furnace exists in the inner space. In other words, they are the carriers of positive toxicity. In the current competitive and VUCA age, most professionals are in this zone, causing damage to the experience of inner-wellbeing at personal and collective levels.

The mind takes the shadow self (lowest and lower self) to the psychological past or future for a sustained duration as a hostage. During this hostage, the mind dwells between aversion and cravings. In other words, it unconsciously brings up the resonating lower energy fields (pain and pleasure) to the surface and is experienced by the outer self.

Mr. Eckhart Tolle calls this accumulated energy field in the causal body a pain body. He defines the pain-body as *"the human tendency to perpetuate old emotion" accumulated in their "energy field."* He says - *"Once the pain body has taken you over, you want more pain. You become a victim or a perpetrator. You want to inflict pain, or you want to suffer pain, or both. There isn't much difference between the two. Of course, you are not conscious of this and will vehemently claim that you do not want pain. But look closely, and you will find that your thinking and behavior are designed to keep the pain going for yourself and others. If you were truly conscious of it, the pattern would dissolve."*

When self or being at LOC < 200), the pleasure hormone gets like dopamine, and Oxytocin gets released from the body even if you just fantasize about your craving. For example, you will have dopamine when you fantasize about awards and oxytocin when you fantasize about sleeping with your favorite star. The most entertainment industry and motivational speakers are busy helping you fantasize unconsciously to give you temporary and fleeting pleasure. Hence getting carried away with this temporary and ephemeral pleasure is an absolute ignorance, obsession, and sickness unless you are conscious of these ephemeral phenomena and have a quest for everlasting pleasure and happiness.

In summary, the unpleasant and pleasant feeling tone is the shadow experience. In other words, the shadow self (<200) entangled with the shadow experience of body and mind cannot access the intrinsic and causal experience associated with the true self unless it moves to higher consciousness (>200) and functions as a "seer of the shadow self."

Experience of the Higher Self (H, 200 – 400).

The same "seer" of shadow self and "knower" of shadow or Lower Q's (PQ, IQ, and EQ) is also the "knower" of lower experience (i.e., unpleasant & pleasant feeling-tones). With this "knower," you can now handle your lower experience consciously; i.e., you will be able to transmute (or re-purpose) the suffering and pain (i.e., negative and positive feeling tone) to a neutral energy field or feeling tone. My life situation related to dental issues, expressed at the beginning of this chapter, exactly deals with this aspect. In other words, I transmuted or repurposed my suffering and pain body (i.e., negative and positive feeling tone) to a neutral energy field or feeling tone. This feeling tone is free from the duality trap of pain and pleasure. Hence this level of experience by self is meditative; i.e., it is independent of extrinsic experience from sense objects and sensory perception. At this level, both "experience" and "knower of experience" co-exist; i.e., you, as the "knower of experience," can observe the sensational drama performed by your shadow self (<200). You can exist both as a shadow and a true self at this level.

As long as you are identified with shadow self, you will depend on perceptual experience based on body, mind, and senses. However, once your "seer of shadow self" (i.e., true self) emerges, you will derive your sense of self from a meditative state's non-perceptual, causal, and intrinsic experience. Once you have this experience, you can even walk into hell with grace, as hell is an external and perceptual experience through body-mind and senses.

While we will deal with the technique of embracing and transmutation (or repurposing) from the pain body to the neutral energy field in a later chapter, it is important to note that this embracing and transmutation (or repurposing) point is also a shifting point for mind-based intelligence to heart-based intelligence; i.e., intuition, thinking to a feeling. Also, this shift brings a shift in our vibrational-conscious energy (i.e., LOC), as the heart generates a 5000 times stronger electromagnetic field than the brain. As we know, electromagnetic impulses are a key factor in our gross and astral experience. Hence this state creates a perfect harmony between life and life situations and the inner and outer purpose (i.e., Sage-ness and Smartness). To be very specific, it allows one to live a life of possession without possessiveness; pain without painfulness, feeling without thinking, passion without obsession, quest without desire, being angry without having anger, facing criticism without an inferiority complex, inspiring without superiority complex, staying in the present and visiting past or future as a guest, putting effort with effortlessness; working without being tired and so on. It allows involvement in life-situation without being entangled with them, hence freedom full of actions, accountability, and responsibility. Such can be achieved in our professional life and day-to-day work as well. In psychology, this state is called "flow."

According to positive psychologist Mihály Cskszentmihályi, flow is *"A state in which people are so involved in an activity that nothing else seems to matter; the experience is so enjoyable that people will continue to do it even at great cost, for the sheer sake of doing it,"* (1990). The **"knower of experience"** emerges in flow-state.

What Happens In The Brain During This Flow State?

The prefrontal cortex is a part of the brain in charge of higher cognitive tasks like self-reflective consciousness, memory, temporal integration, and working memory. It's the area in charge of our awareness and explicit mental states. This area is thought to momentarily down-regulate in a state of flow, a phenomenon known as transitory hypo-frontality. This momentary inactivation of the prefrontal area may result in emotions of time distortion, loss of self-consciousness, and loss of inner critic, i.e., lack of judgment, discrimination, aversion, yearning, and so on. Other studies have proposed that the flow state is linked to the brain's dopamine reward system because curiosity is heightened during flow (Gruber, Gelman, & Ranganath, 2014). Hence in this state, people become so engrossed in a work that the rest of the world appears to untangle and drift away, and nothing else matters. When people are in a flow state, time seems to fly, their concentration sharpens, and they lose control. In this state, the sense of self derives not from shadow self and perceptual experience but from meaning and purpose. We can say the experience in this state is beyond gross and perceptual experience. Everyday activities like becoming lost in a good book or working passionately on a challenging project can all lead to a flow state. Hence this state is achieved only when you are involved but not entangled.

This is precisely the point Krishna said to Arjuna during Mahabharata as per Bhagavat Gita (2.47); *"कर्मण्येवाधिकारस्ते मा फलेषु कदाचन;"* which means – *"You have a right to perform your prescribed duty, but you are not entitled to the fruits of action. Experience of Flow creates intrinsic or eudemonic happiness."*

In this type of happiness, the sense of self is achieved through experiences of neutrality, meaning, purpose, self-actualization, and inner purpose (i.e., Sage-ness). In simple, it is an experience beyond sensation and perception. In the case of the higher self, the flow with eudemonic happiness or associated experience does not remain consistent; i.e., it's not like a constant stream of water from a faucet but more like raindrops that fall one by one. In yogic literature, this state is referred *"Dharana."* And, when the state of flow with eudemonic happiness or associated experience becomes a constant stream of water from a faucet is referred to as *"Dhyana,"* i.e., a meditative state. The way intuition is a transition point from higher to highest- self concerning intelligence (*Chit*); *"Dhyana"* or **"meditative state"** is the transition point concerning experience (*Ananda*). When professionals have even a smidgeon of access to this dimension, i.e., feeling the inner space with their day-to-day job, it opens the door to peak experience, and effort becomes second nature. Sweat transforms into recreation, labor transforms into worship, and work transforms into a source of delight. Cowardice transforms into bravery. Stress is transformed into tranquility. Considering the need for inner well-being and human sustainability, this is the dimension every organization must promote and integrate with the work.

Experience of Highest Self (H+, 401 - 1000)

Perceptual experience is fleeting. For example, place a grain of salt or sugar on your tongue. After the first spike in sweet taste experience, notice how the flavor begins to fade and vanish forever after some time. You may bring this perception and experience to your imagination through visualization. Still, it will be feeble and vanish once your mind is occupied with something else. This makes you aware of how fleeting the experience is. Again, we examined how individuals perceive different objects, concepts, and "truths" in the universe: we all live in separate worlds, each of which may have things in common due to our unique perspectives on our worlds. This is also known as subjective reality since it is "subject" to a complex series of perceptual filters. Sensory apparatus (e.g., the rods and cones in our eyes), sensory processing (e.g., the visual cortex), higher-level brain activity, and psychological factors are all capable of altering our sense of reality (e.g., expectations). As a result, what one person perceives is always distinct from what another person experiences, although in subtle ways.

We are so enamored with objective experience — ideas, pictures, feelings, sensations, and perceptions that we never notice the experience of just being aware. In other words, we struggle to exist just as a knower of fundamental and pure reality, which is played as a life situation for us. This is because of limitations and filters in perception. In truth, most individuals spend their whole lives without ever being aware of the dimension of "seer-knower-observer;" that underpins all intelligence, experience, and existence; which is in pure consciousness; *Sat-Chit-Ananda*. This pure consciousness has its source in space, silence, and stillness. Intellectually, it is beyond spiritual intelligence (SI); experientially, it is beyond neutrality, i.e., emptiness or transcendental, metaphysical reach beyond the causal body; the great causal body and scientist refers to this dimension as a quantum field with infinite potentialities. Before any other expression occurs in time and space, it has the potential for mental activity.

For the duration, you concur the Higher (i.e., LOC > 400); you are from perceptual experience. Once you attain a LOC range of 600-800, you become permanently independent of perceptual experience. It means when you can experience bliss (i.e., *Ananda*), even if you do not have your body and mind (i.e., after death). Hence, wise people say, look within to get pure happiness. At this level, the "experience" merges with the "knower of experience." In other words, the shadow self gets merged with the true self. Also, for the highest self, there is no difference between outer and inner purpose (i.e., Smartness and Sage-ness), and the purpose becomes singular.

In yogic science, this experience is termed *"Turiya."* Also, as per yogic literature, the background pervades the experience of lower states of consciousness (awake, dream, and dreamless sleep). In other words, the *"Turiya"* state can objectify, see, know, and experience the lower states of consciousness (awake, dream, and dreamless sleep). One can achieve this when the meditative state becomes permanent, i.e., the state of *"Samadhi."* Hence *"Turya"* is an experience of the *"Samadhi"* state or highest self. In the *Dhyana* state, the self is still involved in its outer- purpose without being entangled with it. However, in the state of *"Samadhi,"* both the outer and inner purpose (i.e., Smartness & Sage-ness) merge and become a singular purpose; that is purposeless. Another point to note is that the *"Samadhi"* state has two incremental sub-steps, i.e., *"Savikalpa samadhi"* and *"Nirvikalpa samadhi."* While with *"Savikalpa samadhi,"* self can still return to time and space; however, *"Nirvikalpa samadhi"* is a state of no return. At this stage, the experience gets merged with "knower of experience." In the last chapter, we saw, this is also the level, where all "known" got merges with "knower." In other words, the shadow self merges with the true self. In other words, the shadow self merges with the true self. Hence this must be the level where all expressions merge with timeless existence; manifested *"Sat"* merge with non-manifested *"Sat,"* which we will discover in the next chapter.

Suffering is the creation of the shadow self, and joy is the creation beyond the shadow self.

Call to Action

When you are just sitting in a garden, the traffic is passing, and there are many noises and sounds around you, i.e., a crow is cawing. Just focus your attention on the cawing sound intensely, even if it is very subtle than the traffic noise, and feel it without thinking about its quality of sounds. You will see the whole traffic noise will go away from your awareness, as all your awareness is consumed in feeling the cawing sound. In other words, the feeling of cawing is at the center of your awareness. Develop your sensitivity and feelings; when you eat, shower, and watch TV.

Let's take a life situation where you are watching a competitive show on TV, and try observing the experience of your mental and psychological world. Let's say your favorite party is on one side of a discussion or game; notice how your mind pattern has a craving or hunger for your preferred party to win and an aversion for the opposing party. Observe or pay attention to the feeling-tone and sensations in your inner body, along with your thought and inner narrative pattern. When your favored party is in a winning situation, you will get a pleasant sensation (i.e., positive excitement). Try to observe and objectify it non-judgmentally; just feel it without thinking until it reaches a neutral tone. If you succeed, you have already elevated your conscious vibration matching to higher-self vibration (201 – 400). If you cannot succeed and it is beyond your tolerance limit; you may call your best friends to inform your excitement; i.e., you are at your pride (175); which belongs to the lower self (craving shadow self)

Similarly, when your favorite party is in a losing position, you will get an unpleasant sensation (negative excitation). Try to observe and objectify it non-judgmentally, i.e., feel it without thinking until it reaches a neutral tone. If you succeed, you have already elevated your conscious vibration matching to higher self-vibration (201 – 400). If you cannot succeed and it is beyond your tolerance limit, you may start blaming the situation or environment of competition or any other; i.e., you are at your grief (75), experiencing your lowest self (aversive-shadow self). You might also get angry about the non-performance of your favorite party; i.e., you are at your anger (150) and experiencing your lower self-vibration. This brings a different perspective to how we should look at different life situations to transcend our experiential dimension. Regularly elevate your conscious vibration in bliss ("*Ananda*" essence).

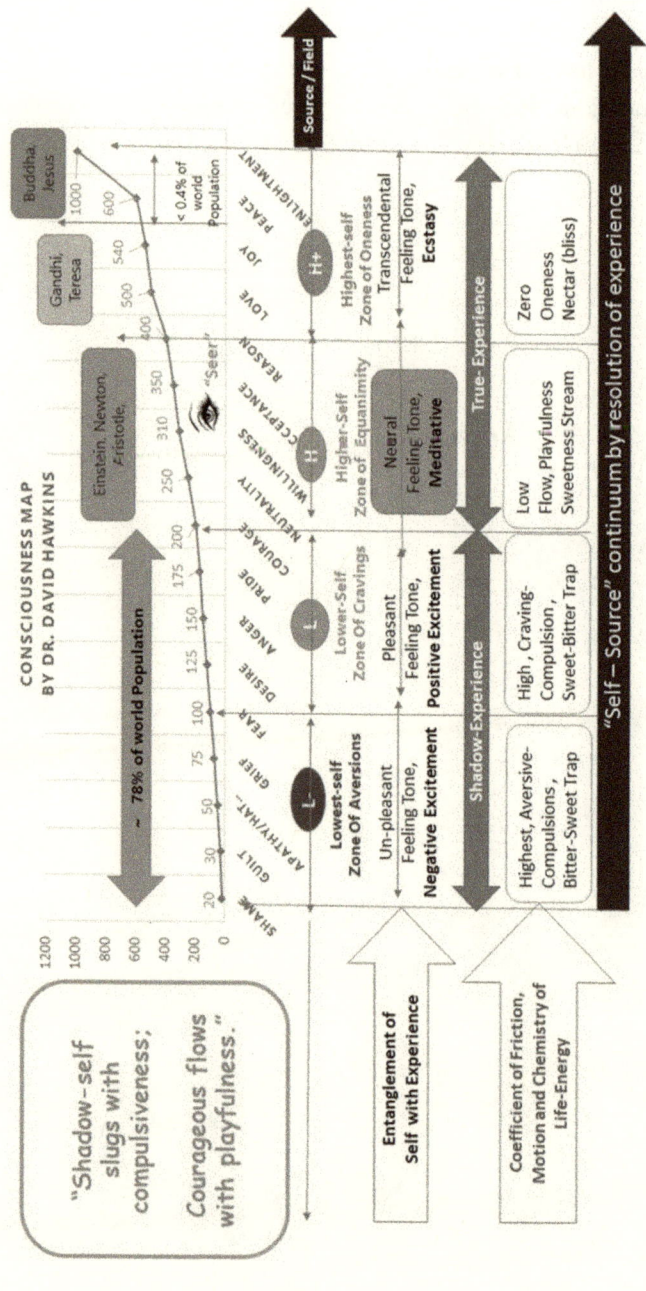

6

EXISTENCE & EXPRESSION
High-Resolution Existence and Expression Happens Beyond Courage

"There is One unchanging indivisible Reality which, though unmanifest, reveals Itself in infinite multiplicity and diversity."

— Anandamayi Ma

You might have seen two brothers with the same upbringing express their life differently; one life with playfulness and the other with anxiety. Similarly, to friends with the same level of understanding joining one company at a time, one has both inner and outer well-being while the other has only outer well-being. What is the root of our expression?

Sat: The Existence and Expression, Two Things at Once

Our physical existence, the shadow self and "I am" (i.e., ego), is "out there" is all because of the outer journey of our being or "innerself." The concept of the outer journey of the self, i.e., philosophy of manifestation or causality, is found in the *Sankhya Upanishad* of Vedic

Science, which was discovered by the sage *Kapila Muni* much before Buddha's time. Yoga and Ayurveda both recognized this philosophy for creating energy and health. According to this philosophy, which does not exist cannot be created, and what is present cannot be absent.

> The Latin phrase- *"ex nihilo nihil fit"* translates to *"That which does not exist cannot come into being."*

In other words, **"You can't make something out of nothing."** The cause conceals the consequence before it is formed. In this sense, creation denotes the manifestation of the hidden, whereas destruction denotes the concealment of the manifest. In this manner, both creation and destruction denote the abandonment of one form or quality in favor of another. This doctrine also says; there is no separate existence of the cause and the consequence. Particle-Wave Theory of dualism in quantum physics also states that light behaves simultaneously as a wave and a particle. In short, both ancient philosophy and modern science contend that there is no difference between the energy that grows a walnut and the walnut itself. All of existence (*Sat*) is two things at once; existence and expression.

Among the great, fascinating scientific triumphs of our century, the emergence of the unified field is undoubtedly the most notable. The hunt for the origin of fundamental particles and the search for the ultimate source of our universe points to the unified field theory. Here we get an objective view of how our universe and humankind came to be for the first time. This scientific research has revealed that "fields" or non-manifested quantum potentialities are as real as the material world. Fields are a fundamental existential reality, more than the material world, because the material world is nothing more than an expression of the underlying quantum fields (existence). Although the fields are undeniably existent, they cannot be seen or touched; i.e., it is beyond human perception. For example, we cannot feel or touch the field of gravity, yet we know it exists; all we have to do is leap to verify its presence. As per this doctrine, the spirit co-exists with matter (through energy), or the spirit is the only reality that prevails. Also, "seer" co-exists with "seen". Hence, the world comprises at least two radical and primitive substances: spirit and matter in different levels of vibrational energy, where the spirit is existence and matter (through energy) is the expression.

It reminds us of what Krishna said in the *Bhagvat Gita* (7.24); *"The less intelligent do not understand my impersonal, imperishable and formless nature is co-existing with my form (personality)."*

Here the personal form (personality) represents the expression (manifested *Sat* essence), and the impersonal formless represents the soul (non-manifested *Sat* essence). Our formless and non-manifested causal body co-exists with our astral and gross body with continuous transformation, reconciliation, and expression. Our microcosm is in continuous transformation and reconciliation with the macrocosm.

The non-manifest can manifest their presence only when they operate on material objects with which they are coupled or co-existing. Hence conscious imagination and visualization, which can simulate this coexistence, is one of the primary aspects of laws of manifestation. Also, this is why the inner purpose (i.e., Sage-ness) of a human being is the primary purpose that has to co-exist with the outer purpose (i.e., Smartness) for manifesting abundance.

Self is an Agent to Express the Existence (*Sat*)

Over the last decade, advances in theoretical physics have led to a more unified understanding of nature's principles, culminating in the recent discovery of unified field theories based on superstrings. These theories propose that all forms and phenomena in the universe are based on a single universal, unified field. Simultaneously, cutting-edge neuroscience research has shown that the 'unified field" exists as the fourth state of human consciousness. This state is physiologically distinct from waking, dreaming, and deep sleep, referred to as the state of *"Samadhi"* with the *"Turiya"* experience. In this state, the observer, the observed, and the process of observation—are united in one indivisible wholeness of pure consciousness. According to John Hagelin, a distinguished scientist and Transcendental Meditation leader, the discovery of the unified field of physics and consciousness provides a real certainty that a unified field of physics is similar to a unified field of consciousness. During the *Samadhi* state, human awareness (i.e., *Chit* essence of self) directly experiences the unified field (i.e., *Ananda* essence of self), which is at the root of existence (i.e., *Sat* essence of self).

Suppose we summarize the creation process as per science. In that case, the only conclusion that makes sense when we put all the experiments of quantum physics and metaphysics together is that – "quantum wave frequencies are downloaded from the unified field (i.e., *Sat* essence of self) to the brain in the form of awareness (i.e., *Chit* essence of self), which are then translated into a particle by collapsing wave function that is projected "out there" to perceive through our mind/senses. Finally, it is available to experience (i.e., *Ananda* essence of self) as the reality of the physical world. In other words, the higher consciousness conceives, the human brain receives, the mind perceives, the intellect & ego decides, and a reaction or response happens. So, when human consciousness participates at the quantum level, conscious events and phenomena propel downstream evolutes, expression, or creation at astral or gross levels as an outer journey of self.

According to *Sankhya*'s philosophy, there are two instincts at the basis of the conscious creative process: *Purusha* and *Prakriti*. *Purusha* and *Prakriti* are not entangled in any action and are also not prone to destruction because they were not born from anything. These instincts are said to have existed from the beginning of time, long before evolution began. *Purusha* never grows into sub-entities; instead, it is a witness as a "seer" to the interplay of entities created by *Prakriti*. Like two birds in one branch, while one eats as "seen," the other observes or witnesses as "seer." Hence, while *Prakriti* evolves and gets manifested as "seen", *Purusha* observes and witnesses as "seer". The *Purusha* is referred to as the masculine part of the source or 'prime source', and *Prakriti* is referred to as the feminine aspect of the source and is called 'nature'. Also, to be very specific, *Prakriti*'s non-manifested state is called root nature, and manifested state is simply known as "nature."

From the perspective of self, even if everything gets destroyed, *Purusha* and *Prakriti* will still exist as non-manifested *Sat-Chit-Ananda*. Also, for evolution to occur, both must be together. For non-manifested *Prakriti* to start producing its evolutes and making the universe, it needs a previous cause. Anything can be manifested through a previous cause that necessitates its manifestation. The nature of *Prakriti* in non-manifested form (i.e., root nature) is causeless, eternal, and in absolute harmony and equilibrium with the prime source. The downstream evolutes of *Prakriti* are not active by their own choice, but the *Purusha* guides their activity; as *Purusha* is on a quest to observe and hence *Prakriti* needs to satisfy *Purusha*.

The nature of the manifested state of *Prakriti* (i.e., nature) is impermanent, non-pervasive, active, interrelated, multiform, dependent on the cause, and has an identity with name and form.

The reflection of *Purusha* and *Prakriti* are found in all living beings in the causal self or the bliss sheath. The initial evolute or expression from the interaction between *Purusha* and *Prakriti* is "*Mahat*," which consists of two components. One is the "*Chitta*" of self; i.e., the intelligence of cosmic order, and the other is *Buddhi*; i.e., the intellect or decision maker in self to protect the interest of *Purusha* (i.e., observation) and that of *Prakriti* (evolution). In other words, the responsibility of *Buddhi* is to protect inner and outer purpose (i.e., Sageness and Smartness). While *Chitta* sits in the bliss sheath or causal self along with tendencies of the past, *Buddhi* sits in the Intelligence sheath of the astral body. As the second evolute of nature, *Buddhi* evolves into shadow self (<200) or true-self (>200) depending upon whether it protects the interest of individual-self or collective-self.

The emergence of intelligence (*Buddhi*) from *Prakriti* is followed by the emergence of astral elements (i.e., mind and five sensations) and gross elements (i.e., five sense organs, five motor organs, and five fundamental elements). All these evolutions mirror the stages a newly conceived individual will pass. Here, *Chitta*, or intelligence of cosmic order, is the initial evolutionary step that gives the newly fertilized cell the ability to organize, grow and allow the organism to sense its surroundings, and so on. While the true self influences the evolution of the developmental or spiritual gene, the shadow self-influences the evolution of the selfish gene in our biological system. Also, while the developmental gene stores the good *Karma*, the selfish gene stores the bad *Karma* in the form of low-vibrational-conscious-energy (i.e., LOC) (<200) and feeling-tone or sensation at the causal layer. *Karma* is at the root of all happenings and phenomena of human life. Finally, other events of consciousness like thinking, imagination, visualization, choices, decision-making, and reaction or response occur. These events propel other downstream evolutes, expressions, or creations at astral or gross levels.

Also, there is strong evidence that this consciousness pervades across all levels. It is also why our genes get switched on and off according to how we think and feel; i.e., there is an interaction between the mind and the matter. Hence consciousness is condensed as astral and gross, as a stream is condensed as water and ice. Sri Krishna also confirms these evolutes of nature as his manifestation and expression as material energy (gross and subtle or astral).

> Sri Krishna says in *Bhagvat Gita* (7.4), "*Earth, water, fire, air, space, mind, intellect, and ego—these are eight components of my material energy (i.e., manifested or expressed as material energy).*"

Variations of Existence and Expression with Levels of Self

All these evolutes, except *Chitta*, have three fundamental existential essences, being or qualities called *"Trigunas."* Hence our existence is rooted in these qualities. These are *Sattva* - Pure, *Rajas* - Stained, *Tamas* - Impure. The movement of the two former ones (*Sattva and Tamas*) is dependent on *Rajas*. *Sattva* and *Tamas* are inactive without *Rajas*. Three existential qualities (*Sattva, Rajas, Tamas*) are not limited to humans alone but apply to practically all living organisms, including the food we eat, the animals around us, and all other elements in our surroundings. Each living being is considered to have a predominance of one or more qualities that distinguishes that being or matter. Also, as per the dominant quality, we may roughly map our levels of self; i.e., lowest self or aversive-shadow self (0-100) is dominated by *Tamas* (or impure) with heaviness, lethargy, darkness, and ignorance and victimized surrender, lower self or craving-shadow self (101-199) is dominated by *Rajas* (or stained) with desire and aggressive dynamism, higher self (200-400) is dominated by *Sattva* (or pure) with purity, clarity, brightness, and steadiness. Finally, the highest self (401-100) is not dominated by any of these qualities and is also known as *Nirguna* (beyond the boundary of qualities). This *Nirguna* is signified by oneness and enlightened surrender. The way the dominance of intelligence (Q's) and experience (feeling-tones) varies with the level of self; similarly, the dominance of existential qualities (*Sattva, Rajas, Tamas*) varies across the level of self. Here the *Tamas* (impure) and *Rajas* (Stained) existence and expression are irrelevant, whereas *Sattva* existence and expression are intrinsic. Hence the expression as well varies across the self. As we know, quantum wave frequencies are downloaded from the unified field (i.e., *Sat* essence of self) to the brain in the form of awareness (i.e., *Chit* essence of self), which are then translated into a particle by collapsing wave function that is projected "out there."

Any expression or manifestation in this world happens first at the level of thought (including imagination and visualization) and then the expression as further evolutes. Also, there is a direct correlation between the disposition of our experience and expression. Hence according to the disposition of our experience; we have different kinds and densities of thoughts.

- ***Samadhi*, or deep-sleep state** with mental disposition as oneness, is dominated by delta brain waves (less than 4 Hz); which leads to *Nirguna* expression, expressing around <10 thousand thoughts per day.
- **The meditative state** with mental disposition as equanimity is dominated by theta brain waves (4-8 Hz), and the

concentrative problem-solving state, with stability, is dominated by the alpha wave (8-12 Hz). This leads to *Sattva* expressing around 10 to 30 thousand thoughts per day.

- **Active problem-solving state** with mental disposition as craving is dominated by alpha and beta-waves (13-30Hz), which leads to *Rajas* expression, expressing around 30 to 60 thousand thoughts per day.

- **The reactive problem-solving state** with mental disposition as aversion is dominated by gamma waves (> 30Hz), which leads to *Tamas* expression, expressing around 60 to >80 thousand thoughts per day.

The way shadow intelligence (PQ, IQ, EQ) in silo works for shadow self (<200) in the absence of SQ; similarly, low amplitude brain wave (gamma, beta, and alpha) works for shadow self (<200) in the absence of theta and delta; i.e., it results in unconscious and selfish participation in the creation process. This selfish manifestation process also produces the by-product of aversion and cravings, leading to suffering and human affliction. However, the brain-wave theta and delta activate the "seer of shadow self" and hence qualify for conscious expression, creation, and manifestation. Also, we may say our capability of manifestation increases with our level of conscious participation at the quantum level. Hence all teachers of the law of manifestation encourage participation in the creation process by elevating the consciousness beyond body-mind identification and shadow self. This conscious manifestation process doesn't produce the by-product of aversion and cravings hence leads to joy, peace, and meaning in life. Hence it can be called as green or sustainable creation. To attest to this aspect, there is one beautiful quotation in Vedic Science, which is *"Yat Pinde Tat Brahmande."* This means whatever is in the microcosm is also in the macrocosm. In other words, as the "existence," or being so is the "expression".

Expression of Lowest Self or the Aversive Shadow Self (L-, 0 - 100)

People at this level are very far from an ultimate neural pattern for peak existence, intelligence, expression, and expression (i.e., *Sat-Chit-Ananda*). Hence, their brains are dominated by gamma waves and *Tamas* or impure characteristics like ignorance, illusion, inertia, cautiousness, and apprehensiveness. While they have good physical intelligence, they are poor in other intelligence. Also, their inner space is filled with an aversion to unpleasant feeling-tone. Biologically they lose control of their autonomic nervous system. They lose their tolerance limit to embrace a life situation with unpleasant feeling-tone at the gross or physical level. Hence their response to a stimulus is the fight-or-flight response at the gross level. They perceive their surroundings as dangerous. When confronted with possible danger, their nervous system is poised to flee or engage in physical aggressiveness, as the name implies. They create physical violence to take revenge and are prone to suicide. To compensate for an unpleasant tone, they eat *Tamas* foods (e.g., alcohol, meat, processed food) or overindulge (e.g., overeating, oversleeping).

In organizational or professional workplaces, this appears in the form of becoming non-mobile, not being physically available with the team during a crisis, and not attending to moral and ethical responsibility voluntarily if it is not monitored. In extreme cases, it appears as sexual harassment as well. *Tamas* professionals defend and preserve their boundaries even if there is an opportunity for growth and transformation. They waste time and energy with confusion and indecisiveness. They often cannot appreciate the positive stuff around them; instead, they find a negative perspective with their *Tamas* filter in psychology. They stay blind to reason with a hostile personality. They live fragile lives by pursuing happiness by constantly avoiding pain and unpleasant situations. They try to achieve this by withdrawing, pouting, sulking, and pursuing their business in a cheaper and *Tamas* way without caring for integrity or with an attitude of "fake it till you make it'. They are primarily motivated by their cleverness in exploiting the world with available loopholes in the system and keeping others blind or by backstabbing.

Such is the story of Elizabeth Anne Holmes (born February 3, 1984), an American former biotechnology entrepreneur. She created and served as the CEO of Theranos. This now-defunct health technology business claimed to have revolutionized blood testing by creating technologies that could use remarkably small volumes of blood, such as from a finger-prick, in 2003. Based on the $9 billion value, Forbes declared Holmes the youngest and wealthiest self-made female billionaire in America in 2015. As discoveries of suspected fraud regarding Theranos' claims began to surface the following year, Forbes reduced its estimate of Holmes' net worth to zero. Fortune named her in its feature piece "The World's 19 Most Disappointing Leaders."

Theranos' demise began in 2015 when journalistic and regulatory investigations raised questions about the company's technological claims and whether Holmes had misled investors and the government. In 2018, the SEC charged Theranos and Holmes with "massive fraud" for making incorrect or overstated statements about the company's blood-testing accuracy. Later, Holmes settled the charges by shelling out a $500,000 fine, returning 18.9 million shares to the company, relinquishing voting control of Theranos, and accepting a ten-year ban from holding a position as an officer or director of any public enterprise. For Holmes, making the world better was motivated by making growth with an intent of self-glorification in a cheaper and *Tamas* way (101-199). When it became evident that her inventions were ineffective, she concealed data, fabricated information, and bullied whistle-blowers.

In summary, *Tamas* is a shadow-existence and they have the lowest capability for sustainable expression, manifestation or creation. Hence, these people are the least playful. The outer purpose (i.e., Smartness) is the primary purpose of their life. Also, many times they are passive and not bothered with any purpose. The self or life of *Tamas* people is tightly entangled with life situations; i.e., the slightest up and down in life situations makes them negatively excited.

Expression of Lower Self, the Craving-Shadow self (L, 101- 199)

People at this level are away from an ultimate neural pattern for peak existence, intelligence, expression, and expression (i.e., *Sat-Chit-Ananda*). Hence their brains are dominated by gamma-waves and *Rajas* quality, such as being driven by self-centered passion, excitement, and desire, which can lead to avarice, activity, taking up work, and restlessness. People with *Rajas*-dominant personalities are attached and want to be acknowledged or credited for their efforts without a miss. Making the world a better place motivates them to grow with the intent of becoming famous and glorifying themselves. Because of the dominance of self-interest in these persons, they lack self-control and the ability to perceive, objectify, and understand what is right and wrong, and hence have a biased opinion on such situations. While IQ and EQ dominate them, they lack SQ. Their inner space is filled with cravings for pleasant feeling-tone. They lose their tolerance limit to embrace a life situation because of their craving for a pleasant feeling-tone, which leads to desire, anger, and pride (101-199). Hence their response to a stimulus is the fight-or-flight response at an astral or psychological level. Rather than acting to protect their body, they behave to protect their ego and their boundaries. Anger, criticism, cynicism, and disrespect are the psychological versions of the fight response. They also displace toxic positivity to manage their self-glorification (toxic inside and positivity outside). *Rajas* and self-centered leaders are common in the VUCA world, but they might be difficult to spot. They may find it easy to portray themselves as organizational supporters, mission-driven persons, or even people who care about the well-being of those they manage. However, as their subordinates have discovered over time, these leaders tend to make decisions and take acts that benefit their welfare, career, or reputation. They are also largely driven by their ability to exploit the weaknesses of others. There are numerous examples of activities that such self-centered leaders may conduct.

Favoritism: They will comply with outside requests to profit personally or professionally, even if it means burdening their subordinates or ignoring problematic ethics. Self-centered leaders care about their subordinates' performance.

Reactive and Impatience: At first appearance, these leaders appear to be laid-back. However, this is only true until their image or reputation is jeopardized. Then, despite being uneducated or inexperienced with the circumstances, they make a hasty decision based on self-interest. When these leaders believe that a problem will negatively influence them, they have little or no patience for the issue or the people involved. Often, their concern for themselves causes people to become enraged when they are subjected to perceived inspection or questioning.

Self-glorification: These individuals skillfully can claim credit for others' successes and distance themselves from challenging situations. They try to paint a colorful picture of their effort without hesitating in demeaning contributions from others. Furthermore, to advance their careers, self-centered leaders will blatantly appease higher intellectual or important figures to defend and preserve their fame. They dwell in the past and are vulnerable to the weaknesses of others.

Intimidation: Self-centered leaders frequently use their position to frighten and influence subordinates into responding to commands or demands. They may even threaten unjustified disciplinary proceedings. This is crucial for these leaders since their staff will only respond to them out of respect and a good relationship. They try to control people by any means as they cannot inspire.

Passing Toxicity: These leaders may frequently emphasize the difficulties of their work and the associated stress to others, even holding meetings for this reason. Instead of establishing an environment conducive to creative brainstorming, problem-solving, and design thinking, they seek the scapegoat in the ecosystem. Employees get a sense of compulsion and tension in their inner well-being simply by watching or dealing with these self-centered executives.

In summary, *Rajas* are also a shadow-existence, and they have a lower capability for sustainable expression, manifestation, or creation. Hence, *Rajas* people are less playful. Also, outer purpose (i.e., Smartness) is the primary purpose of their life. The self or life of Rajasic people is also entangled with life situations; i.e., the slightest up and down in life situations makes them proud and angry.

Expression of Higher Self (H, 200 - 400)

When we moved to our own house, we planted twelve flower plants in a row. After a few weeks, I saw the last one in a row was not growing at par with others. From that day, I started giving intimate attention to it, not in terms of nurturing with physical labor but just motivating it through silent *Sattva* dialogues to feel empowered and express its full potential. Also, sometimes I express my love through gentle, empathetic touch. I was keeping my wife updated about this. To our astonishment, the last plant grew better than the others, with more flowers. When life becomes *Sattva*, our expression in life situations also becomes *Sattva*.

"Self" plays its role in "life-situation," i.e., between stimulus and response. Also, it plays a role in "life," i.e., between our existence and expression. Hence, when the "self" vibrates at the energy of courage (200) or beyond, the potentials of life get repurposed, bringing transcendence in "life". Also, the "life situation" becomes vibrant, effective, and efficient. In other words, the shadow self (<200) entangled with the shadow existence of the body-mind cannot make a real expression.

As we know, the "seer of shadow self" emerges when LOC is greater than 200, and it co-exists with shadow self-till LOC = 400. Accordingly, here the "seer" co-exists with the "seen" and can observe the misdoing and low expression of the shadow self. In this state, people start truly confessing themself and move forward courageously.

They start seeing life as a movie, the world as a theater, and themselves as an actor and express their existence fully and truthfully. They do not derive their sense of self from this movie but rather use it to refine and transcend their "self" to its fullest, as they are completely aware that they have to go home (i.e., merge with the infinite) once their move is over. They derive their sense of self from the primary product of life (i.e., meaning, and existential purpose) rather than by-products in life situations (i.e., wealth, power, position, name, fame). People at this level are closer to the ultimate neural pattern for peak existence, intelligence, expression, and expression (i.e., *Sat-Chit-Ananda*). Hence, their brains are dominated by alpha and theta brain waves and *Sattva* characteristics, like being motivated by ecosystem-centric passion, courage, curiosity, possibility, creativity, and quest; (i.e., natural desire with willingness, acceptance, and enthusiasm). In such people, the mind and senses are at ease with neutrality and non-judgmental observation, i.e., no place for aversion or craving for pleasantness. In other words, they are meditative and remain silent unless their word is more valuable than silence. They have self-control and the ability to comprehend, objectify and understand to differentiate between desirable and undesirable and undutiful and dutiful action. They perform work with calm understanding, free of doubts, and without ignoring society's and humanity's welfare. They have a high SQ and other intelligence like PQ, IQ, and EQ.

Let's understand this through a story. This is the story of three IT professionals (Tapas, Rajesh, and Suresh) working in the same organization at the same grade with similar performance levels and pay. They owned and resided in the same apartment thirty miles away from the office, in consideration of their friendship and affordability. They used to take a rented three-wheeler taxi for some distance and then a local bus for the remaining distance to commute to the office. There were no other convenient means to alter the arrangement in the city. This commuting mechanism wasted their valuable time and energy and created inconvenience and imbalance in their work and life. The three discussed working toward earning the next possible but competitive promotion at the year-end, which may enable them to buy a four-wheeler and change their situation. Tapas was not content with his current situation; however, he was lethargic and wanted to achieve the target with the bare minimum effort. Hence, he was not embracing any challenges that came while fulfilling responsibility. He kept living in the comfort zone of his stagnant life and left the promotion to destiny. Rajesh was not content with his current life situation and was embracing the challenges; however, it was based on his craving to change his status restlessly with obsession. Because of fear of failure in competition, he was not openly sharing his best practices at work with a wider audience. His mind was agitated at the arrival of challenging work situations or in case any outcome was unfavorable. While he was feeling proud of any appreciation at work, he felt jealous when his colleagues were appreciated. Suresh was content with his current life situation; however, he had a quest to serve the interest, expectations, and needs of stakeholders around him in the best possible way without any expectation of appreciation. Hence, he accepts outcomes calmly and moves on to the next opportunity by courageously embracing whatever challenges may come. He was openly sharing his best practices and celebrating others' success. Finally, the promotion results were announced at year-end; there was no update on Tapas, but Rajesh's promotion was moved to the next cycle. Suresh got the promotion along with a handsome annual performance bonus. While *Tamas* Tapas blamed destiny, *Rajas* Rajesh accused Suresh of getting a promotion with unfair practice. *Sattva* Suresh got a metallic black Jaguar and offered Tapas and Rajesh help for commuting. Also, his embracing nature ensured no entanglement in any life situation but only involvement with meaning and fulfillment.

Inner-purpose (i.e., Sage-ness) of the *Sattva* people is the primary purpose of life. Hence, the expression, creation, or manifestation of the *Sattva* people is more conscious, playful, and sustainable. Therefore, the coaches of laws of attraction or manifestation advocate an increase in conscious level to this *Sattva* and higher self-level (200 to 400) to accelerate manifestation, where there is a high probability of conversion of opportunity from possibility to reality.

Jesus also announced the same; when he said, *"Whoever has will be given more, and they will have an abundance. Whoever does not have, even what they have will be taken from them."*

Now the question is - Whoever has what? While there are numerous answers to this, i.e., love, gratitude, etc., I would say, "Whoever has a 'higher consciousness' will be given more."

The way SQ repurposes other Q's, neutral feeling-tone repurposes lower feeling-tones (unpleasant and pleasant); *Sattva* quality repurposes the *Tamas* and *Rajas*; i.e., they embrace the aversion and craving with courage. This embracing courage helps transmute (or re-purpose) the self-centric to natural ecosystem-centric growth and transformation, motivation from the result of action to motivation from curiosity, possibility, creativity, and so on.

The creative and inspiring business outlook of Ratan Tata is an example of a leader dedicated to the "triple bottom line," implying that businesses should plan for three distinct outcomes. The traditional metric of business profit, driven by earnings, is one. The second is a company's people account bottom line, which assesses how it contributes to and interacts with people inside and outside the business. The third is the company's planet account, which shows how socially and ecologically responsible and sustainable it has been. While Tata accomplished all three bottom lines as outer purpose (i.e., Smartness), his inner traits reflect an evolved, courageous, curious, calm, creative, and compassionate leadership in silence, distinguishing him from the rest. When Tata introduced the Nano," the people's car", it expressed a leader's inner ideals and *Sattva* existential quality reverberating with courage, creativity, social responsibility, love, and compassion, which were visible by his outward expression. Also, Mr. Ratan Tata is a rare business personality of the 21st century who has the ultimate clarity and ability to objectify inner purpose (i.e., Sageness) as primary purpose; when he says, "I admire very successful people. But if that success has been achieved through too much ruthlessness, I may admire that person, but I can't respect him." Here he reserves admiration for outer success and respect for inner success.

If we look into his life or read his biography, we will realize the significance of what Swami Vivekananda said; *"Power will come, glory will come, goodness will come, purity will come, and everything excellent will come when this sleeping soul is roused to self-conscious activity."*

Hats off to this Sattva leader. Many of his philanthropic expressions are also reverberating with his highest self.

In summary, *Sattva* quality is a true existence, and they have the higher capability for sustainable expression, manifestation, or creation. Hence, *Sattva* people are very playful. Also, inner purpose (i.e., Smartness) is the primary purpose of their life.

At the junction of the higher and highest self, while intelligence becomes intuitive and the experience meditative with unconditional love and expression-wise, the brain produces theta wave. Also, as per the research from HeartMath institute, at this stage, the heart serves as a key access point through which information originating in the higher dimensional structures is coupled into the human physical system, including brain waves and DNA, i.e., the theta brain wave gets transmuted (or repurposed) as gamma wave and selfish gene spiritual gene.

Expression of Highest Self (H+, 401 - 1000)

People at this level resonate with the ultimate neural pattern for peak existence, intelligence, expression, and expression (i.e., *Sat-Chit-Ananda*). Hence, delta brain waves and *Nirgun* characteristics dominate their brains, i.e., "everything is OK" and "nothing matters." We discussed in earlier chapters; the highest self has ultimate cosmic intelligence to objectify the illusion of the outer self. It also has the ultimate experience of source (*Purusha*), i.e., *Turiya* or *Samadhi*, or non-perceptual bliss like running water instead of the internment of drops of water. Additionally, it also realizes that both ultimate intelligence (*Chit*) and ultimate experience (*Ananda*) exist timelessly forever, which is the ultimate existence (*Sat*). The way all academic streams converge at a higher level of studies like a Ph.D. (i.e., doctor of philosophy); in the same way, all three essences (or potentialities) converge at the highest self as one singular essence *"Sat-Chit-Ananda"* or *"Sachidananda."* At this level, the existential quality is beyond *Sattva, Rajas,* and *Tamas.* All three qualities merge and lose their significance, known as *Nirguna*. People at this level become the synonym for the highest order of human values, i.e., Gandhi for nonviolence, Mother Teresa for selfless service, Jesus for forgiveness, Krishna for love, etc. When the self becomes *Nirguna*, it merges with the source (*Purusha*). In other words, all "manifested" get merged with "non-manifested", all expressions get merged with existence, and the shadow self-get merged with true-self. Also, for the highest self, there is no difference between outer and inner purpose (i.e., Smartness and Sage-ness), and the purpose becomes singular.

We extensively discussed human potentials (intelligence, experience, and expressions) and how they evolve along the map of consciousness. It also discussed how the inner purpose (i.e., Sage-ness) becomes primary beyond courage (200).

Now the big question is, even if we know this intellectually, **why are we not able to adopt the inner purpose (i.e., Sage-ness) as the primary purpose easily and automatically to have higher intelligence (*Chit*), expression (*Sat*), and experience (*Ananda*)?**

Why does around 78% of the population are below the courage line (200) and suffer from aversion and craving for shadow self (<200)?

Why do they face poverty in inner purpose (i.e., Sage-ness), despite their advancements and abundance in outer purpose (i.e., Smartness)?

A gentleman was walking through an elephant camp and spotted that the elephants weren't being kept in cages or held by chains. A small piece of rope tied to one of their legs was holding them back from escaping the camp. As the man gazed upon the elephants, he was completely confused about why they didn't just use their strength to break the rope and escape the camp. They could have easily done so, but instead, they didn't try to. Curious to know the answer, he asked a trainer nearby why the elephants were just standing there and never tried to escape. The trainer replied, "When they are very young and much smaller, we use the same size rope to tie them, and, at that age, it's enough to hold them. As they grow up, they are conditioned to believe they cannot break away. They believe the rope can still hold them, so they never try to break free." The only reason the elephants weren't breaking free and escaping from the camp was that, over time, they forgot that they had a higher potential now and carried an old limiting belief that it just wasn't possible.

Both reasons are true for 78% of people suffering from shadow self (<200), i.e., they have forgotten their current potential and have some old limiting belief or misperception of self. In simple, they are in ignorance.

Call to Action

Now, readers, reading the stories, theories, and explanations of higher expression is inspiring, leading to playfulness. It is now your chance to put them to the test. Every day, try doing at least one expression of your "self" (thought, word, or action) that does not serve your shadow self with aversion or craving; i.e., you derive your sense of self from radiating neutrality, purity, love, and compassion in silence instead of having a sense of doing a favor, pride, and creating noise about it among family, society, or social media. It might be as basic as filling a water bottle for your co-workers with genuine love and care in the office when you notice they are busy.

Do it in silence, without creating any noise about it. In a few weeks, it will enhance your mood, vibration or consciousness, intelligence, and experience and attract positive events and phenomena around you. Try to preserve it in silence.

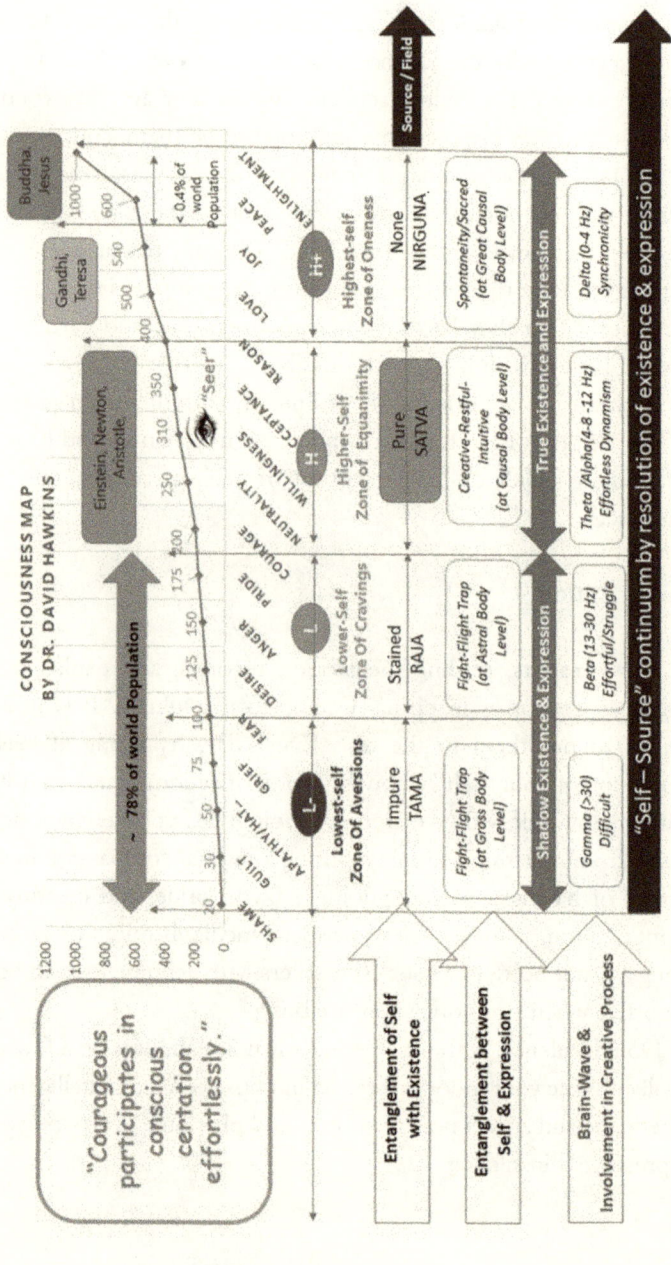

PART III: PROBLEM

7

IGNORANCE
Misperception of Self and Consequence

"Most people are drowning in their delusional ignorance without knowing that their suffering was created by themselves."
— Jakusho Kwong Roshi.

There was a businessman named Ravi. He had an abundant and affluent life - including a profitable business, a royal bungalow, social influence and power, well-educated children, etc. While prosperous, he was restless and dissatisfied most of the time. Suddenly, he realized that life should not be like this and sought containment and bliss (*Ananda*). Once during an evening walk in a nearby forest, he noticed a saint meditating under a tree. He approached him gently and waited for the saint to open his eyes. He was pleased to spend some time with the saint. He resolved to remain there till the saint opened his eyes. After some time, the saint gradually opened his eyes. He was shocked to see a man sitting calmly near him.

"What do you want?" the saint inquired meekly.

"Can you tell me the route to bliss (*Ananda*)?" "Where can I discover containment?" Ravi wondered

"Go to the next pond and ask the fish the same thing," the saint suggested with a smile.

"She will provide you with the solution." The ignorant man, Ravi, then proceeded to the adjoining pond and asked the same question to the fish.

"O nice guy!" exclaimed the fish.

"First and foremost, get me some water to drink." Ravi was taken aback.

"You live in water," he explained. "But do you still want to drink water? How peculiar!"

At this point, the fish said, "You are correct. And now you have the solution to your inquiry. A human's heart and soul contain the love, containment, joy, and bliss that you are looking for. But, since he is dipped in ignorance, he looks for them in the outside world. Instead of roaming, search within yourself to discover them." This brought Ravi a lot of happiness. He thanked the fish and returned home wiser. He altered his perception of the world and himself and started looking at his inner world. Gradually Ravi found himself out of discontentment and restlessness. He did everything he could to spread this message to the rest of his fellow humans. All his pals embraced him as their master and sought his advice on changing their perception, reducing their ignorance, and having a healthy self. Like Ravi, most people are still in a misperception that the ultimate experience, bliss (*Ananda*), is available outside the self. Hence the rat race for an outer purpose (i.e., Smartness) has become a primary purpose for all.

In earlier chapters, we discussed how human perception is filtered at different levels of mind and senses, making it personalized and subjective and finally limiting us to have a subjective experience of reality (*Ananda*). The prime reason for misperception is ignorance, which is a veil on our intellect (*Buddhi*) and can corrupt our intelligence (*Chit*), compel our cognition to follow the ego-self (*Ahamkara*) - ignoring the true-self and limit our objective experience (*Ananda*). Most people are intellectually aware that "love (500)" is appreciative involvement in life with life-situation. However, they unconsciously pursue, act, or respond to life-situation with possessive (125) entanglement, which limits them to remain in "like (125)" instead of "love (500)". In other words, while they are intellectually aware of love, they can't vibrate at that energy level when the situation arrives. This difference is due to unsettled or non-reconciled intelligence in life. i.e., ignorance.

Two types of people live life to the fullest. One is completely ignorant, and the other is wise. If you are totally ignorant of the happening in the world, you can live life to the fullest. A sheep or a goat lives to the fullest even when taken for slaughtering because it does not know it will die soon. In the same way, if you are ignorant of the consequences of your actions and the laws of the world, you will enjoy your life to the fullest. Hence it is called ignorance is bliss. However, this bliss is till such time. You are hit by a calamity or die. However, if you are wise, you know the world's deepest secrets.

Hence, you know what is to be done and what is not to be done. You don't do anything that can bring you suffering; hence, you don't suffer in life. You only perform actions that bring you joy; hence, your life is filled with joy, and you live fully. If most people in the world suffer from numerous pains, it is because they are neither ignorant nor wise. They are only semi-knowledgeable and half-wise. They have little knowledge of the world, yet they believe they know it all. Hence, they keep doing things for happiness and joy, but that brings them suffering and pain. In today's world of abundance of information, it is impossible to be ignorant once you have acquired some knowledge. Hence, the only way to live fully is to become wise and virtuous.

Ignorance is a universal force that affects everyone. The Sanskrit term "*Avidya*" refers to it, and it is formed by combining the root vid, which means "to see, know, comprehend, or understand," with the negative "a," which has the opposite meaning. This ignorance (*Avidya*) and misperception present us with a distorted reality and impact our intelligence, emotions, and potentialities of self in a downward direction, limiting us from bliss and freedom. The tragedy of this misperception is that it negates each potentiality of our true self. While our life or true existence is timeless (*Sat*), this ignorance creates a misperception that our existence is limited to this life only. Again, though our gross existence of this incarnation is till our death, we forget the same while living the day-to-day life, and we live in this body as if it will exist forever. In other words, we perceive the span between birth and death, which consists of life situation as life itself.

Similarly, while our true nature is bliss (*Ananda*), we misperceive the ups and downs in life situations and become unnecessarily excited and disturbed by them. What you think of as happiness is just a kind of excitement with pride (175). Let's say you have won the lottery and feel great happiness. Your happiness means you are so excited that you can't even sleep at night. Your pulse goes up, and your blood pressure goes up. So, what you call happiness is a kind of excitement with pleasantness and pride (199), and unhappiness is also an excitement with unpleasantness, fear, and anxiety (100). Then what is the difference between these two? This is why it also happens that what is happiness today becomes unhappiness tomorrow, and what is unhappiness today can become happiness tomorrow. This is a cyclic loop of every duality that exists in this time & space, i.e., today's aversion to bringing craving for tomorrow and vice versa.

The corporate coaches call this positive or healthy tension to create outer well-being for the organization and offer you to take inner un-wellbeing (<200). Perhaps, you may not have thought about it, but what you call happiness or pleasure is very tiring and impermanent or temporary – hence nobody can live with this kind of happiness and pleasure all the time. Hence this kind of happiness is not bliss (*Ananda*). While ignorant call positive excitation happiness, Yoga says that the unexcited state of the body is happy. Hence, what you call happiness and unhappiness, Yoga calls both as *Nir-Ananda* or i (i.e., non-bliss state). However, ignorance makes you choose happiness (*Nirananda*) instead of bliss (*Ananda*); i.e., you crave pleasantness and become averse to unpleasantness. In other words, your shadow self chooses suffering (<200).

Finally, while one consciousness (*Chit*) is our true comprehension, we misperceive the diversity of the material world as our ultimate reality. We cannot perceive our true-self as *Sat-Chit-Ananda* and hence assume a life that is derived, limited, time bound, less intelligent, and full of suffering. Hence, ignorance, illusion, and misperception are the primary dimension, so nearly 78% of our population is still below the courage consciousness (<200). Let's explore some more fundamental misperceptions caused due to ignorance in each of our potentialities; *Sat* (existence), *Chit* (Intelligence), and *Ananda* (bliss).

Vedic Science and Modern Science

Let's have a close look into a few scientific facts about electrons. In 1907, J J Thomson received the Nobel prize by saying the electron is a particle, and his son P J Thomson also got the same Nobel prize in 1937 by saying the electron is a wave. In 1933 Erwin Schrödinger got the same Nobel Prize by saying an electron is a wavicle (neither wave nor a particle). Then in 1933, Werner Karl Heisenberg got the same Nobel Prize by saying in one moment, an electron behaves as a particle in other moments, and it becomes a wave (i.e., a quantum particle and wave). However, Vedic Science and *Bhagvat Gita* (11.54) already told all these 5000 years that the fundamental particle of the universe exists in both states; visible & invisible, manifested and un-manifested. In other words, modern experimental science is seeing different parts of the same elephant incrementally. However, the Vedic experiential science saw it at one go. Hence, modern science seems to be more illusory than Vedic Science. Vedic science is the oldest but more advanced than modern science. While modern science is based on experiments at gross (i.e., physical) and shuttle (i.e., psychological) levels, Vedic science is based on experience covering the causal level and the shuttle and gross.

It is less well-known that the pioneers of quantum physics were students of Vedic science; hence, the connections were not discovered by chance. They were looking for it and came across it. Quantum science and Vedic Science are completely aligned that physical reality is a fleeting illusion.

Neils Bohr, one of the founding fathers of quantum theory, is famous for saying, *"Everything we call real is made of things that cannot be regarded as real. If quantum mechanics hasn't profoundly shocked you, you haven't understood it."*

Another quantum scientist Werner Heisenberg stated that, *"Those who have read Vedic Science will not find quantum theory ludicrous."*

Irwin Schrödinger stated that, *"The unity and continuation of Vedic Science are reflected in the unity and continuity of wave mechanics."*

The Root Cause of Ignorance and Upsetting the Human Condition.

At the beginning of human evolution, the self-reverberated with high conscious vibrational frequency (~ 1000); human beings were cooperative, selfless, peaceful, joyful, playful, and loving instincts, i.e., original normal programmed intelligence, the voice or expression of our true self.

Charles Darwin said, *"The moral sense affords the best and highest distinction between man and the lower animals."*

During those times, the life situation and its stimulus were only perceived and responded to by this original human instinct. Hence there was oneness, equality, and interconnectedness. Gradually, human beings developed the biological nervous system based on intelligence based on learning from the natural phenomenon of cause-and-effect relationships from life-situation around human beings. Hence human beings gradually started perceiving beyond the original program and responding differently, i.e., not completely complying with the original moral instinct. The original program of moral instinct was deprogrammed, leading to a drop in consciousness. This aspect is also amplified by the instinct of "survival for the fittest," which is the origin of aversion and craving, i.e., shadow self (<200). Hence, it is said, "when Adam and Eve (i.e., we humans) took the 'fruit' (Genesis 3:3) 'from the tree of knowledge' (Gen. 2:9, 17), and became 'disobedient and were thrown out Eden Garden".

In our context, we deviated from our true self, *Sat-Chit-Ananda*. Due to the drop in consciousness, there was a miss in objectifying the deviation with **"seen" vs. "seer"** intelligence of moral instinct. In other words, there was an absence of truthful rationalization of deviation with intuitive intelligence. The human intellect deviated from the original instinct. This was also the point when human beings lost their connection to causal self and got entangled with the body-mind. Hence the meta-cognition is reduced to cognition.

This cyclic war of criticism and defense between original instinct and human intellect became a disease of psychosis. The defensive rationale from intellect was artificial, superficial, pseudo idealistic, which made the human being (self) selfish, arrogant, depressed, deluded, pessimistic, hateful, cynical, mean, sadistic, immoral, guilt-ridden, evil, psychotic, neurotic, and alienated. All these aspects got expressed along with human actions (outer *Karma*). Also, the associated low-vibrational-conscious-energy (i.e., LOC) (<200) got accumulated as bad *Karma* (inner *Karma*) as well. We can categorize all these outcomes of the war between original instinct at the astral level; it will either fall under aversion or craving; i.e., shadow self (<200); which leads to a cyclic loop between duality. This war has continued for two million years and continuously degrades the human consciousness. To our surprise, the Bonobo family (a human species) in the South African Forest is still living the original instinct of pure self majorly, without corrupting it much. In other words, we can say they are living beyond-shadow self (>200). However, they may not be complete with their Buddha-self (~1000); which refers to the level of consciousness (LOC) maintained by Siddharth Gautama after his liberation till his death; i.e., from the age of 35 to 80. However, they are very limited in numbers per 2020 estimates (within an approximate range of 10 to 20 thousand). Australian biologist Jeremy Griffith defines this corrupted shadow self as an **"upset-human condition"**; in his book "FREEDOM: The End of The Human Condition." This unreconciled, unsettled, residual, and defensive behavior gets deposited in the causal body as ignorance or tendencies and passed to subsequent generations. Jeremy Griffith says further that this is upsetting the human condition, and hence the ignorance is doubling in every new generation. Without this "upset-human condition" or ignorance, we are the Buddha-self (1000). Additionally, if we try to understand this war in genetic science, in that case, the hereditary genes drive the human or biological intellect, also called a selfish gene representing the connection between any carryover of past Karmic energy from two million years. In other words, our residual bad-Karmic energy (Sat essence) is nothing but our accumulated ignorance (*Chit* essence). However, the good thing is that we have another type of gene in our body that can rescue us from this "upset-human condition," ignorance, and bad-*Karmic* energy, which we will discuss in the subsequent chapter.

Impermanent Is Perceived as Permanent: Ignorance in Sat

In earlier chapters, we discussed the permanent nature of Pure Consciousness (*Sat-Chit-Ananda*), which combines *Purusha* and Root-*Prakriti*. However, the rest of their evolutes are temporary and impermanent. In other words; all five elements (earth, water, air, fire, ether), five sense organs, five perceptions, and five motor organs; human intelligence, ego, conscience, mind, sadness, fear, anger, pride, cells in our bodies and all downstream evolutes are temporary and impermanent. Hence any human existence, including incarnations of gods, is temporary and impermanent.

> Ram Dass, An American psychologist and spiritual teacher, says, *"Death is not an error, it is not a failure, it is taking off a tight shoe."*

Death makes us realize that just as life is finite, suffering is also temporary. Even though people intellectually know that their existence is impermanent and that nothing lasts, they cannot align their life span and life situations to correct perception. This is because the ego self looks for permanence in impermanence. We suffer when we fail to comprehend this simple yet profound fact properly. When we appreciate this fact, we can also experience true serenity, just as the monks do when they meditate.

In truth, there are no permanent jobs; only regular ones exist. I wonder why we're so obsessed with permanency since nothing in the world is permanent. Not our employment, our relationships, our friendships, our nationality, our status, or even life itself. Our shadow self (<200) wants things always to be just as they are, as permanence equates to security. The wealthy attempt to avoid impermanence by having their names engraved on buildings and organizations with the expectation that their legacy will live on. Some see it as a branding exercise, while others see it as pure ego enhancement. Permanence is an illusion in all instances.

> When asked - **what surprised him the most about humanity?**
> Dalai Lama replied: "*Man? Because he sacrifices his health to make money. Then he sacrifices money to recuperate his health. And then he is so anxious about the future that he does not enjoy the present, the result being that he does not live in the present or the future; he lives as if he is never going to die and then dies having never really lived.*"

In other words, man is not able to act as "seer" and objectify the impermanence of life-span as "seen." We can also say life-situations of a man taking his consciousness and pushing him to stay as shadow self (<200), i.e., below the courage line (< 200).

Buddhist philosophy teaches that everything in material or relative existence is transient. Everything has a beginning, a middle, and, most importantly, an end. Flowers, trees, autos, houses, businesses, institutions, political views, relationships, human beings, mountains, rivers, seas, planets, suns, and even galaxies are all transient and will perish.

The Greek philosopher Heraclitus reminds us, "*No man ever steps in the same river twice, for the river has changed, and he is no longer the same man.*"

Our tangible existence is defined by impermanence. Despite its pervasiveness and irrefutability, it is the notion that we have the most difficulties incorporating this into our worldview. Why? Because impermanence forces us to confront our death, which is terrifying, and our shadow self (<200) does not want to accept the same. We get identified with these things; these are the items that give our object-referential reality meaning. We are plunged into disembodied limbo if we lose such identities. Many of us avoid or postpone activities that bring impermanence to the forefront, such as visiting people in the hospital, attending funerals, or estate preparation, since they cause discomfort and cognitive dissonance. This method simply serves to delay the inevitable and cause agony. Our misery is caused by our attitude towards impermanence, not the impermanence itself.

Impermanence, sometimes known as the philosophical question of change, is a philosophical concept addressed by various faiths and ideologies. One of Buddhism's fundamental principles is impermanence (*Anicca* or *Anitya*), which states that "everything changes and nothing lasts forever." This is expressed in Buddha's final words: impermanence is unavoidable. Everything disappears. As a result, nothing is more crucial than perseverance in the journey. All other solutions either deny or minimize the issue.

According to Ashwaghosha, a first-century Buddhist philosopher-poet, *"All manifestations in the world are nothing but the illusory manifestation of the mind and have no existence of their own."*

Rumi, a 13th-century Sufi mystic, said, *"This place is a dream."*

However, without realizing this, if the illusory sense of permanence dominates us, our effort, energy, and resources will be directed towards craving for an outer purpose (i.e., Smartness) at any cost beyond the necessity, which will then invite unconscious aversion to separation from outer-purpose (i.e., Smartness). If outer purpose (i.e., Smartness) is not fulfilled, it will lead to apathy (50), grief (75), and anxiety. If the desire is fulfilled, it creeps into the development of pride (175). There will always be fear of uncertainty (100). In this way, the illusory sense of permeance compels the self to remain in the suffering of the shadow self (<200).

Psychological Time Is Perceived as Clock Time: Ignorance in Sat

We live in a dynamic environment that is always evolving. Our interior environment is equally dynamic, constantly changing biological and mental processes. Life on Earth would not exist without these changes in exterior and interior surroundings. "**Time**" refers to the subjective dimension of all these changes. Without considering time, no explanation of human behavior and life situation can be complete. As a result, people developed methods of measuring time (minutes, days, years, and so on). If we examine nature, the sun and moon rise and fall, and the four seasons cycle with each sun rotation.

Even animals go through life mostly in the Now, living and dying without regret or anxiety about the future. They are constantly focused on the task at hand. They learn from history but only dwell on it for a short time. As a result, most of their time is focused on with a brief conscious journey to the past and future for learning and planning purposes as a guest. Nature is purely on clock time, and animal life is closer to clock time. Our daily lives are packed with time as well. We are surrounded by time from the moment we wake up till we check the alarm clock in the evening. There are appointments and tight deadlines at work. Every full hour, the news is broadcast. There is always the risk of becoming stuck in time when we divide our mental attention in this manner. We divert our attention away from the current instant and lose ourselves unconsciously in memories of the past or imaginary fantasies of the future without being aware or conscious of life situations in clock time; this is called psychological time. The shadow self (<200) loves this psychological time as the past gives us a sense of identity, and the future holds hope. It's a very safe zone for shadow self.

According to the account, a senior monk and a young monk were traveling together. They arrived at a river with a high stream at one point. As the monks prepared to cross the river, they noticed a young, attractive woman attempting to do the same. A young woman approached them and inquired if they could help her cross the river. The two monks exchanged glances because they swore not to touch a lady. The older monk then took up the woman, carried her across the river, and carefully deposited her on the other side before continuing his quest. What had just transpired astounded the younger monk. He remained dumbfounded after rejoining his friend, and an hour passed without them speaking. After two more hours, then three, the younger monk couldn't take it any longer and said, "As monks, we are not supposed to have a woman; how could you then carry that woman on your shoulders?"

"Brother, I laid her down on the other side of the river. Why are you still holding her?" the older monk said, looking at him. Similarly, you might become a senior or junior monk depending on whether you consciously or psychologically use clock time in your life situation.

Suppose you found out you did not get a job you interviewed for. Suppose you reflect curiously and courageously on your application process and interview to determine the opportunity for improvement to enhance the success probability for the next opportunity without repenting, complaining, and blaming anyone. In that case, you are visiting the past consciously as a guest and remaining in clock time. In other words, you (as a "seer") can objectify and observe your past (as seen). However, if you repent for your mistakes, chastise yourself for tripping over an interview question, or blame the firm for not understanding your worth, you are unconsciously in psychological time. In other words, you cannot act as a "seer" and objectify your past as "seen." Here the life situation is taking over your consciousness, pushing you to stay as a shadow self (<200).

Supposing another life situation where you set a career goal to become the CEO of a company. If you define and pursue the steps curiously, courageously (200) to get there over time, with quest but without any aversion and craving (<200) — like the development of leadership skills, strategy skills, networking with other professionals, following the demand and supply chain dynamics in your industry and pursuing promotions that help you climb the ladder toward that top position — you are using clock time. However, if you get consumed by the dread of failure, unconscious fantasies of celebration, or the anticipation of each new step, the destination comes to define you, and you are no longer experiencing the process; you have entered psychological time, i.e., you have lost the ability to objectify your result from the process. Here the life situation is taking over your consciousness, pushing you to roam the zone below the courage line (< 200).

The shadow self (<200) treats the present moment in one of three ways: as a means to an end, an impediment, or an adversary. Let us examine them individually so that you might recognize and determine again when this pattern works for you. It is nearly impossible to misidentify from one's thinking. It has engulfed us all. What is the best way to train a fish to fly? Here's the deal: Put an end to the illusion of time. Time and the mind are inextricably linked. If you take time out of your mind, it will cease working until you choose to utilize it. To be associated with your mind is to be stuck in psychological time: the need to live almost entirely via recollection and anticipation. This leads to a continued obsession with the past and future and a refusal to appreciate, acknowledge, and allow the current moment to be. The compulsion emerges because the past provides you with an identity, and the future promises redemption and satisfaction in whatever shape. Specifically, the mind of the lowest self (<100) has a permanent residence in the psychological past, and it goes to other times as a guest.

The mind of the shadow self (100 -199) has a permanent residence in the psychological future and clocks time as a guest. They're both deceptions. Nothing ever happens in the past or future; everything happens now.

You conceive of the past as a mental memory trace of a previous Now. You reactivate a memory trace when you recall the past and are doing it right now. The future is a mental projection of the present moment. When the future arrives, it does so in the form of the Now. Past and future do not exist in their universe. They are similar to the moon, which has no light and can only reflect the sun's light. However, we call the light reflected by the moon "moonlight" instead of "sunlight." Its illusion us and take our ability to objectify the light as "sunlight." Similarly, past and future illusion us and take our ability to objectify the time "clock-time or now" and push us to the suffering of shadow self (<200). Also, this illusion pushes humanity to its psychological past and future.

Interconnectedness is perceived as Separated: Ignorance in Chit

At a micro level, we have a conscious (within the astral body) and unconscious mind (within the causal self). The conscious mind is a part of our mind that we use to think daily. We utilize it daily for efforts such as moving our arms and legs, speaking, smiling, singing, dancing, and changing our breathing patterns. With the movement of your body with your conscious mind, your cells are moved with your unconscious mind. It also regulates your pulse, hormones, and the generation and flow of neuropeptides. It is frequently out of reach of our conscious mind since it controls so many more things. Hence, it is referred to as the unconscious. Observing how nature has provided us with an inbuilt interconnectedness between our conscious and unconscious minds to operate in harmony is amazing. At a macro level, we also have a "collective unconscious" mind that unites everyone. So, we all share a collective unconscious mind at the macro level. It works similarly to how computers connect to the internet. And, just as anybody can access the internet (with the appropriate technology), anyone may access the collective unconscious with an appropriate level of consciousness. Also, the way we have the Internet of Things (IoT), we can visualize our collective unconsciousness as the Internet of Unconsciousness (IoU), also referred to as a universal causal body we all share per our degree of consciousness.

Our intuitive feeling of being is connected. More and more medical experts realize our mental and emotional attitudes are connected to diseases, influencing our and others' healing processes. The number of practitioners combining alternative and allopathic medicine is rapidly increasing. People perceive the world in new ways than they were only a few years ago, and their decisions are altering for humanity.

When we get down to quantum physics, it starts to have actual impacts. For example, it's been established that if you do something to one of two subatomic particles, such as electrons, it will always affect the other. This shows us that once the matter is physically connected, the energy remains connected even when its parts are separated. In this expanding cosmos, all matter is made up of particles. We're all entangled in the same particle science. According to science, if you could go into the cosmos right now and collect all the particles of matter, as well as all the space in between, and compress it all into the size of a single atom, that means that every one of us was once a part of the same particle that created the universe as we know it today. Even if those particles have separated and expanded, investigations demonstrate that we are all still energetically bound to an atom as its electron multiverse objects, which quantum mechanics describes.

In 1935, Schrödinger coined the term "entanglement" to explain the phenomena of non-locality. In a pure, coherent state, two particles are entangled. "Entangled" is a fantastic term to depict this inextricable oneness. The two particles do not need to be created together from one source to form one system at first. Any two particles of matter, even large particles like neutrons and protons, can be created at distant and unrelated sources in an experiment. As soon as they come together and interact, they become entangled with each other long after clashing and splitting. They've merged into a single quantum system. Couldn't the same be said for macroscopic particles such as humans?

There's also something else. It makes a difference in who performs the observation and how they do it. Both the prospective observer and the observed are inextricably linked. The so-called observer is a member of the decision-making process. The entanglement begins once the intention to observe is present. Even if two individuals are on opposite ends of the world, the moment they decide to attend a meeting, they have been entangled with one another when they decide to attend a meeting. If they decide jointly, the entanglement is at the astral level, but if they decide unknowingly, accidentally, or as Karmic intuition, the entanglement is at the causal level. And once they've interacted, they'll be entwined or connected at different levels for a long time, maybe forever. Telepathy represents intuition from Karmic energy precisely from the same frequency and amplitude as Karmic energy.

There are two distinct perspectives on how we experience the world in general. The first viewpoint holds that all creatures exist independently and that the universe comprises such entities. The life and death of one creature are unconnected to the life and death of another from this perspective. The second worldview holds that all entities exist in connection to one another rather than being independently or separated. Our contemporary thinking and learning habits are built on witnessing a world of 'things,' which we consider discrete or separate building pieces. This worldview allows us to count and measure items without regard for their intrinsic value, giving us clear definitions and a sense of control over our lives. This method, however, separates humans from one another and nature. And this view is an illusion due to our ignorance of Chit essence. In truth, everything in nature is related in a fluid, dynamic manner.

Most of us are familiar with the concept of six degrees of separation - the idea is that anyone on the planet can be connected to anyone else in just six steps. So, you are effectively connected to the Queen of England, Tom Cruise, or even a Mongolian sheep herder through just five other people. The huge volumes of data collected by the game allowed sociology researchers to analyze exactly how interconnected Hollywood actors are. They found that six degrees of separation do indeed appear to exist. Still, people's random acquaintances, not their friends, are the key to all of this.

'Separateness' is a misconception we've created, and it's quickly becoming a hazardous hallucination affecting how we interact with business, politics, and other critical aspects of our everyday lives. This narrative of separateness at the astral and causal levels develops the mindset of duality and diversity with unhealthy competition, jealousy, hatred, revenge, mistrust, divorce, and violence and thereby pushing the self to roam around the zone below the courage line (<200) at the micro level and cause the suffering of shadow self (<200). Also, at the macro level, in the current context, this separated mindset created issues like sustainability and non-inclusiveness, which is alarming for each of us.

Ephemeral Happiness is perceived as Permanent Happiness: Ignorance in *Ananda*

A farmer plowed his fields with the help of an old horse. The horse bolted and galloped away. When the farmer's neighbors commiserated with him about the bad news, he said, "Good? Or Bad"?

A week later, the horse reappeared with a herd of horses! This time, the farmer's neighbors congratulated him on the excellent news. "Good? Or Bad?" he said, "Who can say?" The farmer's son then fell from the horses' back and injured his leg while attempting to tame one of the wild horses. This came as a shock to everyone. "Good? Or Bad? Who can say?" said the farmer. The troops marched into the community a few weeks later and enlisted every kid they could find. They let the farmer's son go when they saw his fractured leg.

Is it good or bad? Who can say?
If there is no absolute good or bad in a life situation, i.e., all good and bad are relative and temporary, deriving a sense of happiness or unhappiness from life situation is foolishness.

Like this farmer did not know which ephemeral life situation is good or bad, do you clearly understand what is positive and negative in your life situation? Do you have a complete view of the situation? Many people have found that constraint, failure, loss, disease, or pain in any form has been their greatest teaching. It taught them to let go of distorted self-images and ego-driven goals. It provided them with a sense of profundity, humility, and compassion. It gave them a more realistic feel.

Poison is often considered harmful but may also be beneficial in some circumstances: many lifesaving medications are poisons. Vitamins can be beneficial, even lifesaving, but when ingested in excess, they can be lethal. As a result, the terms "good" and "evil" are merely relative. Wisdom teaches us that if there is a connection, a transient pleasure may be rapidly replaced by pain. The shadow self (<200) is oblivious to the fact that there is serenity in the cycle of pain and pleasure. Pain is a physically unpleasant sensation brought on by sickness or damage or by negative perception by our sense organs.

Similarly, pleasure is a physically pleasant sensation brought by positive perception by our sense organs. Suffering is a type of mental pain (aversion or craving) that manifests as an unpleasant bodily experience brought on by a thought. While pain is an unavoidable or inevitable aspect of life, suffering is a decision or optional. We are taught in the parable of the two arrows that Weeping and wailing after being struck by one arrow is the same as being struck by a second arrow, the first being a bodily sensation and the second a mental sensation or suffering. We also know from personal experience that accumulating physical pleasure does not guarantee mental contentment.

The pursuit of craving for pleasure and aversion or avoidance of painful ones can be reduced to the history of humanity, especially for the shadow self (<200). For the same reason, the lowest self (0 -100) is stuck at aversion to pain, and the shadow self (101 -199) is stuck in craving pleasure. Both of these pursuits are fragile. In the subtle levels of the mind, pleasure may be just as destructive as suffering. Suffering is a close friend of the shadow self (<200). In other words, like other ignorance, this ignorance also keeps the "self" roaming around the zone below the courage line (<200) and prevents you from becoming higher-self. Choosing not to pursue pleasure initially appears counterintuitive, but closer examination reveals that it is not. Peace is achieved when we live in non-suffering.

Peace is beyond pain and pleasure, happiness and unhappiness, good and bad, and unpleasant and pleasant sensations.

Ignorance Entangles You with Shadow Self (< 200)

So far, we understood that the prime reason for misperception is ignorance which is a veil on our intellect (*Buddhi*) and corrupts our intelligence (*Chit*), which compels our intellect (*Buddhi*) to follow the egoism (*Asmita*) within the shadow self (*Ahamkara*) ignoring the true self, whenever we are faced with a stimulus to respond. This pattern of affiliation between the shadow self and intellect based on illusory misperception and ignorance makes the shadow self-remain in the comfort zone of continuous aversion to non-favorable and craving to favorable for ego. This pattern of aversion and craving in the astral body gets translated into pleasant and unpleasant sensations in the gross body. Considering that every duality (positive and negative) forms a cyclic loop, pain, and pleasure become a cyclic trap of suffering and entanglement for the shadow self. This is just like the boiled frog gets entangled with the warmth of the gradually elevated water temperature till death. In summary, this illusory ignorance (*Avidya*) is the prime reason for suffering and being stuck with shadow self (<200).

If the lighted bulb is covered with a cotton cloth, its glow or intensity of light will be lower. Similarly, the veil of ignorance obstructs our pure awareness and hides the truth and our true selves. Hence ignorance increases from the highest self to the lowest self.

As per Bhagavat Gita (14.13), "*When there is an increase in the mode of ignorance; there is an illusion, darkness, heedlessness inaction.*"

So, one in ignorance does not work by a regulative principle of consciousness; he acts whimsically and unconsciously for no purpose. Even though the self can work, he does not endeavor. This is called an illusion. Although consciousness is going on, life is inactive.

The lowest self (0-100) has the thickest layer of ignorance.

If ignorance is thickest, you survive predominantly with the cognition of aversion to unpleasant sensations. You mostly remain in a psychological past and have the lowest perception of the stimulus you receive in life. Accordingly, your response becomes unconscious and weakest. Your existential quality becomes *Tamas*, and you vibrate in your lowest self (0-100). In Vedic Science, the thickest layer of ignorance is called "*Avarana*"; i.e., intelligence is completely covered and lazy, like vision obstructed when the window is covered with a curtain. Hence you survive as a shadow self (<200) only; unless there is a conscious effort to dissolve the ignorance.

The Lower Self (101-199) Has A Thicker Layer Of Ignorance.

If the ignorance is thicker, also you survive predominantly with the cognition of craving for pleasant sensations. You mostly remain in a psychological future and have a lower perception of the stimulus you receive in life. Accordingly, your response becomes unconscious and weaker. Your existential quality becomes *Rajas*, and you vibrate in your lower self (101-199). People in this zone spend most of their time in the psychological future. In Vedic Science, the thicker layer of ignorance is called "*Vikshyepa*"; i.e., the intelligence becomes crazy with agitation in mind, like the vision to the bottom of the sea is disturbed by the waves on the surface. Hence here also, you survive as a shadow self (<200) only; unless there is a conscious effort to dissolve the ignorance.

Both thickest and thicker ignorance represents our shadow self.

The Higher Self (100-400) Has A Thinner Layer Of Ignorance.

If ignorance is thinner, you live predominantly in meta-cognition aligned with the original human instinct. In other words, your disposition becomes a non-judgmental, equanimous, neutral sensation. Hence have a higher perception of the stimulus you receive in life. Accordingly, your response becomes conscious and stronger. Your existential quality becomes *Sattva*, and you vibrate in higher-self (200-400). People in this zone spend most of their time in the present or now (i.e., no psychological past or future). In Vedic Science, the thicker layer of ignorance is called "*Mala*"; i.e., intelligence becomes slightly hazy than reality, like a mirror shows a hazy image when there is little dust. Here you go beyond your shadow self (<200) and have the ability to activate your "seer" very regularly, however slightly away from the true reality. People in this zone are in their present or now most of the time (i.e., no psychological past or future).

Highest-Self (401-1000) Has The Thinnest Layer Of Ignorance.

If ignorance is the thinnest, you always remain in meta-cognition aligned with the original human instinct. In other words, your disposition becomes love, joy, peace, oneness, and beyond neutral sensation. Hence you have the highest perception of the stimulus you receive in life. Accordingly, your response becomes conscious and stronger. Your existential quality becomes *Nirguna* (beyond all three qualities), and you vibrate in your highest self (401-1000). Here you go beyond your shadow self (<200) and have the ability to activate your "seer" all the time and see the true reality. People in this zone spend their time always in the present or now (i.e., no psychological past or future).

This illusory ignorance from the last two million years has its residence in our causal body (i.e., unconscious mind) through the hereditary route. This ignorance gets stored (or recorded) in the form of temptation, low-vibrational-conscious-energy (i.e., LOC) (<200), or bad *Karmic* energy mapping to aversion and cravings. Accordingly, the self continues developing non-heroic personal preferences (<200) and forms many limiting beliefs in the astral body, making our perception and response to stimulus sub-optimal. When our response emerges from ignorance, it becomes unconscious, unsettled, un-transmuted, and unreconciled. Hence, its residual impacts are stored (or recorded) in our causal body as temptation, lower vibrational energy, or bad *Karma*. Hence; Rishi Vasistha; the first sage of the Vedic Science of Hindu philosophy and teacher of Lord Rama, said; there is no liberation without wisdom; i.e., no flow, freedom, meaning, and fulfillment in life. Like ignorance and bad *Karma* are the companions of the shadow self (<200), we also have wisdom and good *Karma*, which are the companions of the true self.

Call to Action

At least once a week, live a day as if it were your last day. This will make you more aware of the impermanence and futility of your physical and psychological self. Hence you will spend each moment on something more important, meaningful, and purposeful. You will not say any hurting statements to anyone. Maybe you'd finally get the courage to do what you love because you have nothing to lose. This practice of impermanence of your gross body will automatically allow you to make decisions free from aversion and craving, i.e., thinner ignorance and higher intelligence (*Chit*). Hence, there will be no further *Karma* deposit, and you will feel a sense of flow, freedom, meaning, and fulfillment on the day.

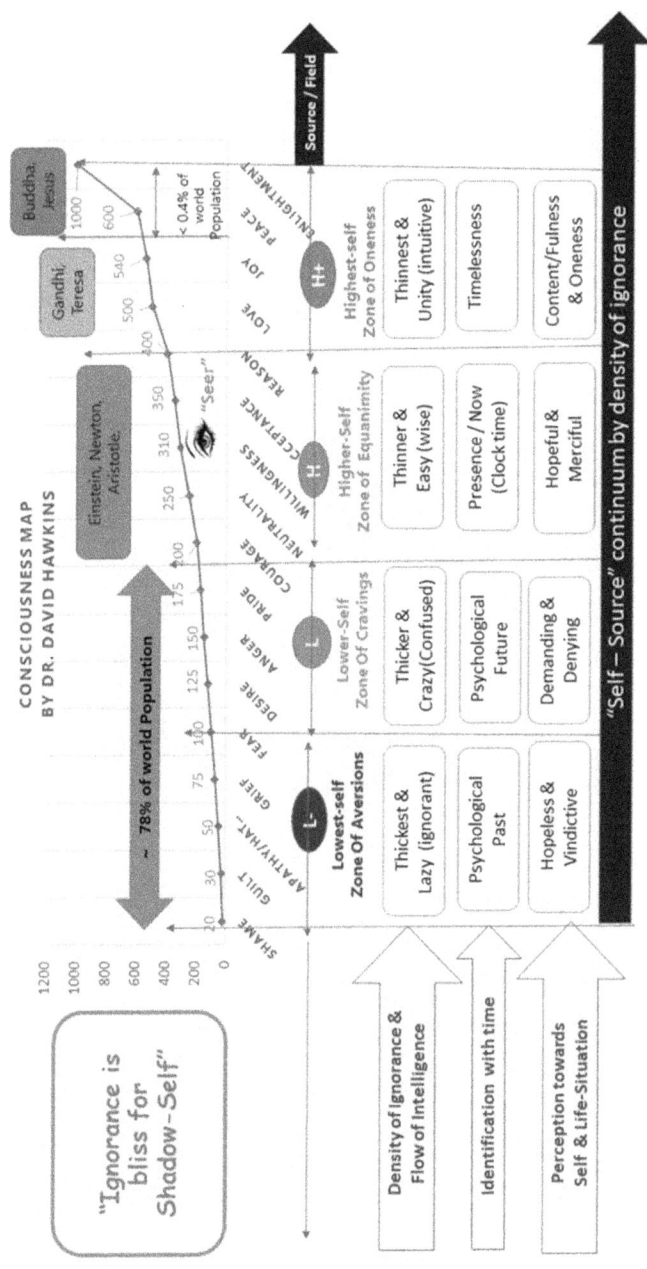

PRASHANT PANIGRAHI

8

KARMA & FREE WILL
In-Control and Out-of-Control of Self

"When you truly understand karma, then you realize you are responsible for everything in your life."

—Keanu Reeves.

Have you ever felt, "Why is it me that always has to suffer"? Not just you but most of the humanity feels this way. The moment they see things go out of control, they stand in the middle of an unfortunate situation and always question, "Why me?" And they start hating the source and nature.

A concept of common sense passed down the generations is that 'if we cause the good thing, then good things will happen to us. At a simplistic level, it would seem a wonderful path to follow. However, we do not know what is good, though we may know it subjectively or relatively concerning the context, as per our limited perception. Due to this hidden misperception or ignorance, this concept has baffled us from the beginning of time. So, the fundamental question remains: What is the right thing to do, and how do we know when we are doing the right thing? Hence, we always get different views and schools of thought at the outer level, i.e., as per the level of consciousness (LOC).

"Stimulus in Now" Is Inevitable and Destined

We discussed in earlier chapters that everything in this universe is nothing but energies with different frequency levels. The human being or the microcosm consists of three bodies: The physical body, the subtle or astral body, and the causal body. Each body is an energetic field of different densities that vibrate at different frequencies. Similarly, the universe or macrocosm and all its constituents, including our actions, also consist of three bodies vibrating at different frequencies. Also, all energy bodies are in communion, transmutation (or repurposing), or transformation. As per Vedic Science, the physical world in time-space is a three-dimensional immersive projection (i.e., movies) of energies below absolute consciousness (1000).

Let's say you act (outer *Karma*) of public speaking. If you like it, this experience will generate associated astral energy of pride from appreciation, desire to perform again, and anger for criticism. All these experiences and memories are the energy of craving type (101-199) with a pleasant tone and will get stored (or recorded) first in subconscious memory or astral self. Once this becomes a trend, it finally gets stored (or recorded) at the causal self as tendencies and potentialities. To become a trend, one need not have the same life situation repeatedly, but the repeated imagination and mental commentary of the same are enough. Similarly, if you do not like your performance, you will get disappointed and fear performing next time. Hence energies of aversion type (0-100) will get stored (or recorded) as tendencies and potentialities in the causal layer. We call this low-conscious-vibrational-energy (<200) from your action (outer *Karma*) as bad *Karma* (inner *Karma*), which has a resonance with the energy of (<200). However, if you took it as a neutral experience without aversion or craving, i.e., you have only a quest to serve the audience to your best with enthusiasm if an opportunity comes, then it will store a conscious vibrational energy of neutrality or equanimity (>199); which we refer as good-*Karma* (inner *Karma*). As bad *Karma* is undesirable, it is widely discussed and referred to simply as *Karma*. Also, even if the outcome of the action (outer *Karma*) looks to be bad unless it generates low-conscious-vibrational-energy (<200) in self, it will not store as bad *Karma*. *Karma* gets stored (or recorded) in a causal layer along with tendencies of self. Also, as long as we have residual bad *Karma*, we have regret, i.e., no meaning in life.

Any action in life-situation below the vibrational energy of courage (200) stores aversion and craving in life as unsettled or non-reconciled existential energy, called bad *Karma* (inner *Karma*). Let's consider a life situation where a patient died while the doctor was operating with good intentions of care and love. In this case, there is no low-conscious-vibrational-energy (<200), hence no question of bad *Karma*. Let's consider another life situation where the victim survived while a murderer attempted to kill him. In this case, even if the victim is not dead, the murderer will have bad *karma*, as he had ill intent with low conscious vibrational energy (<200). While the doctor and murderer failed in the outer purpose (i.e., Smartness), only the doctor succeeded in the inner purpose (i.e., Sage-ness). Hence inner-purpose (i.e., Sage-ness) is closely related to the intent behind the action. Hence The Bhagavad Gita says, "*The meaning of karma is in the intention. The intention behind action is what matters.*"

Now let's go one step back. Why did the murderer get a stimulus or life situation to kill the victim?

As per the law of energy conservation, the total energy of an isolated system remains constant—it is said to be conserved over time. Energy can neither be created nor destroyed; rather, it transforms from one form to another. Hence the unsettled inner Karma (or bad *Karma* energy) recorded as tendencies and potentialities in his causal layer from some of his past actions (outer-*Karma*) pupped-up in the form of life-situation as the three-dimensional immersive movie "out there." And the purpose behind this life situation or stimulus is to allow him to embrace and transmute (or repurpose) the bad-*Karma* to high-conscious-vibrational-energy (>200) so that it can move towards absolute consciousness (1000) or get transcended.

Hence, the way the law of conservation of energy is inevitable, the pupping-up of a stimulus or life situation in front of us in "now" is inevitable, as *Karma* maintains the general ledger of energy till the previous moment. The Law of *Karma* not only stores the energy as potentialities but also does general ledgering with absolute precision and projects three-dimensional immersive movies as life-situation at the right time. Hence it is said, *"Not even a leaf can move without his permission."* *Karma* is an intelligent energy like life-energy (i.e., *Sat* essence). The way *"Chitta"* manages our physiological and psychological system 24X7X365 with utmost precision as a smart-intelligent-cosmic-platform, the law of *Karma* (inner) is also a smart-intelligent-cosmic-platform for accounting of Karma. In summary, this platform maintains the purity of "now" and governs the inevitability of "now," considering the general ledger of *Karma* till the previous moment of "now." Hence, we cannot change "now." That's why it is said; even highly conscious beings are subject to the "inevitability of now" or "law of *Karma*" without any escape. In other words, "none of our stimulus or life-situation are problematic. It is perceived as so due to our shadow self." But also, our response is problematic due to the shadow self." Once we ignite the "seer of the shadow self," we can realize the beauty and purity of "now," and our response can be of conscious contextualization instead of compulsive habituation.

Once there was an interesting conversation between two warriors in the war of Mahabharat- Krishna & Karna. Krishna was the warrior in chief on the side of the Pandavas (five brothers), and Karna was a key warrior on the side of the Kauravas (hundred brothers), who were against Pandava.

Karna asks Lord Krishna - "My mother left me the moment I was born. Is it my fault I was born an illegitimate child? I did not get any education from Dhronacharya (one of the great teachers of that time) because I was not considered a Kshatriya (the royal cast). Parsuraam (another great teacher) taught me but then gave me the curse to forget everything when he knew I was the son of Kunti, mother of Pandavas, but against Pandavas. My arrow accidentally hit a cow & its owner cursed me for no fault. I was disgraced in Draupadi's Swayamvar (Ceremony to choose the groom). Even Kunti finally told me the truth only to save her other sons. Whatever I received was through Duryodhana's charity. So how am I wrong in taking his side?"

Lord Krishna replies, "Karna, I was born in a jail. Death was waiting for me even before my birth. The night I was born, I was separated from my birth parents. From childhood, you grew up hearing the noise of swords, chariots, horses, bows, and arrows. I got only a cow herd's shed, dung, and multiple attempts on my life even before I could walk! No Army, no education. I could hear people saying I was the reason for all their problems. When all of you were appreciated for your velour by your teachers, I had not even received any education. I joined the school of Rishi Sandipani (another great teacher) only at sixteen. You are married to a girl of your choice. I didn't get the girl I loved & rather ended up marrying those who wanted the ones I rescued from demons or me. I had to move my whole community from the banks of Yamuna-river to a far-off seashore to save them from Jarasandh (a demon). I was called a coward for running away!"

If Duryodhana wins the war, you will get a lot of credit. What do I get if Dharmaraja wins the war? Only the blame for the war and all related problems. Remember one thing, Karna, "everyone on this earth has to face and settle their past Karma in "now" without any escape, as it is inevitable and destined by the law of *Karma* (LOK)." Hence all philosophers in the world have advocated accepting "now" univocally.

"Response in now" or "Choice" has three possibilities:

The law of *Karma* (LOK) is in absolute compliance with the natural law of energy conversion and laws of action and reaction. Hence every stimulus in "now" is the truthful projection of inner *Karma* from the causal self, which is inevitable and destined. This stimulus consists of an outer event and an inner tendency or temptation. And there is no other option than to accept both of them in "now." However, you can do many things during life-situation, i.e., between stimulus (and inner temptation) and response to the outer event. You can bring variation to the next version of *Karma* in three broad different ways, depending on your level of consciousness (LOC) in your outer self, with which you are responding to life situations.

To understand the response trigger, we need to understand three sequences happening in different layers of self (i.e., causal, astral, and gross) and the involvement of elements beyond the causal self. First of all, stored (or recorded) potentialities emerge in the causal layer as a life situation sensed by our relevant physical senses. Once sensed, the tendencies stored (or recorded) in the causal self-emerge as temptation. This tendency encapsulates ignorance and *Karma* as well. This way, ignorance obstructs pure intelligence *(Chit essence)*, and *Karma* obstructs pure potentialities *(Sat* essence*)*. When these obstructions touch the astral body, it reappears as an attachment (aversion or craving). In the gross body, it reappears as a sensation (experiential essence, *Ananda)* in the gross self. If the tendency is aversion, the sensation will be unpleasant; if the craving sensation is unpleasant (opposite excitation of unpleasant), else the sensation will be neutral (i.e., without any aversion or craving). Accordingly, the intellect (*Buddhi*) of the astral self perceives the sensation and chooses (intelligence essence, *Chit*) to like it, dis-like-it, or be neutral about it. Finally, the "like" promotes the intention of craving, "dis-like" promotes the intention of aversion, and "being neutral" promotes the intention of neutrality and stability. At any moment, the disposition or level of consciousness (LOC) of your shadow self is equal to that of your life situation. Here the elements of your shadow self-include your tendency, temptation, sensation, perception, and intention. The life situations in front of you are just the three- dimensional -immersive-movies of your pre-recorded *Karma* energy.

Let's consider a situation where your boss angrily scolds you (150) for your mistake. This life situation has pumped off to bring out your pre-recorded Karma energy of LOC = 150 (i.e., anger temptation) to the space between stimulus and response. Now let's discuss a few possibilities.

Firstly, if you are operating as your Shadow self (<150), you will not be able to objectify your inner temptation or tendency of anger (150) as a "seer." Your intelligence (*Chit* essence) is low to recognize or objectify your anger temptation. Hence you will intend to avoid embracing the unpleasant sensation or feeling tone due to inner temptation at any cost. Then, you will perceive the intent of life-situation as attacking and your boss as the villain. Hence, in this case, your response (outer-*Karma*) will be with fear (100). So, at that moment, you might start attacking back or defending with all tactics and weapons of your shadow self (<100). Hence, the *Karma* energy associated with your response (<100) will be recorded back into your causal self. In other words, there is a degradation in your *Karma* energy (inner *Karma*) from 150 to 100. Meaning, you have failed in inner purpose (i.e., Sage-ness). You might also fail in your outer purpose (i.e., Smartness), as your boss will not like it and take revenge during performance evaluation.

Secondly, if you are operating at LOC < 200, you will be able to objectify and recognize your inner anger-temptation or tendencies (150) as "seer"; however, you do not have inner courage (200). In this case, you will intend to embrace the unpleasant sensation or feeling of tone compulsively. Hence you will perceive the intent of the life situation as not attacking but only as offensive. Hence, your intention will follow and will respond with anger (150); as an outer *Karma*. So, at that moment, you might say "yes-boss" with anger inside (<150). However, you may plan for an act of revenge (<150) in another life situation triggering anger from him in the future. Hence there is no change in the next version of your *Karma* energy (inner *Karma*); i.e., the same anger (150) tendency and potentialities will get recorded back into your causal self without any change in it. In this case, also, you have failed in your inner purpose (i.e., Sage-ness). However, if your boss is also ignorant, i.e., not having enough EQ to understand your tactics, you may succeed in your outer purpose (i.e., Smartness).

Thirdly, if you are operating at LOC >200, you will be able to recognize and objectify your inner tendencies of anger (150) and also you will intend to embrace the anger consciously and courageously

(200). In other words, you will be willing to cross your comfort zone. Hence, you will perceive the intent of life-situation as enabling and merciful (i.e., not as attacking or offensive). So, you will accept (350) the situation and say, "sorry-boss" (outer *Karma*). Also, you will not plan any revenge (<150), even if another life situation triggers his anger in the future. Hence, your next *Karma* energy (inner *Karma*) version is upgraded from 150 to 350. In this case, you have passed in inner-purpose (i.e., Sage-ness) or transcended. Also, you will succeed in your outer purpose (i.e., Smartness).

In summary, both Karma (inner and outer) represents our shadow self. When you act on your outer purpose without the "seer of the shadow self," you become only Smart. However, when you do the same in the presence of a "seer of the shadow self," you become a Smart-sage.

In the last scene of the above life situation, your response follows the intention of transcending your shadow self. The shadow self has taken instruction from the "seer" or true self. However, in the other two scenarios, neither there was "seer" nor the transcendence of your shadow self. In other words, in the first two scenarios, you failed in inner purpose (i.e., Sage-ness).

Sadhguru Jaggi Vasudeva says, *"For you to be at peace, at least your shadow self has to take instruction from you as "seer."*

Another point to note is that, in the first two scenarios, while you couldn't see your "shadow self" and its recorded *Karma* energy as a "seer," you saw the same indirectly by perceiving your boss negatively. Hence it is said; when you perceive your enemy is hateful towards you, it means your "shadow self" is also resonating or vibrating with the energy of hatefulness. Hence be thankful to your enemy as he enables you as an indirect "seer" by acting as a mirror. Also, to transmute (or repurpose) your hateful energy through conscious embracing instead of rerecording the same back to your causal body.

Our life span between birth and death is a big life situation which is a three-dimensional immersive movie with forms and phenomena as per the matured potentialities and tendencies in our causal self. Within this, many small, smaller, micro life situations are bounded by a *Karma* stimulus from the causal self and response to the stimulus by the gross & astral self. Here both stimulus and response are conscious vibrational energy below pure potentialities (1000). Hence the process of transcendence of energy continues till it reaches the absolute potentialities of *Sat-Chit-Ananda* (1000). In other words, one has to settle all his *Karma* by embracing as "seer" to reach the absolute potentialities (1000).

We are not the doer

We think "We are acting or responding" as a doer of the action *(i.e., outer Karma)*. However, once we activate our "seer of Karma-energy in shadow self," we realize that we are not the thinkers and doers of our world. We are not in control of anything. To understand this Just lift your right hand. How did you raise your hand?

Here we are not interested in the story of how the brain sends signals that make the muscles contract. That's a useful scientific theory to explain *what* is happening, but it doesn't address the question of *how* you do it. Rather, what we are looking for here is, just try explaining *how you did it*, to a child who didn't know how to raise his or her hand with a set of clear instructions.

What you will inevitably find is that you cannot even **begin** to explain it. You cannot explain it because in reality you don't have any clue how you do it. Neither does anyone else. We can all make our hands do all kinds of things with ease, but the truth is, we don't have any idea *how* we actually make any of it happen. No one knows. If we examine our direct experience, we will inevitably discover that we don't know *how* we do *anything* that we do – how we read this book, how we talk, how we talk, how we learn, or even how we think. It's all just happening.

> Buddha said, *"Events happen, deeds are done, but there is no individual doer thereof."*

Everything happens due to the replay of prerecorded inner *Karma*. In simple terms, without the "seer of *Karma* energy in shadow self," all human beings cannot realize the illusion that they are only puppets of their inner *Karma*.

"Outcome in now" is of infinite possibility:

Depending on your degree of conviction in *Karma*, the complexities of life situations, your level of consciousness (LOC) moment to moment, accuracy in your perception towards life situations, degree of intent from you to embrace the life situation, and so on, there might be infinite possibilities of "response in now." Hence depending on the "response in now," there will be infinite possibilities in new tendencies and potentialities entering the causal layer replacing the same, which exited as the stimulus of life situation. In simple, there will be gross addition in tendencies and potentialities in the causal layer and reconciled as net tendencies and potentialities.

These reconciliation and general ledgering in gross and net addition is done by the laws of *Karma* (i.e., smart-intelligent-cosmic-platform-accounting platform). This platform continuously looks for opportunities to get expressed and transcended as well. As part of the expression, inner tendencies are projected (or replayed) as temptations and inner potentialities as outer events "out there," i.e., a three-dimensional immersive movie with forms and phenomena. The outer event decides success in the outer purpose (i.e., Smartness), and outer temptation decides success in the inner purpose (i.e., Sage-ness). While the outer purpose (i.e., Smartness) deals with abundance and admiration from society, the inner purpose (i.e., Sage-ness) deals with authenticity, respect, and devotion in society.

Another point to note is that the outcome of a response is a projection of gross tendencies and potentialities created in life-situation as there is a maturity period to gross elements. Hence the outcome of life events depends on matured tendencies and potentialities in the causal layer. So, there are three states of *Karma* or tendencies and potentialities, i.e., gross, net, and matured. In Vedic Science, the net

Karma is called *"Sanchita Karma,"* i.e., saving all gross *Karma* in installments till maturity. This gross *Karma* is called *Agami Karma* in Vedic Science, which means *Karma* for the future. The matured Karma, which gets dispensed in a favorable situation, is called *"Prarabdha Karma"* in Vedic Science.

In summary, the laws of *Karma* or smart-intelligent-cosmic-accounting platform follow the logic of an insurance policy.

All stimuli and outcomes in your life situations are a projection of your *Karma* or *Karma* energy. Also, all responses are either taking instruction from your inner tendencies (i.e., temptation) or your transcended self (i.e., seer). Hence you and only you are responsible for everything in your life. In other words, Karma is getting what you deserve and deserving what you get. Hence, being responsible and accountable for your *Karma* energy. This was the sole reason a bandit became a saint after he realized *Karma* energy could not be shareable with the other self; it can only be transmuted (or re-purposed) to make *Karma* free within himself. Any residual bad *Karma*, i.e., unsettled, or non-reconciled aversion or craving, is experienced as a life of meaninglessness, emptiness, regret, and remorse. However, when the same is reconciled, it is experienced as life with meaning and fulfillment. The critical question is, what is the starting point of gross and net calculation or metering and storing the historical Karma energy deposit?

Ignorance is the Cause of Karma

As we discussed in the chapter on "ignorance," in the initial days, i.e., before two million years, the conscious-vibrational-energy of human beings was at absolute *Sat-Chit-Ananda* (1000). We call this "original instinct." This original instinct or absolute consciousness started getting deviated, corrupted, or degraded once the human response followed the intelligence based on the biological nervous system-based intelligence, which is based on learning from the natural phenomenon of cause-and-effect relationship from life-situation instead of original instinct. In other words, while ignorance is an impurity or blocker of intelligence (*Chit*), *Karma* is an impurity or blocker for existence (*Sat*), and both are holographic. Due to this, humanity has impurity or blockage in experience and hence suffering. This deviation and impurities are getting passed to the next generations through hereditary and transmigration of the causal self.

> Swami Vivekananda says, *"So, once the body dies, what guides the soul? The end outcome of all the effort it has made and all the ideas it has had."*

If the outcome is such that it needs to create a new body for further experience, it will go to those parents willing to supply it with appropriate material for that body. Following are the viewpoints from other personalities on reincarnation.

> *"The soul comes from without into the human body, as into a temporary abode, and it goes out of it anew it passes into other habitations, for the soul is immortal."*
>
> - Ralph Waldo Emerson

> *"Has it occurred to you that transmigration is at once an explanation and a justification of the world's evil? If the evils we suffer result from sins committed in our past lives, we can bear them with resignation and hope that if in this one we strive toward virtue, our future lives will be less afflicted."*
>
> - W Somerset Maugham

So, the metering of Karma storage or gross-net calculation was two million years ago. Now the next question is, where exactly does the Karma and causal storage start its impression in the human biological body after transmigration from one incarnation to another?

Karma Is Genetics

Dr. Tater's study suggests that karmas are the cause and genes are the outcomes of karmas, instructing and motivating genetic codes and genes to operate and mutate appropriately. Hence, the genes not only carry their parents' genetic features but also store the impression of an individual's *Karma* with tendencies and potentialities superstructure, i.e., the blueprint of one's future route. Comparing *Karma* and DNA can shed much light on this crucial part of life. "We are what we are because of our DNA," genetic science claims. "We are what we are because of our karmas," our *Tirthankaras* have said from the beginning. We all have a physical body. The body is made up of organs that are organized into systems. Organs are made up of tissues, tissues are made up of cells, and cells are made up of genes. This much is known to science. Beyond DNA, what is there? Is there a feeling of emptiness? Where do non-molecular ideas and emotions come from? The solution that genetic research will eventually discover is that genes are accompanied by a metaphysical causal body with consciousness and intelligent *Karma* energy as potentialities, which is the blueprint for pre-human beings sent and future life situations. These intelligent and conscious potentialities construct the body and guide the many functions of organs, such as a living creature's brain and neurological system. While there is acceptance from scientific communities of the *Karma* deposit at the gross and astral level because of its basis on cause and effect, there is still no strong scientific acceptance of the causal deposit of *Karma* because science always looks for reduction and experimental evidence. We have always seen this roadblock in science when it encounters experiential and objective evidence. It finally accepts compulsively by pointing the finger at a concept called the "hard problem of consciousness."

There was a beautiful debate between Kevin Mitchell, an American neuroscientist, and Swami Sarvapriyananda, an Indian monk, around the "Genetics Is *Karma*." This debate explored Karma, which has intriguing connections with evolutionary influences on human nature, genetic effects on our unique personalities, and learning and memory brain pathways. However, the discussion ranged from neuroscience reductionism to subjective experience, the self, perception, qualia, free will, morality, artificial intelligence, and consciousness. Although Kevin Mitchell does not believe in Eastern faiths (or any religion), he found many features of the underlying philosophy to be a welcome alternative, particularly the focus on flux over stasis, process over essence, and wholes over parts. He preferred it to the more rigid, essentialist, and reductionist approaches that pervade much of Western scientific thought and, in his opinion, trap us when attempting to grasp the relationship between brains and minds.

In response to Kevin Mitchel, Swami Sarvapriyananda said, "I believe we are in accord there but from different perspectives. But there's practically a *Karma* language - that we've inherited a lot of Karma from our ancestors and certain proclivities and personality qualities."

It will not be unreasonable if we say the intelligence of *Karma* energy governs genetic codes and manages them for future births/modes. It gives them a serial system that allows the soul to move in quest of a new body after it has departed its own. The soul is drawn to such a body to grow it based on *Karma*, genetic codes, and fate. This can be read to mean that a *Karma* body of that sort is made, which can easily fit into such established genetic codes, and the soul begins a new existence in a new body with the soul. A cow, a lion, an insect, a bird, or any other creature can be made after meeting the genetic codes of a living being. Another natural law is organic matter's biological and genetic law, such as the natural evolution of seeds (cause) and fruits (result). An apple tree seed, for example, cannot produce oranges as a fruit, but only apples. The sugar cane seed has a sweet flavor rather than a bitter one. This encompasses the law of heredity in plants and animals via cells, genes, and genetic information encoded inside the DNA.

Destiny Gene vs. Developmental Gene

DNA, genes, and chromosomes work together to make you who you are. Chromosomes carry DNA in cells. DNA is responsible for building and maintaining your human structure. Genes are segments of your DNA that give you physical characteristics that make you unique. Your body has a complete instruction manual that tells your cells how to behave. Every living being's body structure and function are determined by its chromosomes. Every life situation (the span between stimulus and response) necessitates producing some protein, which only a particular gene can accomplish. Hence, these genes are always changing, which is called "mutation." Now the question is, what governs the direction of the mutation process?

At birth, each of us is handed a hand of cards over which we have no influence. We do not pick our parents, place of origin, birth date, or anything else. Those choices are chosen for us based on a sequence of causes and effects that dates to the dawn of time. Also, what distinguishes us from one another, and what gives us our personality features? Do we identify as introverts or extroverts? Are we cautious or rash? Are we driven or relaxed? All these features contribute to who we are throughout our lives. Mr. Kevin Mitchell explains in his book "Innate" very beautifully why our traits are more innate than we think. He says, "All those traits have some physical basis in how our brains are wired. And then the question is if that's true – if it's how our brain is wired right now that is influencing our personality traits – then what is the origin of that? Why our brain is wired the way that it is? And so, one of the reasons is genetics. We all have a program in our genome, in the human genome, to make a human body with a human brain. So, our shared human nature is part of our evolutionary heritage.

If we had chimp DNA, we would have a chimp brain and behave like chimps. The differences between species can be narrowed down to the differences in their DNA and the brain development program encoded in that DNA. And the same principle applies within a species. So, between individuals, we all have variations in our genes. We have millions and millions of differences if we look at our DNA compared to each other. And some of those differences affect how our brains develop and our psychology. So, the circuits that control how outgoing we are or how risk-averse or threat sensitive or sensitive to rewards – all of those things that manifest as patterns of behaviors in any given scenario – ultimately are wired into our brains somehow. So, there is a large genetic component to variation in these personality traits. We can measure that, and it's very easily demonstrated in things like twin studies and family studies and even studies across the whole population where we can see people who are more genetically similar to each other are more similar to each other, not just physically, which we all are very aware of, but psychologically as well."

So, we have the *Karma* gene, which governs the brain development, psychology, behaviors, and destiny aspect of our life. Hence, we call this gene a destiny gene. Many people call this gene a selfish gene as well. So, what about the free-will aspect of life? Are we totally to drift as flotsam on the stream without ever being able to change the course of life? Mr. Kevin Mitchell explains further, "But the relationship between our genes and the way our brains work is very indirect. It's not the case that you're extroverted because you've got genes for extroversion that are doing something in your brain right now. They're not genes for extroversion or genes for intelligence. They're genes for building a brain, and the process of development actualizes it. There's a potential in the genome that gets realized through the processes of brain development, which are extraordinarily complex. There are trillions of connections in the brains of thousands of different areas. There are thousands of different types of neurons. They all have to connect in very, very specific ways. So that means that the relationship is not a static one; it's not a deterministic one. It's played out through those development processes and introduces another source of variation, which is the opposite of destiny. The original potentialities and tendencies of the genome, which follow the direction of *Karma* energy, can be altered through conscious alteration in psychology and brain development.

In summary, whenever there is a transmutation (or repurposing) in conscious-vibrational-energy, through embracing tendencies or temptation, there is an associated change in direction in brain development and mutation in the gene. We have also seen evidence of switching on and off a particular gene based on our thinking, beliefs, and behaviors. Hence, the intentional or conscious transcendence in the outer self (i.e., astral and gross self) brings transcendence in the inner self (causal self). Hence, a pseudo free will is available only when you objectify the *Karma* gene's lower energy (i.e., tendencies and potentialities) as "seer." In other words, as a "seer," you can embrace and choose beyond the tendencies and temptation and transmute (or re-purpose) the *Karma* and destiny gene to a developmental gene that governs this free-will aspect of our life. Dean Hamer, who is working in this area, terms the developmental gene a spiritual gene and says by exercising our free-will aspect in our response, we could change the nature or quality of our *Karma* genes. Through our effort, the dormant, *Karma*, or destiny gene could be transmuted (or repurposed) and activated to change the course of our destiny. For example, the creative gene can stay dormant till one comes out of the comfort zone, exercise courage and transmute (or re-purpose) the future. Again, there is a fight between unconscious evil (*Karma* or destiny gene) and conscious good (spiritual or developmental gene). Hence courage to go beyond the comfort zone, and objectifying the *Karma* or destiny gene as a "seer" is the gateway from destiny to free will.

Deterministic vs. Probabilistic Causality

Our life situation is a series of stimuli and responses. While the stimulus is always destined and inevitably affects our *Karma*, governance of response is subjective to the consciousness of the respondent. To understand this, let's go through the story of Michel de Nostradamus, a famous French astrologer. According to one narrative, while residing at his castle in the Lorraine area, the visionary Nostradamus was confronted by the royal skeptic, the Seigneur de Florinville. Nostradamus was shown two black and white suckling piglets. Florinville then asked Nostradamus to foretell what they would have for supper that night. They would consume the black pig, according to Nostradamus. Florinville then instructed the chef to cook the white pig. At supper that night, Nostradamus again asked which pig they were eating, and he said the black one. Floresville excitedly requested the cook to identify the pig they were eating. According to the cook, a tame wolf cub had strayed into the kitchen and devoured the white pig. The cook then butchered and cooked the leftover black pig for dinner.

It was not about the predictions or the probability of the pig being slaughtered but about Nodtradamus's consciousness and higher perception of direct destiny as "seer." However, the misperceived free will aspect of Seigneur de Florinville became an indirect destiny for him. So, while stimulus to human life is impacted by intelligent *Karma* energy, the human response to stimuli depends on its level of consciousness, which governs either destiny (or *Karma*) or developmental (or spiritual) genes.

In any endeavor of cause and effect, if you analyze the reason, there will be infinite causes, including macro and micro. Depending on your ignorance and conscious level, you will have perception and comprehension of only a few limited reasons. You are unaware of most causes and their complex interrelations and variations. Again, while you know a few cases, you have no control or influence over most of the known few. For example, while you are breathing, you have knowledge, awareness, and control over only a few parameters on the gross and astral layer, and you are not aware and have no control over many causes at the inner and causal level, which has a direct or indirect effect over it. To name a few, your social, environmental, and economic uncertainty may alter your mental state and affect your breathing pattern. Your genetic code may disturb the structure and capacity of your lungs and impact your breathing pattern. Many of these unknown and uncontrollable causes are under ignorance and misperception and governed by intelligent *Karma* energy. Let's say you have to respond to a "fill the blank" question, where the blank represents the root cause of an effect, and you have a hundred options. Out of which, you are confidently aware and able to perceive or comprehend only five to ten choices. In this case, the probability of getting the correct response will be very low. Hence, in this VUCA world, very few outcomes are utterly deterministic, depending on your awareness, intelligence, and consciousness level.

Therefore, it is said; that deterministic fortune hardly exists. However, accepting *Karma* stimulus and responding courageously as a "seer" are only friends to maximize success in the chaotic zone between deterministic and probabilistic casualties. Let's explore how different levels respond to challenges, a Karma stimulus.

Lowest-Self (0-100) with Lazy intention.

The lowest self is *Tamas* in nature and far below the courage line (< 200). With the thickest layer of ignorance, they have an extremely limited or lazy perception of reality and *Karma* stimuli. Hence whenever a *Karma* stimulus arrives in a life situation, they ignore it passively. In other words, their *Karma* (or destiny or selfish) gene limits them from crossing their comfort zone. With their whimsy and compulsive aversion to life situations and the world around them, it misses exploring the opportunity and potential around them. Let's try to understand this with the help of a story.

For almost thirty years, a beggar has sat by the side of a road. A stranger passed by one day. "Do you have any spare change?" murmured the beggar, holding out his old baseball cap. "Unfortunately, I have nothing to offer you," the stranger said. Then he inquired, "What are you sitting on?" "Nothing," the beggar said. "It's just an old box." I've had that on my mind for as long as I can remember." "Have you ever peered inside?" inquired the stranger. "No," the beggar said. "So, what's the point?" There isn't anything in there." "Look inside," the man insisted. The beggar was successful in prying open the lid. He discovered the box was full of gold, much to his surprise, doubt, and delight. To summarize, the beggar could not perceive the advice of many such strangers in the past and has thus avoided opening the box lid for many years because of lazy tendency, temptation, and intention from his *Karma*-gene.

The people in this zone of consciousness ignore the *Karma* stimulus, and hence the *Karma* (or destiny or selfish) gene always loses the battle with the developmental (or spiritual) gene. Also, due to lower perception or misperception of life-situation, they live with fear and fragility and become Losers. In summary, the stimulus is *Karma* for the people in this zone of consciousness. The *Karma* gene also influences the response; without any aspect of free will, their ignorance may make them perceive and give a false sense of free will. They neither accurately perceive outer purpose (i.e., Smartness) nor inner purpose (i.e., Sageness). In summary, these people respond to stimulus with a temptation of aversion and lazy intention from their *Karma* gene, with a false sense of free will; i.e., their choice and response are constrained by the compulsion of shadow self (<200).

Lower-Self (101-199) with crazy intention.

People in this zone are *Rajas* and below the courage line (<200). With a thicker layer of ignorance, they have a disturbed perception of reality and *Karma* stimuli. Also, their primary purpose is outer-purpose (i.e., Smartness). Hence whenever a *Karma* stimulus arrives in a life situation, they compulsively go beyond their comfort zone, with the whimsy impulse from craving, desire, greed, anger, and pride. Though people in this zone are in a better position than the lowest self and may achieve success in outer purpose (i.e., Smartness), it is non-sustainable. Also, they remain away from the inner purpose (i.e., Sage-ness) of life. Let's try to understand this with the help of a story.

There were two friends, Ravi and Satish. Both were from middle-class families and joined an IT firm with engineering degrees. They were much disciplined, and their energy and enthusiasm were limitless. Both became famous for their extraordinary performance and got early confirmation as an employee with a promotion and bonus. After three of their careers went for higher studies, did an MBA in a reputed organization, and started a start-up with an initial investment capital of $1000. Within three to four years, their business grew exponentially, and a market capitalization of $2.5 million. Satish was a *Sattva* and wanted to share the profit with other contributors in their organization. However, Ravi was naturally *Rajas*, and hence this success made him arrogant, proud, and greedy. His *Karma* gene was compelling to grab the credit alone with craving temptation. With this unvirtuous intention, he made all evil plans, including organizational politics, by taking an internal crowd with a similar mindset and manipulating organizational policy. With a hidden agenda, he convinced Satish to introduce Taran (one of Ravi's followers) as a third partner in the name of business expansion.

On the other hand, Satish was calmly creating exponential value for the organization by embracing all challenges with courage, curiosity, quest, and integrity. With the notion of craving and greed, influenced by the comfort zone of destiny gene, Ravi and Taran suspended Satish from a partnership with a well-crafted unfair practice complaint. While Satish went to court for justice, Ravi and Taran withdrew the profit and made the organization financially weak. Satish embraced all these dirty dramas for around one year with the power of his developmental or spiritual genes. On the previous night of the final hearing, Ravi, Taran, and their lawyer met one Saint to understand the direction of the wind in the legal case. The Saint said the negative *Karma* energy is too high for the wind to flow toward you. The court directed splitting the company into two with a massive penalty to Ravi and Taran. With their inability to pay the penalty, they both had to surrender their business to Satish. Now Ravi is a divorcee and addicted to drugs. In summary, Ravi had to face the music of bad *Karma*, as he could not embrace the crazy tendency, temptation, and intention of his *Karma*-gene. However, by doing so, Satish is now the single owner of the most innovative and profitable organization in the industry sector and leading a happy family life.

Every relationship and connection with others is not just a chance or coincidence. It is designed by the law of *Karma* to settle the unsettled *Karma* account. Hence, it will create an uncomfortable situation unless we intend to settle the *Karma* temptation by embracing and activating spiritual genes. In summary, the people in this zone of consciousness respond to a stimulus by craving temptation and crazy intention from their *Karma* gene, with a false sense of free will; i.e., their choice and response are constrained by the compulsion of shadow self (<200).

Higher-Self (200-400) with easeful intention.

Like Satish, people in this zone are *Sattva* in nature and above the courage line (>200). With only a thin layer of ignorance, they perceive reality more and *Karma* stimulus as "seers". Courage brings additional intelligence (SQ) to people in this zone. Hence, they repurpose their lazy and crazy intentions, if any, into easeful intentions. In other words, whenever a challenging *Karma* stimulus arrives, they accept it nonjudgmentally and respond with courage and curiosity by embracing the situation and going beyond their comfort zone. This courage, going beyond the comfort zone and embracing, transmutes (or repurpose) the bad *Karma* to good *Karma*, producing easeful intention. Once matured, the good *Karma* flows as a reward and outcome. That's why it is said that; "Fortune favors the brave. In other words, Karma energy rewards the bold and higher self.

> As Robert Frost clearly articulated, *"Two roads diverged in a wood, and I chose the one less traveled by, and that has made all the difference."*

We have seen how the easy intention and courageous decision of Mr. Ratan Tata took Tata Motors from a non-performing to a peak-performing organization by embracing the arrogance of Bill Ford, the then-chairman of Ford. Similarly, we have seen how the easy intention and courageous decision of Sudha Murthy during the inception of Infosys made her a role model for generations by embracing her temptation to join Infosys.

> Similarly, a mighty empire had crumbled under the courage of Mahatma Gandhi, who brought freedom to India with non-violence and said, *"It takes courage to forgive someone who has wronged you."*

The world is indebted to those men and women who have faith in their courage and executes them. Whatever the fields- science, art, literature, culture, entertainment, sports, or politics- people dared to step away from the norms and make a difference by embracing and re-purposing any lazy or crazy intentions from their *Karma* gene to easeful intentions. In summary, these people have free will beyond shadow self (<200); i.e., their choice and response are not constrained by the compulsion of shadow self (<200).

Highest Self (401- 1000) has the Intention of Ecstasy.

People in this zone are beyond all quality with fearlessness. With no ignorance and full of wisdom, they have an ultimate perception of reality and *Karma* stimulus as "seer." In fact, with access to higher intelligence, they respond to stimuli intuitively. As they are ever ready to embrace anything, they do not see the difference between destiny and free will and deterministic and probabilistic causalities. They feel life situations are happening through them, i.e., they do not take credit in their doer-ship, so they do not create *Karma*. Hence, Buddha said, "Events happen, deeds are done, but there is no individual doer thereof." When the human consciousness is elevated, humans automatically realize *Karma* stimulus flow and *Karma* response flow intuitively in their doing or action, without their doer-ship in action. If there is no doer-ship, there will not be any gross *Karma* by them. They are always in a flow of dissolving all their net *Karma* in their causal store, which takes them towards absolute *Sat-Chit-Ananda* (1000). So, while we perceive what they are doing at an outer level as lazy, crazy, and easeful, their inner intention is ecstasy. Hence, Swami Yogananda Paramahansa explained in his autobiography that the law behind ordinary events and miracles is alike.

Do you have Free-will?

Free will is the power of choosing and acting without the constraint of anything beyond "self." Though the shadow self perceives that human beings have free will, a deeper scientific study reveals that the Human biological brain makes decisions much before it even knows it.

Dr. Stephen Hawking states, *"It is hard to imagine how free will operates if our behavior is determined by physical law, so it seems that we are no more than biological machines and that free will is just an illusion."*

John-Dylan Haynes, a British-German brain researcher, led the study "On the button," where he and his colleagues imaged the brains of fourteen volunteers while they performed a decision-making task. When the participants needed to decide, they were instructed to press one of the two buttons when they needed to decide. Each button was controlled by a separate hand. Simultaneously, a stream of letters was displayed on a screen at half-second intervals. The volunteers had to remember which letter was displayed when they hit their button. When the researchers reviewed the data, they discovered that the earliest signal the team could detect began seven seconds before the volunteers recalled making their decision. Because there is a few seconds delay in the imaging, brain activity could have started up to 10 seconds before the conscious decision. The signal came from the frontopolar cortex, which is found near the brain, right behind the forehead. As a concluding remark, John-Dylan Haynes says, "We think our decisions are conscious, but these data show that consciousness is just the tip of the iceberg." This study challenges our 'conscious decisions" and may even challenge ideas about how 'free' we are to choose at a particular time.

It seems there was a long conversation between Einstein and Ramana Maharshi to reconcile the idea of free will from the perspective of consciousness.

> Einstein mentioned, *"Man can do what he wills, but he cannot will what he wills."*

So, the root of the will (or intention from temptation) originates in consciousness driven by intelligent *Karma* energy, which is beyond low-conscious human perception. Now the question is, should we leave everything to nature and destiny? The debate between free will and destiny stems from the arrogance of the shadow self (<200) with lazy and crazy intentions.

> According to Ramana Maharishi- *"The only freedom, man has to strive for and acquire jnana."*

Here, *Jnana* means the dimension of knowledge, awareness,

consciousness, and the opposite of ignorance, representing the intelligence (*Chit* essence) of the Self. This is because intelligence is at the root of seeing reality as a "seer" (*Sat* essence) and bringing easiness in intention, providing courage to embrace and transmute (or repurpose), playfulness in expression, and joy in experience (*Ananda* essence).

As we are solely responsible for our life and can perceive the world through our "self," it is simple and effective to concur our "shadow self" to concur all life situations with ease, playfulness, and purpose. However, we must realize that the expression of potentialities (existence, intelligence, experience) is challenged by our inherited problems (i.e., ignorance and bad *Karma*). In other words, our success is not in tune with purpose. We cannot cut the fruit effectively and enjoy the cutting process because we have a blunt knife. Hence, we have to sharpen the knife to conquer the challenges in achieving both purposes; inner and outer; i.e., transcendence and transformation.

Call to Action

Whenever your boss or spouse gets angry at you, try to observe and recognize the stimulus as your *Karma* energy is being presented in Infront of you as an opportunity to transmute (or re-purpose) it in your response. Also, try to be non-judgmental about the medium of anger, i.e., your boss or spouse. Just know that you are meeting your inner self (*Karma*-energy), where your boss or spouse is just a mirror in the metaphoric simulation. This realization will help you to take full responsibility for your *Karma* or *Karma* energy. Hence there will be no residual friction, unpleasantness, hurt, regret, or remorse from this life situation. In other words, you will feel a sense of flow, freedom, meaning, and fulfillment in this life situation.

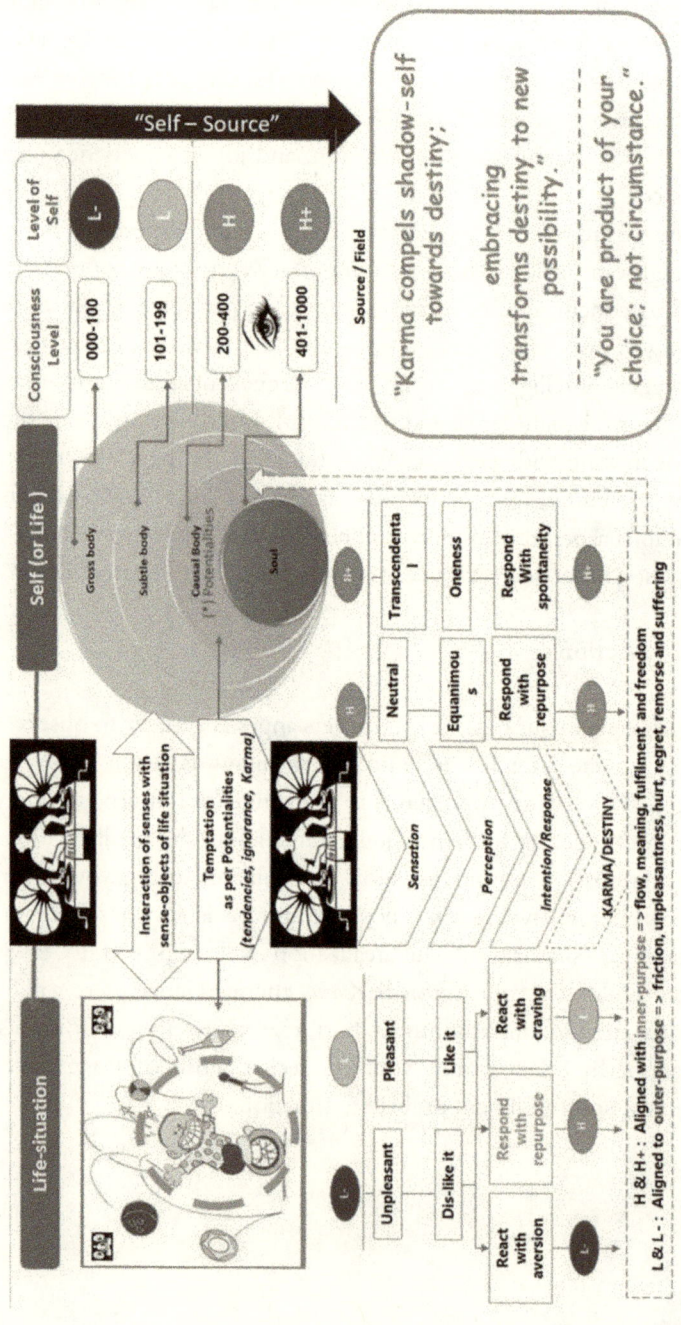

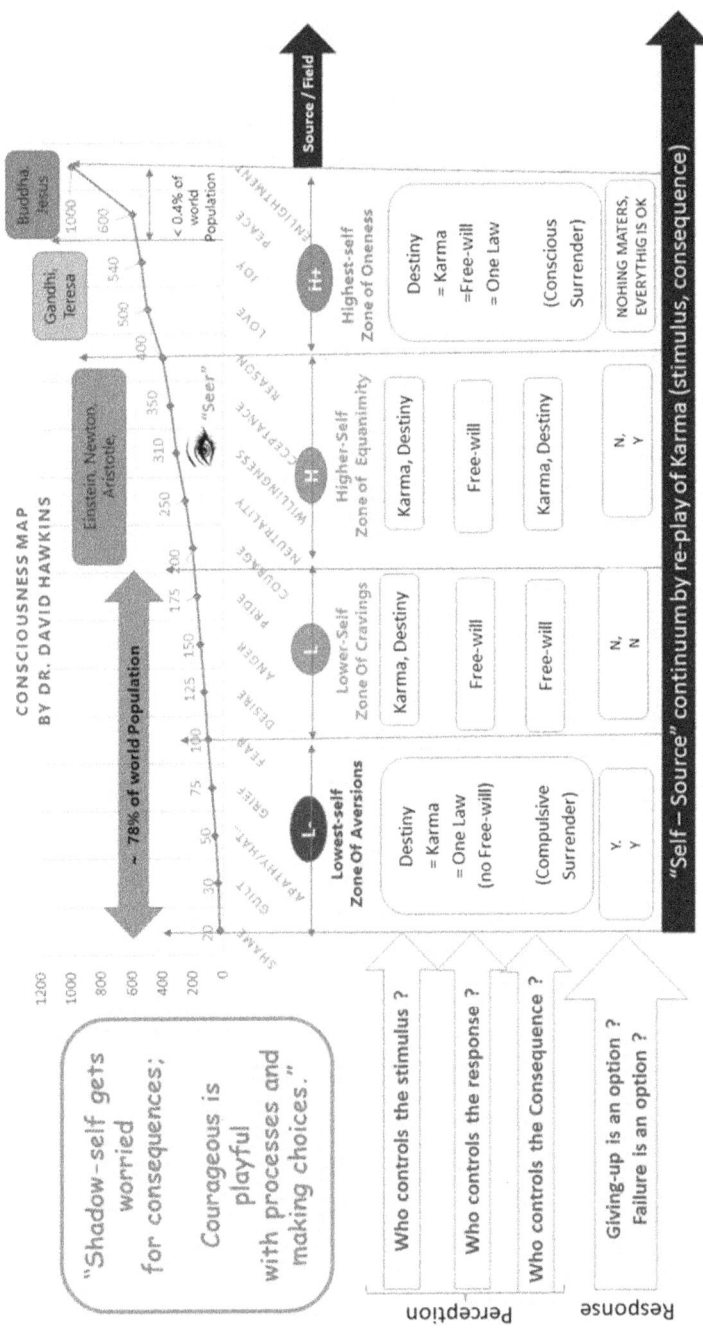

PART IV: PERSUASION

9

MUSCLES FOR SAGE-NESS
Causal Muscles to Sharpen the Self

"It is better to conquer yourself than to win a thousand battles."
                                                          -Lord Buddha.

Smart-Sage though Conquering

According to David Hawkins, around 78% of the world population is below the courage line level (< 200), and a typical person's level will fluctuate around five points throughout a lifetime (this is not a statistical derivation but an average determined by Dr. Hawkins' kinesiologic studies). However, an individual's level of awareness (such as an aspirant of transformation and transcendence) might rise (or fall) hundreds of points in a single lifetime. While transcending to the highest self (401-1000) needs a dedicated aspiration, I feel "actualizing or transcending to higher-self (200-400) should be within the regular rate-race of humanity in the VUCA world. This level of vibrational conscious energy with its associated levels of intelligence (i.e., SQ), experience (i.e., meditative), expression (i.e., Playful or with ease), and inner well-being should be the minimum right for everyone in the 21st century. And it's possible by conquering or re-purposing our shadow self. With this spirit, moving the majority mass (~78%) below the courage line (<200) to above the courage line (>200) and hence higher-self is a low-hanging fruit".

Becoming a Smart Sage is a Low-Hanging Fruit for All of Us.

Maslow's famed Hierarchy of Self-actualization is at the top of the list, followed by esteem, love/belonging, safety, and physiological necessities. As per him, the physiological and psychological needs must be met before actualization and fulfillment. By saying "must be met," he meant "must be conquered," as meeting the "need" is an illusion that has no endpoint. In other words, to conquer the need, "desire with aversion and craving" has to be transmuted (or repurposed) to quest with equanimity." This is because the fulfillment of desire leads to pride, and non-fulfillment leads to anger, which is at the center of entanglement with the shadow self.

Here conquering means going beyond it, not going away from it with aversion or craving but moving ahead. In other words, they have no power to entangle you anymore. For example, men and women have conquered and are no longer attached to their childhood. Given an opportunity, they will jump to become a child, though there will be a bit of shyness. However, they will still derive their sense of self only from their inner manhood or womanhood rather than childhood.

Similarly, when you conquer your outer purpose (i.e., smartness), you will continue pursuing it even with higher intensity, but instead of deriving your sense of self from it. You will derive your sense of self from something bigger than it, i.e., inner purpose (i.e., Sage-ness). In simple, conquering or re-purposing outer purpose (i.e., Smartness) is conducting outer purpose (i.e., Smartness) as "seen" in the presence of "seer. Hence, as the inner purpose (i.e., Sage-ness) is innate, existential, fundamental, and exclusively only for you, you must give prime attention to your Sage-ness. Also, it is said that our happiness is proportional to how much attention we give to ourselves (or life). Hence, we need the techniques for transcendence, which also help us to conquer the shadow self; when outer purpose (i.e., Smartness) becomes a natural by-product of inner purpose (i.e., Sage-ness). To be very specific, we need the technique to live a life of possession without possessiveness; pain without painfulness, feeling without thinking, passion without obsession, quest without desire, being angry without having anger, facing criticism without inferiority complex, inspiring without superiority complex, staying in the present and visiting past or future as a guest, putting effort with effortlessness, working without being tired and so on. Simply, it allows involvement in life-situation without being entangled with them, hence freedom full of actions, accountability, and responsibility. These conditions ensure that every outer purpose's primary purpose (i.e., Smartness) is intact.

Causal Muscle is the Secret Key for Smart-Sage.

We all share the same universal energy, awareness, and consciousness, whether we are Buddha, Einstein, Gandhi, Ratan Tata, Sudha Moorthy, or you and me. The only distinction is that they have conquered their need at their deeper level of self and nurtured the quest by embracing their life situation in their time of need. Hence, we must explore some muscles to embrace life situations with playfulness and ease. Another point to note is that we need to ensure all muscles are helpful to concur with the shadow self at a deeper level rather than a superficial level. Here the deeper level points to the causal self, which is intrinsic in nature. Also, the need for the causal muscles is because of two reasons.

Firstly, the suffering of the shadow self (i.e., aversion, craving, ego, being trapped with cyclic polarity. etc.) is always created due to lower temptation of the gross body (i.e., physiological self) and astral body (or psychological self).

As Albert Einstein said, *"No problem can be solved from the same level of consciousness that created it."*

Secondly; the blueprint of the temptation of the shadow self; i.e., ignorance and *Karma*, are deposited in the causal body. Though the causal body is not easily accessible to the conscious mind, it is always conscious of external life events or situations within the space between stimulus and response. It keeps reacting to a stimulus with its stored tendencies, which become temptation (*Sat* essence) and feeling-tone or inner sensation (*Ananda* essence) at the interface between the causal and astral layers. Here the LOC of stimulus, temptation, and inner sensation is the same. Hence, we have to catch or hack these lower elements (temptation and inner sensation) as "seer" and then embrace, transmute (or re-purpose), and conquer it by repurposing them to higher LOC elements before it is distorted by psychologically filtered perception. Unless we do so, the "lower self" will not get transcended and deliver compulsive responses with lower intention, leading to low-resolution destiny.

However, if we can do it at the causal level (i.e., hack, transmute (or re-purpose), there will be transcendence in self to "higher self" and deliver conscious response with Sage-ness, i.e., with SQ, *Sattva* quality, and playfulness; which will empower you to participate in conscious creation and manifestation (i.e., Smartness) along with the law of nature.

In summary, once you master this art of objectifying, hacking, transmuting, and re-purposing within the space between stimulus and response, it will reverberate with Smartness and Sage-ness. Hence, Buddha said, *"It is better to conquer yourself than to win a thousand battles"*. This is also in line with *"the more you practice, the less you bleed in war."* In this chapter, we will deal with developing causal muscles to be developed in solitude and strengthen our Sage-ness, and in the next Chapters, we will deal with techniques to be applied in work and life. (i.e., the life of rate race) to strengthen our Sage-ness.

However, it is to be noted that; modern science, which is based on factual and experimental evidence, has its reach only to the world of gross (physical or physiological) and astral (i.e., psychological). And hence it cannot access the causal, metaphysical, and experiential worlds and rationalize with the physical and psychological world. Hence till today, modern science has stopped going beyond this point, referring to it as the "Hard Problem of Consciousness. We need to look for causal muscles within the domain of experiential science like Vedic Science, where the hacking of the existential self was available before the days of Buddha, around 7000 years ago.

In fact, after studying Vedic Science, Buddha was the first scientist in the world who discovered that we do not respond according to the energy of stimulus towards us (i.e., anger, hatred, arrogance, jealousy, love, and so on); rather, we respond to the energy of our own life (or self) or the inner-body-sensation emerging or triggered from the causal body as a response to a stimulus.

Let's explore three causal muscles developed in solitude for objectifying, hacking, conquering, transmuting, and repurposing inner-body-sensation from lower to higher. To be very specific, here, transmutation (or repurposing) happens from fear (100) to courage (200), from desire (125) to quest for the possibility (300-350), from pride (175) to Neutrality (250), from jealousy & hatred to love (500) and so on. In simple, you strengthen your Sage-ness.

Mindful-Breathing as Muscle To Conquer "Temptation" (Sat Essence)

We discussed earlier that you can hack, transmute (or re-purpose) your lower vibrational conscious energy and transcend towards its peak; only when you can objectify and get dis-identified from it by activating your "seer" within, which is available for *Sattva* self. Also, Vedic Science says, mindful breathing enhances our *Sattva* energy to objectify our existential tendencies of aversion and craving in our causal body. Once this objectification is done, our life energy (i.e., Sat essence) goes up the level of courage (200) and beyond. Then, we set a favorable ground for crossing our comfort zone. This crossing of comfort-zone activates spiritual genes for transmuting the *Karma* gene. Also, our mindful-breathing pattern is a natural source of life energy (i.e., *prana*) in abundance, which nurtures our energy sheath (i.e., *Pranayama kosha*) and governs the interface between the gross and astral body. For example, if the flow of breath is erratic, the thoughts are erratic, and heartbeats are erratic as well. Mindful breathing. Hence mindful breathing is one of the most important causal muscles to activate the "seer" within and conquer the temptation of body-mind.

The human body is a moving life-energy and intelligent process governed by five life-force (*Prana or Vayu*) and seven life-energy centers (*Chakra*). *Chakras* govern the range of energy from the most fundamental level, such as self-identity, to the greatest degree of spirit, enlightenment, very importantly, to live a life with a purpose. A mindful-breathing technique activates each *Chakra*, called *Paranamaya (Prana & Ayama)*, where "*Prana* means life force and *Ayama* means ascension, expansion, and extension. Hence *Pranayama* is the expansion of the life-energy (i.e., *Sat* essence) through control of the breath."

Also, the *chakra* system plays a special role in connecting us with past lives. The *chakras* contain the memory record of the emotions and experiences in the subtlest form we have accumulated during our previous course of life. Here the subtlest form refers to the fundamental energy of the quantum-field or causal body. Walter Makichen, a gifted clairvoyant, explains in his book "Spirit Babies" that the past life information is transmigrated and integrated into the fetus as it forms in the womb, resulting in the very different personality that each baby has when it is reincarnated.

Hence, if we reread the functions and manifestations of the chakras, we will see that the negative emotions, experience, and *Karma* energy from a past life is translated and printed as "imbalance" in *Chakra* and gets expressed through us. For example, imbalanced root *Chakra* manifests expressions of worry, insecurity, and fear. In another way, this imbalance also represents the ignorance of the self.

Pranayama is the fourth limb of the Yoga system, developed by Patanjali, an Indian spiritual scientist, to elevate pure life energy (i.e., *Sat* essence) and transcendence of consciousness. Additionally, it offers health benefits as well. The life energy (i.e., *Sat* essence) flows up the spine, activating a metaphysical or mystical channel of seven energy centers in the human body called *Kundalini*. The energy centers are called *Chakra* (wheel). This flow fires up the pineal gland, allowing the practitioner to reach higher realms of awareness (*Chit* essence).

Pranayama aims to awaken the metaphysical channels in the body by combining the properties of the masculine (*Purusha*) and feminine (*Prakriti*) natures in the body, i.e., evolution and union, respectively. It balances and harmonizes the brain's left and right hemispheres for comprehensive consciousness and SQ.

Kindly refer to the beautiful mapping between these *Chakras* with David's consciousness scale and Maslow's hierarchy in ascending order toward transcendence.

1. **Root Chakra:** This chakra is called **Muladhara** in Sanskrit and is located at the base of your spine (i.e., at the pelvic plexus). This chakra is activated by alternate nostril breathing (*Anuloma Biloma Pranayama* in Sanskrit) and Child Pose (*Balasana* in Sanskrit) of sun salutation. This also activates the Adrenal gland in our body. Activating this energy chakra helps fulfill the base needs (i.e., the first layer in Maslow's hierarchy) and objectifying, hacking, conquering, or transmuting tendencies and temptations like shame, guilt, and apathy with vibrational-conscious energy < 50. If this chakra is imbalanced, the sense of self is derived from physical safety and security.

2. **Sacral Chakra:** This Chakra is called **Svadhisthana** in Sanskrit and is located at the hypogastric plexus or sacral vertebrae (i.e., above the root *chakra* and below your naval center of the lower abdomen). This *Chakra* is activated by ocean breathing (*Utjayi Pranayama* in Sanskrit). It is a soft, whispering breathing and can be compared to the sound of the wind. This *Chakra* is activated by the Standing-forward-bend (*Hastapadasana*) and Cobra-pose (*Bhujangasana*) of sun salutation. This activates the Adrenal gland in our body. Activating this *Chakra* helps objectify and conquer (or re-purpose) sensual pleasure and psychological needs (i.e., second layer in Maslow's hierarchy) and transmute tendencies and temptations like

grief and fear with vibrational conscious energy between 51-100. In other words, if this *Chakra* is imbalanced, the sense of self is still derived from psychological aversion.

3. **Solar plexus Chakra:** *Manipura* in Sanskrit is located at the solar plexus or naval center. This *Chakra* is activated by Bellows-Breathing (*Bhastrika Pranayama* in Sanskrit), a heating breathing practice that mimics fanning a fire with a steady airflow. During this practice is done by active filling (inhalation) and emptying (exhalation) of the abdomen and lungs. Another mindful breathing for this is Skull- Shining-Breathing (*Kapalabhati Pranayama* in Sanskrit). It is done by active exhalation and passive inhalation. Additionally, it is done through Salute-with-eight-parts or points (*Ashtanga Namaskara* in Sanskrit) under Sun-Satulation, which also activates the pancreatic gland. Activating this energy chakra helps fulfill the psychological needs of love and belongingness (i.e., 3rd layer in Maslow's hierarchy) and objectifying, conquering, or transmuting the tendencies and temptations like desire, anger, and pride with vibrational conscious energy between 101-175. In other words, if this *Chakra* is imbalanced, the sense of self is still derived from psychological cravings. Once you transcend this level, you transcend aversion and craving, and have access to courage (200) and willpower, going beyond your comfort zone. Hence, this energy entry must be activated sufficiently, as courage (200) is the gateway to the higher self.

4. **Heart Chakra:** This *Chakra* is called *Anahata* in Sanskrit and is located closer to the heart (i.e., at the cardiac plexus) and is the integration point between the lower and the higher *chakras*. Hence, once the lower *Chakras* are activated completely. Additionally, it is activated through

Prayer-pose (*Pranamasana* in Sanskrit) of Sun-Salutation. Activating this *Chakra* also helps in conquering the higher psychological needs of love and belongingness (i.e., 3rd layer in Maslow's hierarchy) and provides the capacity to objectify and sustain tendencies and temptations (>200). It sustains neutrality, willingness, enthusiasm, acceptance, reason, empathy, and love with vibrational-conscious energy between 201-500. Once you activate this *Chakra*, you will access heart intelligence, deeper connections with other beings, and meditative experience. In other words, if this *Chakra* is imbalanced, the sense of self is still derived only from self-centric well-being. Hence this *Chakra* is key for activating the "seer" within.

5. **Throat Chakra:** ***Visuddha*** in Sanskrit is located near the throat (i.e., at the carotid plexus). This *Chakra* is activated with Bumblebee-Breathing (*Bhramari Pranayama* in Sanskrit. Here we produce a bee-like buzzing sound while exhaling. Additionally, under sun-salutation, it is activated by Raised-arms-pose, Plank pose, and Mountain-pose (i.e., *Hastauttanasana, Dandasana, Parvatasana* in Sanskrit), which activates the Thyroid gland as well. Activating this energy chakra also helps conquer the psychological needs of esteem (4th layer in Maslow's hierarchy). It can sustain tendencies and temptations of joy with vibrational conscious energy of 501-600. Also, this *Chakra* provides the capacity to have a higher perception of reality, playful expression (*Sat*), and communication. Hence, people with active "*Visuddha*" can connect the reasoning dots from different schools of thought and are intellectually liberated. If this *Chakra* is imbalanced, the sense of self is derived from the arrogance of intellectual ability.

6. **Third eye chakra:** This is called ***Ajna*** in Sanskrit and is located between the eyebrows. It is a meeting point of all-

psychic channels, providing the ability to objectify worldly reasoning and cosmic intuition. Worldly intellectuals look stupid in front of people with active *Ajna*. This state is associated with peace and experiential liberation, with vibrational conscious energy of 601-800. Alternate nostril breathing can help in activating this chakra. Additionally, under Sun-Salutation, it is activated by Horse-riding-pose (*Ashwa Sanchalanasana* in Sanskrit), which activates the pituitary gland. When *Ajna Chakra* is fully activated, the "seer" matures, and it constantly co-exists with the "seen." Hence, this is also called the "third eye." In this state, the action and life situation is executed in the most conscious, sacred, lovable, peaceful, and enlightened way. We discussed this while differentiating conscience vs. consciousness in the chapter Intelligence.

7. **Crown Chakra:** This *Chakra* is called **Sahasra** and is located at the top of the head (i.e., at the cerebral gland) and associated with your connection to cosmic energy through your causal self. This state is also associated with absolute liberation from the physical world with vibrational conscious energy of 801- 1000. Activating this *Chakra* happens automatically, depending on the depth and breadth of other mindful-breathing practices in combination with other limbs of Yoga. Also, under sun salutation, it is activated by Corpse Pose (*Shavasana* or Yoga *Nidra* in Sanskrit)

Significance of Mindful Breathing (Pranayama)

While *Kundalini* energy flows through these energy centers and at causal, metaphysical, or mystical levels, it is well resonated with our Vagus nerve at a physical level, which is a long, sinewy nerve that runs through the core of our bodies. This nerve lies at a most intriguing intersection between our two physical nervous systems of the gross body (i.e., central, and autonomic nervous systems) and between our two psychological-nervous systems of our astral body (i.e., cognitive, and affective nervous systems). Our Vagus nerve is a bridge between the two nervous systems, operating as a bio-informatical data bus that routes electromagnetic impulses in both directions, which influence our sensation (experience essence), which is to be objectified, hacked, and repurposed to higher experience. Then the automatic re-purposing happens in perception (intelligence essence) and response to stimulus (expression essence). Also, the Vagus Nerve serves as a primary connector between our two neurological systems and our conscious and sub-conscious thoughts. Hence, it serves as a link between our gross, astral, and causal bodies. So, when you activate the chakras (energy centers), you activate Vagus Nerve.

The significance of *Pranayama* is mentioned in Vedic Science as well. Firstly, as per Bhagvat Gita (4.29), it dissolves attachment (aversion and craving). Secondly, as per Patanjali's Yoga Sutras (2.52), it removes the veil covering the light of knowledge and heralds the dawn of wisdom. In summary, mindful breathing is a critical muscle that helps you activate the Vegas nerve, the most important organ in our body, to help conquer our aversion and craving by releasing the impurity of *Karma* energy and ignorance associated with your shadow self.

In a disruptive VUCA world, *pranayama* (mindful-breathing techniques) prepares leaders and organizations to be resilient, innovative, and open to infinite possibilities. One of the research papers from St. Catherine University studied how leaders in corporate America feel regular Yoga and *Pranayama* practice has influenced their leadership in their workplace. The paper concludes with findings that regular Yoga and *Pranayama* practice led to the self-transformation of participants in the form of better relationships, increased intentionality, and improved skills to manage stress and inner-wellbeing. After knowing the muscle to conquer tendencies and temptation (*Sat* essence); now let's look on to muscle conquer sensation (*Ananda* essence).

Non-judgmental-Observation as muscle to conquer sensation (Ananda)

As discussed in the chapter "Experience," Feeling-tone or inner body sensation exists and operates at the fundamental energy level of the quantum field or causal body. The positive and negative feeling-tone is like the opposite poles of electric and magnetic fields. A system only survives in peace when there is neutrality. Hence, as long as there is residual non-neutral energy, i.e., the residual is not dissolved or transmuted (or repurposed) with higher consciousness, the bi-polarity nature continues in an infinite loop, which the main cause of human is suffering. However, once it is transmuted (or repurposed), even stress hormones (i.e., adrenaline) get transmuted (or repurposed) to pleasant hormones (i.e., oxytocin and dopamine).

Buddha is the first scientist in the world who discovered that we do not respond according to energy from the stimulus in life-situation (i.e., anger, hatred, stress, and so on); rather, we respond to our inner body sensation of life (or self) emerging or triggered from the causal body along with external-life event or life-situation. As discussed earlier in the chapter "Experience," these sensations are measured in terms of feeling tone, i.e., pleasant, unpleasant, and neutral. If the sensations are pleasant, we react with craving. If unpleasant, we react with aversion; if neutral, we respond with neutrality and stability. In other words, our intentions are very closely interlinked with these sensations, shaping our response within the space between stimulus and response. As we discussed earlier, aversion and craving cause entanglement between self and the outer world through the duality trap of pleasantness and unpleasantness and hence the cause of suffering. However, the neutral feeling tone empowers involvement between self and world without being entangled with the duality-trap of experience of the outer world. In other words, to remain involved with the environment without being entangled, we must re-purpose the unpleasant and pleasant sensations to be empowered for a conscious response.

Let's consider one life situation where you made a mistake in your job, and your boss angrily criticized you in a forum. The moment you sense the energy of the stimulus (i.e., anger) after hearing through your ear, you will have an unpleasant sensation triggered in your gross body due to a negative feeling tone from your causal body. Suppose you cannot activate the "seer" of shadow self (<200) by elevating your *Sattva* energy. In that case, you miss the bus for objectifying, hacking, and re-purposing the unpleasant inner body sensation. In other words, your temptation will take over you instantly, and your astral body will perceive it as unfavorable (i.e., you will not like the life situation). You will react or respond to the stimulus with aversion (0-100). You might amplify your reaction or repose further by blowing it out of proportion in social media. Further, if you get an un-empathized comment from your colleagues, you might get disappointed (<100). Similarly, if your boss appreciates your good performance in your job, the pleasant sensation in the gross body will be triggered due to a positive feeling tone from the causal body. And unless you again objectify, hack, and repurpose it, your astral body will perceive it as favorable (i.e., you will like the energy of the stimulus). Hence, you will react with craving. You may amplify it with a post of self-glorification or pride (175) on social media. You may get angry if you get a negative comment from your challenger colleague or do not get much "thumbs-up," (150). Hence it is not true that your reactions and sufferings are only influenced by stimulus from the external world but by your inherent quality of body-inner-sensation in the causal layer. As we do not have strong causal muscles, we often cannot activate our "seer" within and then objectify, hack, and re-purpose our lower inner body sensation to a neutral one. Hence, our response is compulsive, entangled with life-situation and suffering. However, if we can activate our "seer" within, we can objectify, hack and re-purpose the lower feeling tone to a neutral one. In other words, we will dissolve the Kama and ignorance associated with a lower-feeling tone. Accordingly, the perception, intention, and response will be equal, neutral (>200), and vibrant without aversion, craving, and suffering.

Hence Buddha taught the world to go to the deepest level where suffering arises by observing both suffering and the arising of suffering. Without observing these two, we can never know the cessation of suffering. He also said, *"Sensations give rise to aversion and craving; if sensations cease, aversion and craving cease; when aversion and craving ceases, suffering ceases."* In the Buddhist tradition, *Vipassana* meditation is the key to the cessation of suffering. *Vipassana* is a Pali version of Sanskrit word **Vipasyana**. Here "Vi" means special or super, and *"Pasyana"* means seeing or observing. Also, when we observe non-judgmentally, we feel the inner-body-sensation non-judgmentally to repurpose it.

Generally, when we observe or perceive something, our mind instantly starts judging, i.e., like or dislike, good or bad, beautiful or ugly, introvert or extrovert, and so on. However, when Buddha advised us to observe, he meant to observe non-judgementally (250). Can someone observe without any judgment? The answer is no and yes. When you observe through your lower mind (<200), you are observing as "seen." In that case, your judgment will be there. However, when you observe as a "seer" within (>200), there will be no judgment. "Seer" will not judge even the judgment of "seen" or "shadow self". So, in other words, when you activate your "seer," you will continue judging as "seen" or "shadow self" under the non-judgemental observation of "seer." Hence "seer" observes without any prejudice, thinking, choice, image formation, labeling, or meaning by the subconscious mind, which distorts the quality of observation. This type of observation breaks the barrier between the conscious mind and the unconscious mind and takes your awareness from the surface level of the mind to the deepest level at the causal layer. This transmuted (or re-purposed) the latent impure tendencies, ignorance, aversion, cravings, negative *Karma* energy, and feeling tone (pleasant or unpleasant) lying at the mind's deepest level. In summary, it transmuted (or re-purposed) suffering. The non-judgemental observation is like sunlight; which takes the impure water from the earth and enables pure water through the rain; i.e., auto cleaning, auto-healing, re-purposing, or transmuting. In the absence of non-judgemental observation of the seer, there is a situation of garbage-in-garbage-out (GIGO). The lower *Karma* energy of life situation will produce a compulsive response.

Mr. Eckhart Tolle, the author of "Power of Now," refers to the presence of "seer" as conscious and the absence of it as unconscious, and he says unless you face your suffering (i.e., pain body inside the causal body), you will continue to suffer. He says, *"The pain-body, which is the dark shadow cast by the ego, is afraid of the light of your consciousness. It is afraid of being found out. Its survival depends on your unconscious identification with it and your unconscious fear of facing the pain that lives in you. But if you don't face it, if you don't bring the light of your consciousness into the pain, you will be forced to relive it again and again".* He also emphasizes "feeling" the pain-body completely instead of thinking about it as feeling push us to "now or presence; which is non-judgemental in nature and normalize it.

Also, coming to science, because of this higher power of non-judgemental observation, only a conscious observer can transmute (or re-purpose) a quantum wave into a quantum particle (non-manifested to manifested) in a double-slit experiment.

As per our level of consciousness, each one of us has a conscious range (LOC). For example, you may fail to detect or become aware of the pleasant feeling tone until it reaches a five (+5) on a scale of (-10 to +10) because your conscious mind has low LOC (<200) to detect below the five. Similarly, when it comes to an unpleasant feeling tone, you notice or become aware of it when the value becomes negative (−2). So, for you, this becomes your blind zone of awareness (from -2 to +5). Hence, through non-judgemental observation, you should develop a consciousness of at least 200 to become aware of the whole range of sensation tones (-10 to + 10). In other words, you can objectify or hack your shadow self (<200) or activate your "seer." While the LOC of 200 is sufficient for you to objectify any range of lower sensation, it is not sufficient to embrace or conquer the same, for which you need a LOC of tolerance or acceptance (350). In other words, while a LOC of 200 will empower you to catch the full range of sensation (-10 to +10), to embrace and conquer the same range of sensation, you need your LOC to be 350.

The practice of non-judgemental observation and feeling the lower sensation can activate or sustain the "seer" and enables the ability to objectify, hack and repurpose the lower sensation automatically, leading to non-suffering (*Ananda*). This experience of *Ananda* shifts your intention and response to life-situation and leads your destiny to

Smart-Sage.

Silence as Muscle to Conquer Perception (Chit)

If the sound is the outer noise, thinking is the inner noise. Similarly, the equivalent of outer silence is inner silence. All thoughts happen on the canvas of our awareness and consciousness, which is the *Chit* essence of our self. The mind cannot describe what is beyond it because it has not been there. In other words, the mind can only give some projected clue of true reality. With all possibilities, these projected clues will have some degree of illusion. However, silence has access beyond the astral body, i.e., to our unconscious mind in the causal body, which has access to cosmic or higher intelligence. In other words, silence can also activate or sustain "seer," which can objectify and hack the ignorance aspect pumped-up along with tendencies, temptation, and sensation. Hence improves our perception and understanding of ourselves and the external world. Numerous scientific studies have recently demonstrated that silence rewires your brain to make you more intelligent. One of the most impressive factors is that silence can produce new brain cells in the area connected to memory, and also brain reacts more harmoniously to silence than to noise. Silence also balances the activities between the left and right hemispheres of the brain, harmonizing logical intelligence (IQ) and emotional intelligence (EQ). In other words, it helps repurpose IQ & EQ as SQ. Hence silence empowers us with spiritual intelligence and vibrancy in our cognition, called metacognition.

Krishna said in Bhagavad Gita (10.38), *"Amongst secrets, I am the silence."*

In his book "Stillness Speaks" Eckhart Tolle says, *"True intelligence operates silently. Stillness is where creativity and solutions to problems are found."*

Perkey Avot, a Jewish Sage, says, *"Tradition is a safety fence to Torah; tilting a safety fence to wealth; vows a safety fence for abstinence; a safety fence for wisdom is silence."*

Nature's fundamental sound is silence. In its way, silence can express and communicate many emotions that voice and music cannot. In rare cases, it awakens the latent forces of living organisms. Similarly, human beings' basic strength is silence, which makes them more aware of existential facts and more receptive to their tasks in pursuit of their goals. The force of stillness is most noticeable when you are far from the madding crowd—into the pastoral plains, the vastness of the ocean, or the tremendous heights of the Himalayas. Your mind slows down with its fleeting ideas, and your intellect performs better, sharpening your thinking process and enhancing your decision-making skills. When reading, being in a quiet environment helps you understand and absorb more.

The five senses of human beings greatly influence the mind and take its attention directly to the external world through perceptual experience and indirectly through fantasy. Hence, during any life situation, the mind becomes an extrovert. This has become a major roadblock in removing ignorance and gaining access to higher intelligence. Only when the lake is wave free can we see the bottom clearly. In other words, the extrovert mind and senses are always disturbed by craziness, which is one of the major impediments to higher intelligence. Silence is called Mauna in Sanskrit, and it is one of the most important pillars of wisdom in most traditions like Buddhism, Hinduism, Jewish, etc. Also, one of the important things is that causal muscles become passive, inactive, and weaker with distraction.

Our society has placed extroverts as a golden standard for success. Parents, teachers, coaches, and employers expect a person to be extra vocal and contribute to the discussions, take the initiative, be competitive, and be good at public speaking to have a bright future. Yes, this might give success in our outer and secondary purpose but not in our inner purpose (i.e., Sage-ness).

The Christian poet Khalil Gibran says, *"You talk when you cease to be at peace with your thoughts."*

Also, in the words of Tao Te Ching, a sage in Taoism, *"Those who know do not speak; those who speak do not know."*

Susan Cain, a former lawyer, an alumna of Harvard Law School, and an introvert who turned to homemaking and writing, articulated in her book, "Quiet: The Power of Introverts in A World That Can't Stop Talking," the history of America and how the culture of outgoing, aggressive, extrovert, showmanship prevailed during the 20th century. She tells us the transformation of the culture of character to the culture of personality in a short period. It bursts the myth of charismatic leadership that even quiet people who think before they speak can be good leaders in their ways. Even the world has witnessed the power of introverted and silent leaders with great wisdom like Mahatma Gandhi, Abraham Lincoln, Eleanor Roosevelt, Albert Einstein, Ratan Tata, Bill Gates, Warren Buffett, Satya Nadella, and many more. Modern scientists are intrigued by the connection between leadership and spirituality. They claim that silence can unlock the power of spiritual intelligence and gene, a must-have characteristic for a transformational leader with authenticity.

The space of silence is not a space of vacuum; rather, it has all potentialities of higher-self, like courage (200), resiliency, neutrality, willingness, enthusiasm, curiosity, acceptance, and love. When reasoning (400) in silence happens, it happens in the presence of all these elements of the higher self (>200), which deliver a higher perspective of reality. Hence this experiential reasoning (400) receives intuitive and subliminal clues as a basis for creative response. Pannikar's (1998) book encapsulates the meaning of silence reasoning (400) as;

For silence to be a response,
A silent query must go before.
But any silent query,
Shelter, in silence, every question.
Now if there is no query;
There is no response;

There is only a glance;
A smile;
love;
And forgiveness;
All,
Nothing,
Yes,
No,
Absence.

The first sound of the universe, "AUM," came to this world through such silent reasoning (400) on human wellbeing by the scientist of ancient India, where the query was posed with a quest, curiosity, and experiential confidence. However, in the imaginary world governed by causality, you project the reason and look for a response about empirical evidence of external features without trust in its unity of awareness and experiential confidence. This is simply an arrogant attitude. Silence provides the space for both unities of awareness and experiential confidence.

In the space of silence, where awareness is high, there is a romantic cosmic union between reason (400) and cosmic response (intuitive and subliminal clues). We can also call it a romance between two dual forces of the macrocosm, union, and evolution, where the reason (400) from silence space represents the sperm of nature (*Prakriti*) with a quest to be in union with the source (*Purusha*). To satisfy this energy of quest, the source (*Purusha*) releases creative intelligence (*Chit*), which forms the basis of response after being perceived by a conscious agent. Hence, whatever thoughts or choices the astral layer receives at that moment is the response, prompt, alert, or signal from higher intelligence through the causal body.

As Albert Einstein says, "*The monotony and solitude of a quiet life stimulate the creative mind.*"

In the VUCA world, people and leaders must make the trade-off and choose the best and most relevant option out of many interconnected options to deliver a conscious response. During this time, silence reasoning can help bring creative intelligence (*Chit*). This is probably why intelligent minds like Sadhguru and Steve Jobs embrace the rule of awkward silence of fifteen to twenty seconds when faced with challenging questions from the media. The rule of awkward silence is simple: When faced with a challenging question, instead of answering instantly, you pause to access the creative intelligence (*Chit*) with silence reasoning (400).

Repurposing power of Causal Muscles.

All the above causal muscles operate at the causal level to transmute (or re-purpose) the negative causal-cause (i.e., ignorance and *Karma*) at the psychological (i.e., shuttle) and physiological (i.e., gross) levels. On a psychological level, all lower elements and essences of self (or life) get transmuted (or repurposed) or repurposed into higher. To be very specific - or repurposing happens from fear (100) to courage (200), from desire (125) to quest for the possibility (300-350), from pride (175) to Neutrality (250), from jealousy & hatred to love (500) and so on. In simple, the self (or life) becomes Sage. Another important point to note for the duration you are leveraging your causal muscles, you ignite the "seer of shadow self". Hence, till you are connected to your causal self; this duration becomes your 'me-time', even if your body-mind is involved with other people or situations. Also, this me-time purely intrinsic in nature and provides nutrients for meaning and purpose of life.

Similarly, at the level of life situation, all lower situations get transmuted (or repurposed) or repurposed to higher-situation. To be very specific, transmutation (or repurposing) happens from vulnerability to vision, from uncertainty to creativity, from arrogance to audacity, from ambiguity to adaptability, from greed to a quest for growth, from result to process orientation, from conformity and creativity, from bias to integrity. In other words, the self becomes

Smart with effectiveness, efficiencies, and efficacy in all his expression in the external world. In summary, causal muscles empower the self with Smartness as well as Sage-ness.

In her 2013 interview with Access Hollywood, Oprah Winfrey talked about her experience with weight loss and body image. She shared that, for years, she had tried to lose weight by following fad diets and trying different exercise routines, but nothing seemed to work. Eventually, she realized that her weight was not just about what she ate or how much she exercised but also about how she felt about herself.

Oprah realized that she needed to work on improving her genuine feeling for herself, i.e., self-esteem and self-worth, before she could make any lasting changes to her physical health at a physical and psychological level. Feeling anything genuinely means doing it non-judgmentally, which prevents the distortion of feeling by any perceptual filters (of the mind and senses). The feeling is a causal muscle that happens at the level of consciousness beyond thinking. Once she started focusing on this aspect, she eventually lost over 40 pounds healthily and sustainably. This experience taught Oprah the importance of causal muscles, for she is at the inner self (Sage-ness) level and its impact on expressing anything in her outer life situation (Smartness).

Call to Action

Try to leverage each causal muscle we discussed in this chapter whenever you are engaged in any physical activities, easy or challenging. For example, you are doing Sun-Salutation (or *Surya-Namaskar* in Sanskrit) for the first time, a series of interconnected physical postures involving the spinal cord, muscles, nerves, key glands, and key glands and energy centers (i.e., *chakras*) from head to toes. Each posture has a geometric positioning of outer body parts with a stretch and energy movement in each cell of the spinal cord, muscles, nerves, and key glands. To do it accurately, it needs effort, energy, attention, and motivation to embrace the comfort zone. This is why Yoga Gurus instruct a pattern of deep and mindful breathing and a series of postures, i.e., breathe-in when your body is moving away from its center of gravity and breath-out when moving towards its center of gravity. The instruction also includes embracing the unpleasant feeling of tone produced by stretching in each posture (a geometric shape) and doing it in silence.

In summary, leverage all three causal muscles whenever you are engaged in any activity, whether it is physical (walking, jogging, running, biking, playing, cooking, gardening, pulling, pushing, waiting queue, etc.) or psychological (i.e., reading, watching, listening, articulating, programming, etc.). This will not only make your activities effortless and playful and improve effectiveness, efficiency, and efficacy of outcome. It will help to live a high-resolution life, like a Smart-Sage.

While engaged in one activity, most people leverage their available attention for multi-tasking; instead of leveraging the same for paying attention to the phenomenon happening inside their inner self through the causal muscles. In other words, they make Smartness the only purpose in life, at the cost of Sage-ness, which is the point of derailment in human values and the sustainability of the planet.

Hence Buddha has summarized this beautifully as *"Be aware of what you are doing."*

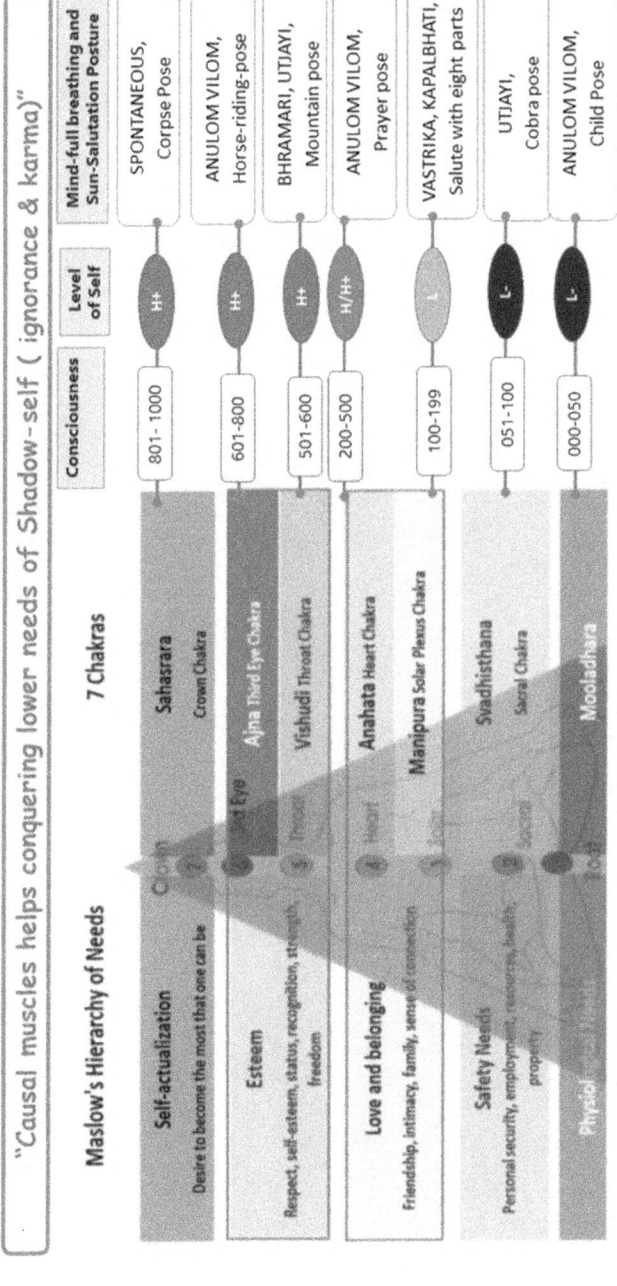

PRASHANT PANIGRAHI

10

TECHNIQUES TO BE SMART SAGE

PEARL Techniques to Respond As Sharp Self

"A sharp knife cuts the quickest and hurts the least."
- Katharine Hepburn.

Once upon a time, there was a newly married royal couple, a king and queen. The queen was very demanding. She asked every night before they went to bed. One day, it was a no-moon day, and she had a peculiar ask for the king; to go alone and get the rarest flower as soon as possible, which was available in the nearby forest. The king lusted with her and went to the forest to fulfill her demand. As there was no convenient street light to navigate the route in those days, in a hurry, the king took the valuable and only Pearl of his kingdom to be used as a torchlight. He also took his cigar, lighter, and his favorite sword. On the way, he became unmindful by the combined temptation of lust, fear of uncertainty of getting the flower, and associated narrative of the shadow self. While unmindful, the Pearl fell on the road, and after a little rolling down, it went into a snake hole, where a giant snake was resting. Once the Pearl entered the hole, the whole area became dark. Recognizing the hole as a snake hole, the king collected some dry wood and used his lighter to create heat around the snake hole, with the intent to kill the snake and collect the Pearl. As expected, the snake peeped out of the hole, and its eyes were also lit up. When the king attempted to kill the snake with his sword, the snake whispered silently; oh king, I had already swallowed the Pearl when it entered the hole, and if you would like to kill me, you will never get the Pearl. I have a divine blessing that no one can kill me. I have two options for you. Option 1; I can give you a similar flower, but it may not be as authentic as the one you want. Also, I will accompany you offering the dim light of my eye, which is the derived light from the Pearl itself, till you reach your palace. And the second option is that; you have to wait and embrace your impatience to witness the moment of the Pearl coming out. Though unsure when I will get the vomiting sensation, I will disappear once I vomit it. The unconscious king was already occupied with the tendency of being impatient, as he had feared facing uncomfortable disapproval from the queen for the delay. Therefore, he opted for option 1, even though the flower was not authentic. The king reached home.

The snake also took the un-mindfulness of the king as an opportunity; it conveniently escaped from the king's attention and stayed in some hidden corner of the palace without his knowledge. The rest of the night became heavenly romantic. When they woke up late the next morning, the queen discovered the flower was not authentic. Then the king explained the whole story of the snake. The queen lost her love, respect, and trust for the king. This distrust translated into constant anxiety and suffering, which impacted the functioning of their kingdom for a long time. During the period of suffering, the king visited one saint for counseling on peace. The king received golden advice to practice conquering temptation, sensation, and perception. The king was practicing the same seriously. One night the queen started demanding the lost pearl by threatening to divorce. At that moment, the snake appeared and again offered two options similar to what he had offered before though this time, it was a duplicate pearl instead of the original. However, the king again chooses option 1 in a hurry. The situation became normal for a few days. However, the queen became furious and left the palace with a divorce note. Then the king went to the saint for further advice. After listening to the narrative, the saint said, you are doing the right things, but you have to do things the right way; i.e., you have sharpened your "self," but you have not used the same in the right way. In other words, you are being hurt by your blunt self, struggling to navigate a challenging life situation; i.e., sharpness is not flowing into life situations. Then the saint gave a few tips on how to use it. When the king returned to the palace, the snake was waiting again with two options. This time option 1 was to convince his wife to stay together without PEARL instantly, and option 2 was the same with PEARL after a few months. This time the king used the tips from the saint and chose option 2, as he realized that the queen would not be happy without the original pearl. The poisonous snake disappeared after making the couple meet and vomiting the pearl. Finally, they lived together with love, joy, and peace. Also, their joint effort brought glory to their kingdom.

Like in this story, the intelligent *Karma* energy offers us inevitable situations with two options. One option is moving ahead with life-situation without sharpening our "self," and the other is by sharpening the self. When you choose to sharpen your "self," you dissolve your ignorance and *Karma*, which leads to abundance with authenticity and transcendence with transformation, i.e., the dual purpose of inner and outer, similar to the renewed life of the royal couple after the reunion. Otherwise, you have to stay with old tendencies in a causal body (like the hidden poisonous snake), with a lower quality of transformation (like a duplicate flower or pearl) and full of suffering (like the fife of the king before reunion). Simply put, choosing to use your sharp "self" leads to reconciliation between life (self) and life situation; i.e., you become sharp and smart. Also, there is flow, freedom, meaning, and fulfillment in life. Here, the sharp self refers to the "seer of the shadow self," which operates at a higher vibrational conscious energy than life and life situations. Hence, without "seer," it is a struggle to face complex life situations authentically, i.e., to achieve the dual purpose of transformation and transcendence.

> As Einstein says, *"No problem can be solved from the same consciousness that created it."*

New Normal in Life-Situation

In the ancient or pre-VUCA days, people's lives were relatively quiet. Hence there was ample time to sharpen their "self." They could do it thrice for an elongated period (in the morning, afternoon, and evening). This elongated practice was enough to ignite the "seer of shadow self" in life situations, even if the life situation was challenging, like an atomic bomb. Hence, they could dissolve their ignorance and *Karma* to live a life of dual purpose of inner and outer transformation, i.e., transcendence and transformation. In other words, they were living life with sharpness and smartness. However, for people in the current VUCA world, life has become volatile, uncertain, complex, and ambiguous. Also, to survive in this world of high social expectations, greedy people have little time to sharpen themselves, which is not enough to ignite the "seer of shadow self" when facing a life situation, even with low stress compared to pre-VUCA days. Hence, they are tempted to live only with transformation, outer purpose (i.e., Smartness), without inner purpose (i.e., Sage-ness).

The people in pre-VUCA days, with "seer of the shadow self" within, had the power to conquer the temptation, sensation, and perception in the internal world first before responding to life situations in the external world.

> Viktor Frankl, one of the famous psychiatrists who survived a Nazi death camp and went on to write Man's Search for Meaning, where he says, *"between stimulus and response there is a space where the power to choose whether to refuse to the call for adventure in internal world first and then responds to the external world. In our choice and response lies our growth and our freedom".*

Now the question is, is it possible to ignite the "seer," i.e., create the space between life and life situation in the super busy life of VUCA world and rate race to objectify, hack and re-purpose the temptation, inner-body-sensation, *Karma* and perceive it without ignorance before responding compulsively to a life situation?

Yes, it is possible! We have to ignite the power of causal muscles, i.e., mindfulness breathing, non-judgmental observation, and reasoning in silence in every life situation between stimulus and response. To ignite the power of causal muscles developed in solitude, I have developed a simple, profound technique that can be practiced within the space between stimulus and response in life with a rat race. This technique consists of four atomic steps, named the PEARL technique.

PEARL-technique and PEARL-space.

The first atomic step, **"P" stands for "Pause,"** which is done at the encounter of the stimulus of the life situation. This first atomic step ignites, nurtures, and leverages the power of a mindful breathing muscle to objectify and concur temptation (Sat or existential essence). The second atomic step, **"EA," stands for "Embrace with Acceptance,"** which is done within the space between stimulus and response of the life situation. This step ignites, nurtures, and leverages the power of non-judgmental observation to objectify and conquer sensation (*Ananda* or experiential essence). The third atomic step, **"R," stands for "Reason in silence,"** done just before responding to the life situation. This step ignites, nurtures, and leverages the power of silence to access higher intelligence for self and perceive the life situation positively (i.e., *Chit* intelligence essence).

The way we ignite the power of stored or reserved energy inside the cracker or bomb instantly; in the same way, the above three atomic steps ignite the power of three causal muscles instantly, which was developed in solitude. It happens in a microsecond, i.e., quicker than the ignition time for a cracker or bomb. As we know, all these three causal muscles also transmute (or repurpose) and repurpose the selfish or Karma gene to a spiritual or developmental gene, helping us choose the option to sharpen the self and deliver the loving response consciously. Hence, the final atomic step is **"L," meaning "Loving response."** This step is done at the exit door from the space within the stimulus and response. This step expresses the self or life with higher possibilities, i.e., higher existential quality, intelligence, and experience, i.e., *Sat-Chit-Ananda*. Hence, the PEARL technique invites the "seer of shadow self" gradually into the space between stimulus and response by igniting the power and potentialities of muscle developed in solitude. For the sake of simplicity, let us call this space (between stimulus & response) with "seer of shadow self" as PEARL space.

In summary, PEARL technique within PEARL space reconciles the essences (i.e., *Sat* 1- existential life energy, *Chit* - Intelligence, *Ananda* - Experience, and *Sat* 2 – Expression) between life and Life-situation. Another important point to note for the duration the "seer of shadow self" is there with you. You are connected to your causal self; hence, this duration becomes your me time, even if your body-mind is involved with other people or situations.

Pause to Repurpose the Tendencies (Sat-Match)

In his book, "Thinking, Fast and Slow," Daniel Kahneman, a world-famous psychologist and winner of the Nobel Prize in Economics, takes us on a groundbreaking tour of the mind and explains how two systems that drive the way we think. System-1 is fast, intuitive, and emotional; System-2 is slower, more deliberative, and more logical. As the researchers say, in an unfavorable situation, most of the VUCA world humans with constant fear and anxiety demand a 30% faster response from themselves regarding thought, word, and action; i.e., they move to system-1 thinking. Psychologically, faster thinking is derived from the temptation of aversion and craving, which are essence symptoms of (< 200). Physiologically, it is a culmination of attachment and entanglement of the shadow self and responding to life situations, supplemented with the inertia and preference of inherited Selfish or Karma Genes. As we know, if we do stuff the same way as our old preference and choice, we will get a similar outcome but never the transformational one. In other words, our past will get repeated and replayed due to recorded Karma energy tendencies and temptation at the causal layer. This is an unconscious landing at destiny. These Karma energy tendencies and temptation represent the existential essence (Sat). Hence, this is the right time to ignite the power and potentialities of the **first causal muscle,** i.e., mindful breathing to conquer the Karma gene of shadow self...

Hence take a conscious pause and a few deep breaths. It will activate and ignite your Vagus nerve (*Kundalini*) and "seer of the shadow self," which will objectify and then start transmuting (or repurposing) the lower-life energy (i.e., *Tamas* and *Rajas*) shadow self at a metaphysical level. In other words, it will empower you to hold high vibration, pure *Sattva* life energy by balancing different nervous systems physically and psychologically. This inner balancing at a level will transmute (or repurpose) the fear, anxiety, and anger (<200) to courage (200). In other words, your reduced temptation will encourage you to cross the comfort zone and shift the direction of your intention and response from the destiny aspect of the *Karma* gene to the free-will aspect (i.e., neutrality, 250) of the developmental gene.

Once this temptation is objectified and repurposed, you own one of three matches, i.e., ***Sat* match.** At this point, there is simultaneous emergence of the "seer of Shadow self" merges, and the space between stimulus and response becomes "PEARL space." In other words, one-essence of the "seer" is now available to you. Hence, this space has become more energetic, confident, vibrant, witness-full, and courageous (200) to play the remaining match. Often this pause may confuse and irritate others but do not worry much now; you and others will witness the power of this pause sooner or later. By now, while you have consciously touched only one essence of trinity-self, i.e., *Sat*, *Sattva*(pure) energy, you have two more steps to touch *Ananda* and *Chit* essences before you choose the right option and deliver the loving response. Till that moment, there is always a probability that you may fall under the trap of the shadow self, which tries to make your PEARL space cluttered and entangled with its psychological drama, propaganda, and counter-tactics. Hence keep your undivided attention and focus on deep breaths.

Embrace with Acceptance to repurpose sensation (Ananda-match)

Your stimulus and life situation awaits your choice, option, and response (thought, word, actions). However, while the earlier step will give you the holding capacity of higher *Sattva* energy (i.e., *Sat*) with courage (200), you still need to get ready completely to deliver a final conscious response. We discussed in the previous chapter that we do not directly respond to the life situation but respond indirectly as per our inner-body-sensation or feeling tone. This lower inner-body-sensation (or unpleasant and pleasant feeling tone) represents our shadow self.

With the elevated Sattva energy of the earlier match, you are now ready for the second match, i.e., the *Ananda* match within the PEARL space. This match transmutes the feeling tone from lower to higher (i.e., negative or positive to neutral). Hence keeping your attention with deep & mindful breaths will amplify your awareness and ability to objectify your lower inner body sensation and feeling tone. Now you can leverage your **second causal muscle** of non-judgemental observation **(i.e., neutrality - 250)**. Once you do so, you will experience the second match of *Ananda* between your shadow self (<200) and true self (i.e., seer of shadow self), where the shadow self will be having a temper tantrum and trying to deny the authenticity & justification of emotional pain. Even it will try to distract and divert your attention to his side of the narrative and justification. To substantiate its advocacy, it will take you to the psychological past and future it is attached to because of this life's *Karma* Gene and past preference. These attachments always have the master disposition of craving for pleasantness and aversion to unpleasant feelings. Hence the shadow self will try not to give you any control to protect its boundary of the lower sensations (unpleasant and pleasant). However, you, as a "seer of shadow self" with higher existential quality of **courage**

(**>200**), continue observing **non-judgmentally (250)**. Try to feel the lower sensation completely with empathy. Sustain it until the transmutation (or repurposing) results in a neutral sensation.

Once this sensation is repurposed, you win the second match, i.e., Ananda, within the PEARL space, like a semi-final match. In other words, now the second essence of "seer" is available for you. Winning this match will empower you to **accept (350)** the life situation with full enthusiasm and **willingness (300)**. Hence, this space has become energetic, confident, vibrant, witness-full, meditative, tolerant, resilient with perseverance, and positive use of adversity. In other words, you will be antifragile and playful to play the final match, i.e., Chit-match. Hence, do not get distracted but continue focusing on deep breaths and non-judgemental observation rather than hurrying to deliver the unconscious response. This is critical, as embracing transmutes (or re-purposes) entanglement between life and life situations to involvement. Hence it brings up flow, freedom, meaning, and fulfillment. Mr. Nassim Nicholas Taleb, in his book "Antifragile," explains how fragile are those who avoid embracing unpleasant emotions. These people want to pursue happiness directly by following pleasure and certainty. However, antifragile people pursue happiness indirectly by embracing unpleasant emotions and uncertainty. They thrive from shocks, volatility, uncertainty, and complexity instead of breaking from them.

Reason in Silence; To Repurpose Perception (Chit-Match)

The two essences already in you, i.e., Sat (Sattva or pure and energy) and Ananda (meditative experience, neutral feeling-tone), have already initiated inner silence. Further intensify the silence by leveraging the **third causal muscle,** i.e., silence. Inner silence means no inner noise (thoughts, sensations, emotions). This silence also means that the PEARL space has access to higher intelligence. As Mr. Eckhart Tolle'ss book "Stillness Speaks" says, "Silence is not only absence of noise, but it is a space where true intelligence operates."

In the past two matches, the gap between shadow and true self was dissolved by repurposing the *Karma* gene and lower sensation.

However, this ***Chit*-match** is to repurpose ignorance, which again represents our shadow self. Once this repurposing is done, there is access to a higher perception of reality and intelligence. In other words, this match is the match to reduce the difference between both selves further, hence bringing intimacy, coupling, union, synchronization, collaboration, and reconciliation through a higher perception of reality. This overall congruence happens in another dimension of two selves, i.e., the masculine source *(Purusha)* and the feminine nature *(Prakriti)*. Now the PEARL space holds all three essences and hence has little scope for the shadow self to survive. Hence, conscious reasoning emerges **(400)** and creation within you, the doorway from unexpressed to expressed, un-manifested to manifested, invisible to visible. Scientifically this is the quantum space where the quantum wave becomes a quantum particle. Philosophically, this space has access to cosmic consciousness and has mercy & blessing of the cosmos. This is the womb of all creation with the potentiality of peak intelligence, experience, and expression *(Sat-Chit-Ananda)* in the physical world. In other words, this is the first step, where potentiality becomes potential.

Here the silence of self is equivalent to your reasoning (400) with quest and curiosity and waiting for the prompt, alert, and signal from the source, which indicates the potential from potentialities. This is like a dating and deepest romantic dialogue between nature *(Prakriti)* and source *(Purusha)*. In the real world, dating and the deepest romantic dialoguing happen in silent gestures without words or very limited words. **Reasoning (400)** is a very existential, fundamental, soft, and feeble query in the context of the life situation – **Why so? What can be done now? How to do it? When to do it?** Etc. Here the reasoning (400) acts as an ovum of nature with a quest to unite with the source. And whatever intention, intuition, or choice comes at that moment is the response, prompt, alert, or signal from the source, acting as its sperm in a quest to be in a romance with nature. This romance and union happen s inside PEARL space, which is already filled with peak existence *(Sat)* and experience *(Ananda)*. Suppose we draw an analogy of PEARL space in the computing world. In that case, it acts as In-Memory database and analytics which can process a high number of input-output or read-write per second, i.e., processing vast quantities of data (i.e., high awareness), fast enough to supply intelligence and insights. This intelligence is far better at making a difference in life-situation without causing aversion, craving, mental noise, stress, and anxiety. In other words, you will be able to differentiate love from like, quest from desire, and positive excitement from bliss in a nanosecond. Also, without aversion and craving, you can repurpose your IQ & EQ to SQ. In other words, you have conquered the perception of Shadow self and won the final match, i.e., ***Chit*-match**. Now all three essences of "seer" are available to you (i.e., *Sat-Chit-Ananda*) within the PEARL space. Many scientists term this intelligence as gut intelligence which bypasses the amygdala and hence the cycle of analysis-paralysis, evaluating pros and cons, i.e., overcoming indecisiveness with sustained stress and anxiety. Also, most of the discoveries and innovations in the world, like gravity, antivirus, telephone, light bulb, radio, and air-plane, happened in silence and intelligence from PEARL space. Every response or action we perform in this world has two characteristics; effectiveness and efficiency.

As management guru Peter Drucker said, *"Efficiency is doing things right, and effectiveness is doing the right things."*

Hence, when you apply the PEARL technique between stimulus and response, while this final match ensures the effectiveness of the response, the first two matches ensure the efficiency of the response. So, the effectiveness of your response makes you smart; the efficiency of your response makes you sharp. In summary, the PEARL technique makes you sharp beyond smart.

Loving response, to repurpose compulsive response

By this time, you have met your shadow self-thrice from three different angles (*Sat-Chit-Ananda*). In other words, your PEARL-space is in absolute company with the "seer of the shadow self," and you are reverberating with high-resolution essences of self (*Sat-Chit-Ananda*), at your body-mind, as compared to the same when the stimulus arrived. In other words, your organized mind is getting inspired by an innocent mind, lower intelligence (PQ, IS, EQ) is getting inspired and repurposed by spiritual intelligence (SQ), lower existential qualities (*Tamas, Rajas*) are getting inspired and repurposed by *Sattva* quality, lower feeling-tones (negative and positive) are getting inspired and repurposed by the neutral feeling-tone, and finally, all "seen" are getting inspired by "seer." In other words, the secondary purpose (outer) is getting inspired by the primary purpose (inner). Now you are ready to deliver a conscious response to your stimulus and life situation from the exit door of PEARL space.

In this state, you will be completely involved with life situations from a timeless being without being entangled with a psychological time of life-line (past and future). Your response will reverberate with neutrality, love, compassion, and forgiveness. The words you will express will inspire, influence, and become melodious for millions of other-selves; the idea you will express will be of creative intelligence elevating millions of other-selves; the action you will express will lead to innovation and will empower billions of others. The effort you will express will be of value-adding service to nature and humanity, and your blessing will heal the other self. Everything you do becomes more effective; your every relationship will become more fulfilling, and life will flow more easily. In summary, you will be in the spirit of antifragile and playfulness or being in *Leela*, uncovering and unlocking the sense of meaning and purpose in life-journey, which constitutes life and living situations.

While the first arrow of external pain is inevitable and governed by inner *Karma*, the second arrow of inner suffering can be diffused with techniques like PEARL within the space between stimulus and response. Also, it will ensure both effectiveness and efficiency in our response and empower us to live playfully like a Smart-Sage with growth, glory, and grace.

PEARL and meaning in life.

Other philosophers and psychologists have also articulated the difference between the higher self and shadow self as; the battle between the "yin-yang," "good and evil," "ego and superego," "Jekyll and Hyde," "heaven and hell," "Adam-I and Adam-II" in their context. The only additional clarity we have brought here is the quantified conscious range associated with shadow self below the courage line (<200) and true-self above the courage line (> 200). In other words, an LOC > 200 can hold both "seer" and "seer of shadow self" within PEARL-space; which is intrinsic in nature and connects us to our existential meaning and purpose.

If you are not developing causal muscles or not adopting the PEARL technique between stimulus and response, activating the "seer of shadow self" or PEARL space will be difficult. Hence, your life situations at gross and astral levels will be driven by the speed thinking of an organized mind, also by aversion and craving of senses of shadow self (<200). Hence, the lower essence (intelligence, existence, and experience) may get amplified by the lower perceptual process without PEARL space. When the living condition and the body's wisdom are dominated by lower essence, the body's orgasm is contradictory. In opposing duality, "positive is for," and "negative is against," "pleasant-is-for," and "unpleasant-is-against." Also, this duality runs in an infinite loop causing a suffering trap. Here, the sense of self is derived from conflicting duality rather than the meaning of life. Therefore, no matter how content you are with outer success, achievements, power, property, fame, and talent, you will remain empty, hungry, and greedy for more and new. In simple terms, without a "seer of shadow self," PEARL space becomes non-existent in your life and hence there will be no nutrients for meaning and purpose of life.

Once your sense of self is tuned to trap, you cannot do anything with fullness or contentment; i.e., you will wake up in the morning with emptiness, walk with emptiness, think with emptiness, imagine with emptiness, eat with emptiness, drink with emptiness, listen with emptiness, speak with emptiness, embrace with emptiness, sleep with emptiness and so on. Even you may die with emptiness, which is a life with regret and without meaning or purpose. Hence, you must invite the "seer of shadow self" or PEARL space to jump out from the infinite loop causing the suffering trap. The trap of suffering with the duality of aversion and craving is also called *VANA*. Once you jump out of *VANA* by inviting the "seer of shadow self" into PEARL space, you are in *nir-VANA*. When you are in *Nir-VANA*, fear (100) gets repurposed to courage (200), selfish desire (125) gets repurposed to willingness for the common good (310), anger (150) gets repurposed to acceptance (350), and pride (175) gets repurposed to love and compassion (600). Now you can do everything with freshness, newness, and fullness; even you can die graciously in fullness; i.e., you will live your life with meaning and purpose.

Wherever attention goes, life energy flows. Hence, at any moment, all your attention should not be devoted only to life-situation, but we must share it between life and life-situation. To be very specific, kindly give attention to temptation, sensation, and perception through deep, mindful breathing, non-judgemental observation, and silent reasoning. This will enable the seer and PEARL space.

Considering attention as the key to uplifting the consciousness, Mr. Eckhart Tolle also says, *"Do not give all your attention away to mind and external life-situation. There is another dimension where perfect enjoyment and peace can be accessed now. A place where nothing can affect you in a negative way—where you are safe. This is the dimension of your inner body. By focusing yo the energy field within, your awareness shifts toward the inner world. As you read this, simply keep some of your attention on the inner body—the heart, stomach, hands, and feet. As you do this, feel the energy increase just as you become more aware of the present moment"*.

The only reason some scientists, artists, musicians, students, and professionals are best in their community is the "attention." Similarly, in our context, attention is the key differentiating trigger to establishing abundant self with authenticity; Sat-Chit-Ananda. In simple, when and where there is:

- Intensity in attention, there will be velocity in life-energy (*prana*),
- Velocity in life-energy, consciousness will be luminous (*chit*),
- Luminosity in consciousness, there will be purity in existence (*sat*),
- Purity in existence, there will be integrity in awareness (*chit*),
- Veracity in awareness, there will be clarity in perception (*chit*),
- Clarity in perception, there will be a novelty in intelligence (*chit*),
- Novelty in emotion, there will be ecstasy in experience (*ananda*),
- Ecstasy in experience, there will be vibrancy in expression (*sat*)
- Vibrancy in expression, there will be authenticity and abundance in the journey of life, i.e., self will become Smart Sage.

In other words, with attention to PEARL space, your responses will reverberate with Sage-ness and Smartness. This is very similar to the *KAIZEN* concept from Japan's quality management system, where the improvement or transmutation (or re-purposing) or change for the better happens incrementally and continuously. I hope you are aware of the 51% rule. If we apply the same rule here, epigenetics are bound to happen once you practice the PEARL technique and empower the Spiritual gene over the selfish *Karma* gene in 51% of your life situation. Also, it will bring continuous improvement in all three dimensions of your PEARL-space, i.e., contraction in time and expansion vibrancy of success. It will make you flow toward a meaningful and successful life journey.

PEARL in Play, Behind the Story of Google Maps

Sundar Pichai, the CEO of Google, had to go to dinner at his friend's house with his wife. Before leaving the house, Sundar Pichai asked his wife to reach the dinner place directly from home, and he will meet them there directly from the office. Sundar Pichai's wife, Anjali, had reached for dinner at exactly 8 o'clock. Sundar Pichai also left on time for dinner but lost his way in the middle. That's why he went to the program at 10 o'clock, but his wife had left by then. Sundar Pichai's wife was very angry with him for not reaching the program on time, which made her occasion inconvenient and uncomfortable. Hence, they had a big fight when Sundar reached his house late at night. It was a tough Karma stimulus or life situation for Sundar to respond consciously. Hence, Sundar prioritized his attention to life with a pause. This pause might have also been accompanied by a few deep breaths, which put him into slow thinking (i.e., System-2 thinking) and connecting to PEARL space. The slow thinking contemplated the response to the Karma stimulus and the life situation. On the same night, he moved to the office and spent the whole night there to embrace the unnecessary temptation and unpleasant feeling-tone; triggered by a tough life situation. Once he embraced the same with complete acceptance and elevated his Ananda essence (experience), his slow thinking reappeared as reasoning in silence, i.e., "what should be done so that no person should ever go astray in such life-situation." With this, he could access higher intelligence (Chit essence) and receive the solution idea as an intuition or prompt from the source. The next day morning, he shared the idea of Maps with the team as a loving response to the stimulus. Earlier, the team was reluctant to work on this idea. With the vibrant, inspiring persuasion from the PEARL space, in 2005, the day came when Google Maps was launched in America. After America, Google Maps reached India in 2008, and now every 7th person in the world travels through Google Maps. The PEARL mapping to inner phenomenon of Mr. Pichai is purely my visualization and articulation of probable happening.

PEARL promotes Yoga

As per Patanjali Yoga Sutra, you are in *Raja* yoga which defines Yoga as *"Yoga is Chitta vritti nirodha"*; i.e., Yoga is stilling the fluctuating mind. When you transmute (or repurpose) the *Tamas* and *Rajas* through "Pause and have a deep breath," your aversion & craving re-purposes to stability, establishing a stable mind and tamed senses. Hence you are in *Rajas* Yoga during the first match within PEARL space.

Secondly, when you transmute (or re-purpose) the lower feeling tones (pleasant & unpleasant) through "Embrace with Acceptance," you establish the neutral feeling tone. Hence you will have a quest and willingness to serve the primary and inner purpose (i.e., Sage-ness) for life (or self as microcosm), which in turn supplements the primary purpose of the microcosm (cosmos). Hence, you are in *Bhakti* Yoga during the second match within the PEARL space.

Thirdly, when you reason in silence, you transmute (or re-purpose) your lower intelligence to access ultimate perception. Hence you are in *Jnana* Yoga during the third match within PEARL-space.

Finally, when you consciously respond to a stimulus or life situation through a Loving Response, it is with an intention and quest for dissolving inner *Karma* and manifesting the meaning in life and life situations without any craving desire on the result, i.e., win or loss, success or failure, fame or defame becomes secondary. Hence you are in *Karma* Yoga when at the exit door of the PEARL space.

In summary, you are handling a life situation within PEARL space means you are in Yoga in that life situation. Once you sustain the PEARL space in every life situation, you become a sharp self. Where there are quick cuts with painting, you achieve transcendence beyond transformation, and inner purpose, i.e., efficiencies beyond effectiveness.

Call to Action

Imagine you are in a long queue for your vaccination dose, which you have not expected. Considering your busyness in this VUCA world, you might become impatient, and your unpleasant feeling tone might go beyond the tolerance or acceptance (350) limit. This stimulus in your life might bring aversion (<200) in you, and your reaction may become angry and blame the inefficient vaccination process and system, leading you to an argument with the vaccine administrator. Recognize that your inner *Karma* energy is in play now. Try creating a PEARL space. Try inviting the "seer of shadow self" into the space between your two arguments through the PEARL technique. You may see the argument will not last for long, i.e., It will end quickly with your sharpness and without much hurt to your inner well-being.

In other words, you will feel a sense of flow, freedom, meaning, and fulfillment in this life situation.

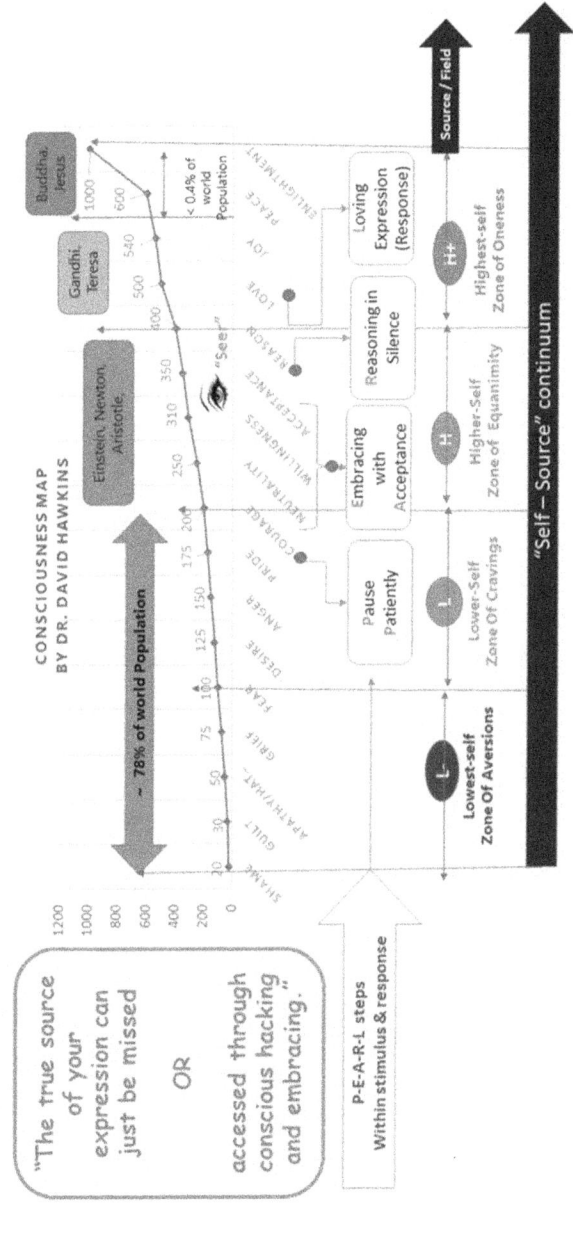

11

JOURNEY TO SMART SAGE
Being Sharp Beyond Smart

"A man must be big enough to admit his mistakes, smart enough
to profit from them, and strong enough to correct them."
- John C. Maxwell

Embracing Is At The Center Of Dual Purpose.

If you closely look at the quote from John C Maxwell while making a profit with smartness is related to our outer purpose (i.e., Smartness); admitting wrongdoing and having the strength to correct it is related to our inner purpose (i.e., Sage-ness); i.e., being sharp. Here, while admitting the wrongdoing needs the energy of courage (200) & acceptance (350), the strength to correct it needs the energy of courage (200), quest, curiosity, enthusiasm, and willingness (300). In simple, it points to embracing the negativity within PEARL space, i.e., embracing with an observation from a "seer of shadow self" Now the question is, what is the wrongdoing in self? Ignorance and bad Karma are tendencies for two million years. Embracing considers the objectified causal substance of tendencies (temptation, sensation, and perception) from the first match. It delivers transmuted (or repurposed) causal substance (intentions and response) to the final match. In other words, embracing brings efficiencies of self (or life), enabling the effectiveness of life-situation. Hence, embracing becomes central to the dual purpose of being sharp and smart.

> As Rob Bell quotes, *"The life that you want begins the moment you embrace the life you have because all of it is a miracle."*

In an earlier chapter, we discussed the current state of self, where most people and professionals suffer from an upset-set human condition, shadow self (<200), and suffering. The prime reason and root cause for the same is; they are still carrying the residual causal substance of tendencies in the form of ignorance and bad-Karma for two million years. This carryover is mainly because of a need for wide and common understanding or reasoning to rationalize the difference between instinct and biological intelligence.

> As Australian biologist, Jeremy Griffith wrote in his book Freedom: The End of The Human Condition, *"While searching for understanding, we can see that three things are unavoidably going to happen. Adam is going to retaliate against the implied criticism from his instincts defensively; he will desperately seek out any reinforcement he can find to relieve himself of the negative feelings; and he will try to deny the criticism and block it out of his mind. He has become angry, egocentric and alienated— which is the psychologically upset state we call the human condition, because we humans developed a conscious mind and became psychologically upset"*.

This understanding is available to and is in practice by the philosophical community, those who pursue the inner purpose (i.e., Sage-ness) as the only purpose of life and stay away from the outer purpose (i.e., Smartness) instead of conquering with it. This gives a wrong message to the rest of the people; that we have to stay away from the outer purpose (i.e., Smartness) to gain and practice the required understanding (i.e., understanding or reasoning to rationalize the difference between instinct and biological intelligence). Hence, a general misconception is that both outer and inner purpose (i.e., Smartness and Sage-ness) are exclusive and separate. i.e., a life situation can be dealt with only one purpose, either inner or outer. In other words, for them, transcendence of life (or self) and transformation in life-situation can't co-exist together. Hence intellectuals and educated get divided at the level of their purpose, i.e., either they become monks to pursue the inner purpose (i.e., Sage-ness) only or become materialist citizens to pursue outer purpose (i.e., Smartness) only. Even though they pursue the inner purpose (i.e., Sage-ness), it is for the sake of compliance and fear.

Unfortunately, this divide is persisting, and some efforts in pockets are visible. Hence, even though people are succeeding in outer purpose (i.e., Smartness); they are out of balance in inner purpose (i.e., Sage-ness) and inner-wellbeing. In other words, most people die with regret and remorse even if they are successful in their outer purpose (i.e., Smartness).

Embracing Compulsively vs. Consciously

People are dedicated only to the outer purpose (i.e., Smartness), correlate their comfort zone with happiness and freedom, and embrace discomfort with suffering. Mr. Victor Frankl, in the book; "Men's Search for Meaning," mentioned the need to go through suffering to have existential meaning. However, by saying "suffering," he meant "pain," as pain is inevitable due to *Karma* and ignorance but suffering is not. Suffering happens only when one embraces discomfort compulsively and unwillingly and without reason, understanding, acceptance, enthusiasm, curiosity, and a quest to discover destiny. This suffering is due to artificial psychological defense and pseudo-idealistic dramatic narrative of the shadow self (<200) due to ignorance, putting stress on the astral and gross body, which Buddha calls a second arrow. While embracing compulsively appears effective in producing outer purpose (i.e., Smartness), it is at the cost of Sage-ness. In other words, it delivers habitual improvement without dissolving ignorance and

Karma in the causal body. Hence it leaves behind hurt, residual regret, and remorse.

There was a poor fruit farmer in an Indian Village. While he unloads his harvested Kalinga fruit into the store, he throws each Kalinga gourd from the bullock cart (loaded with hundreds of it), and his son standing on the ground, catches it and then throws it gently into stores (padded with rice straw). This is their regular affair while storing their harvested fruit. Hence his son gained habitual perfection. His son's habitual perfection of catching by his son was observed by the captain of a football team, who is qualified to play the final match. Then the captain influenced the farmer's son into the team as a goalkeeper in the final match. The final match proceeded with a highly competitive spirit without any goal from any side till the last five minutes. Everyone thought it would end with a tie. Just a few seconds before the end-time, the opponent team kicked the ball with rocket speed to the goalpost protected by farmer's-son. Out of habitual perfection, the farmer's son not only caught the ball with cleverness, but with the same perfection, he threw the ball into his post and finally lost the final. Hence habitation, which is the basis of shadow self and smartness, cannot provide limitlessness to life.

However, applying the PEARL technique in your life situation will shift your embracing from compulsively to consciously; i.e., you will embrace the discomfort willingly with acceptance, curiosity, quest, and enthusiasm. This will automatically break the habituation and transmute (or repurpose) the lower causal substance (temptation, sensation, and perception) to higher, with the dissolution of ignorance and *Karma*. Inner-pain-body or lower feeling-tone will get repurposed to neural feeling-tone, giving you a sense of inner happiness and bliss (*Ananda*); i.e., this will produce a meditative experience beyond the experience from sensation and perception. Hence conscious embracing is just like an adventurous sport where you consciously embrace the effort and energy and go beyond your comfort zone for inner entertainment. In summary, embracing consciously is an efficient or optimum way to produce effective outer purpose (i.e., Smartness) with elite entertainment without hurt, residual regret, and remorse.

For example, when you watch your favorite program on YouTube, and suddenly a compulsory ad comes in (i.e., you can't skip it), you must watch it. Even if it is a 5 seconds ad, it feels like a long time because you're watching something you "have to" and not "want to." And after that, when your favorite program starts again, you can watch the entire program for hours joyfully. Here the "have to" comes from the aversion of lower-self (<200). Once you objectify and embrace the same consciously with PEARL technique, it will get transmuted (or repurposed) and shift to "want-to" with joyfulness. This will be a state which will allow you to walk into hell with joy. Unlike the duality loop of entertainment from sensation and perception, this entertainment brings lasting inner happiness and bliss (*Ananda*) and manifests a dual purpose. Hence it is said that people embracing a holistic purpose "live to die," i.e., live with no residual regret and remorse to die at any moment. In contrast, others "die to live," i.e., live with residual regret and remorse, entangled with aversion and craving.

Eckhart Tolle says, *"Stop looking outside for scraps of pleasure or fulfillment, for validation, security, or love - you have a treasure within that is infinitely greater than anything the world can offer."*

During an interview with Bill O'Brien, the late CEO of Hanover Insurance summarized his most important insights from leading transformational change in his own company. O'Brien said: *"The success of an intervention depends on the interior condition of the intervener."*

In other words, the destiny of our actions as change-makers does not depend on "What we do" or "How we do it" but on the "Inner Place from which we operate". Here the inner place refers to PEARL-Space, and the inner condition refers to embracing. In other words, embracing PEARL space leads to optimum success from a dual purpose.

Hence you must allow this elite entertainment to happen through embracing instead of getting bothered with entertainment from sensation and perception, which is the carving of shadow self (<200).

In other words, you should allow - falling to rise & grow, losing to win, and taking the pain to gain. This is because life's evolutionary spirit and existential meaning are usually buried inside the pain.

When discussing self-development and transcendence, you look into inspirational quotes from wise, moral stories, Scripture commandments, etc. At the same time, all such statements at gross and astral levels vary concerning the context of life situations and specific areas of development. At the causal level, all point to one common aspect of "embracing" life leveraging causal cause. For outer success, the coaches generally advise you to give 100% to a task, including effort, energy, talent, etc. However, they miss the critical component of willingly doing so with acceptance and quest. The answer lies in embracing within PEARL space.

Whenever any challenge strikes in the form of a life situation, only embracing within PEARL space can make you wise, or else you will be hurt and wounded with regret and remorse. In other words, you will have Smartness without Sage-ness.

Also, embracing the life situation within the PEARL space is like trying to break the closed door down to see how many other windows we have open and realize that life comes in life not to tumble you but to humble you. Embracing with the intelligence of a "seer of shadow self" enables transmutation (or repurposing). However, embracing compulsively happens from awareness of "seen" leads to habituation,

A personality like Gandhi, a man with the highest self, always embraced his life situations consciously and completely to know the truth. Wherever he missed doing so, he has confessed the same openly in his autobiography "My Experiments with the Truth" in his one-hundred and sixty-seven life situations. India got independence only because he invoked embracing "non-violence" in the consciousness of Indians.

Every life situation carries some lower *Karma* energy to be settled by the actor. In other words, every life situation allows you to manifest a dual purpose with no hurt, residual regret, or remorse. Hence you need to adopt the PEARL technique in every life situation to encash dual purpose with no hurt, residual regret, and remorse. When you are pleasant and happy, you remain only at the level of music. However, when you are in adversity or challenge, you try to go to the lyrics' levels and look for meaning. Whenever there is adversity or challenge in life, there is a possibility of manifestation of meaning; if we consciously embrace the same. Hence let's look at a few life situations and observe how embracing makes the life situation Smart.

Vulnerability to Vision

"Vulnerability is not winning or losing. It's having the courage to show up and be seen when we have no control over the outcome. Vulnerability is not weakness. It's our greatest measure of courage."

—Brené Brown

Vulnerability is a crisis when we do not have control over the outcome. This kind of situation quickly exposes business leaders' weaknesses and blind spots. If they pretend to have all the answers and are reluctant to admit mistakes or ask for help, others in the leadership pipeline will almost assuredly adopt this same perspective. Because the leader casts a long shadow, this stubbornness will inevitably create a downward spiral of succession failure, as it did at General Electric, Wells Fargo, and Boeing. In this type of life situation, the lower essence and elements of shadow self are a weakness, which controls the outcome with limited knowledge or intellectual resources. Hence to deal with vulnerability, you have to embrace the weakness. When you embrace your weakness, you become transparent about weaknesses in your ecosystem and open to 360-degree feedback, views, and ideas for improvement.

During the pandemic of Covid-19, consider how Donald Trump, Boris Johnson, and Jair Bolsonaro dismissed the virus, displayed fearless bravado, and undermined the calls to wear a mask or socially distance, putting others at risk. In other words, they artificially defended their life situation with pride (175). However, only some other leaders, like Angela Merkel, Jacinda Ardern, and Sanna Marin, embraced the vulnerable situation with complete transparency and became open to a data-driven approach. Hence, they could respond to life situations with courage and curiosity. This saved thousands of lives and mitigated the economic damage to Germany, New Zealand, and Finland. In other words, they transmuted (or repurposed) the urge to defend the life situation with pride (175) to acceptance (350). Hence, they could provide a vision to their country and others, i.e., achieve both purposes simultaneously with a transcendence (from 175 to 350).

Uncertainty to creativity

"If uncertainty is unacceptable to you, it turns into fear. If it is perfectly acceptable, it turns into increased aliveness, alertness, and creativity."

— Eckhart Tolle

Uncertainty is a life situation where we do not know the direction or impact of our actions or decisions. It might be favorable, or it might not. However, many of our best achievements and meaningful experiences come from a trying time of uncertainty. INSEAD professor Nathan Furr and entrepreneur Susannah Harmon Furr argue that uncertainty and possibility are two sides of the same coin. An individual can reach better outcomes by learning to embrace the fear and cope with the grey or unknown area. Nearly everyone initially thought that Elon Musk and his team would fail when they set out to revolutionize electric vehicles and push the world toward a more environmentally friendly, creative, and sustainable future. They couldn't have achieved their breakthroughs if they had not embraced the fear of uncertainty (100) and responded to the endeavor with the quest, courage (200), and willingness (310) for a creative, sustainable cause for the globe.

Similarly, during the pandemic of Covid-19, Khaldoon al-Mubarak, Managing Director and Group CEO of Mubadala, a $230B sovereign wealth fund for Abu Dhabi, spent mornings on the phone with Asia, afternoons with Europe, and evenings with North America. He tapped experts in business, investment, and health leaders around the world before concluding that the world had the resources to beat the pandemic and that it offered a huge opportunity to diversify his country's resources away from oil. Instead of minimizing risk by reducing investments, as many other sovereign wealth firms did during this period, his willingness to embrace the fear of uncertainty has allowed the fund to diversify more creatively than during a standard economy (Jones & Gottfried, 2020).

Arrogance to Audacity

> *"When you discard arrogance, complexity, and a few other things that get in the way, sooner or later you will discover that simple, childlike, and mysterious secret known to those of the Uncarved Block: Life is Fun."*
> -Benjamin Hoff

While Benjamin Hoff uses the word "discard" before arrogance, he means "embrace" the arrogance; else, discard also will bring counter arrogance. Microsoft (MS) was a sinking ship in the age of CEO Steve Ballmer. That period was the age of arrogance and pride (175) in MS, where the culture of innovation with quest and courage (200) was being replaced by bureaucratic control (125-175). Teamwork with a willingness (310) for value delivery was being replaced by internal politics (125-175). Things were falling behind. "The company was sick. Employees were away from their dream, demotivated, tired, frustrated in grief (75), and fearful (100). Satya Nadella promoted embracing arrogance culture (125-175) and established the culture of empathy (250-350) by making the shift in mindset from "knowing all" to "learning all." And took MS to the elite league again with an audacious mindset.

Satya puts this transformation and transcendence by saying, *"Bureaucracy was supplanting innovation." Internal politics had taken the role of teamwork. We were slipping behind." "The corporation was ailing. Employees were exhausted. They were dissatisfied. They arrived at Microsoft with high goals, but it felt like all they did was interact with senior management, carry out time-consuming processes, and quarrel in meetings."*

Unlike best practices that focus on strategy above culture, Satya's top objective was a cultural transformation and transcendence by transmuting lower essences, arrogance, bureaucracy, and corporate politics (all in the range of 125-175) to empathy (250 -350). Inspired by Peter Drucker's idea that the wrong culture eats strategy for breakfast, he said, *"I concentrated on what would be our most difficult task, altering the Microsoft culture."* Nobody would have, even Satya, anticipated the scale and speed of the cultural shift could bring such miraculous creativity and outcome. Microsoft was bursting with creativity in less than a year. Soon, the business results arrived. In the five years after Satya took over, he and his team have accomplished what many thoughts was impossible; they have entirely turned the company's course. In the last few years (2019 to 2022), Microsoft's market value has grown from just over $800 billion to over $2 trillion. With transcendence to empathy at the inner self, Satya could establish an audacious growth and transformation mindset as a recharged foundation of Microsoft.

In the same inline in history, Jamshedji Tata was rejected admittance to one of the greatest hotels in British history, Watson's Hotel, which was confined to 'whites-only. While he saw this as an insult to all Indians, he embraced hotel owners' arrogance (125-175). He resolved to establish a hotel where not only Indians but also foreigners could stay with non-discrimination and harmony (500). What an inner transcendence in life with audacity, which brought Hotel-Taj into life-situation, as India's first super-luxury hotel, welcoming tourists worldwide till today.

Ambiguity to Adaptability

> *"Take advantage of the ambiguity in the world. Look at something and think what else it might be."*
>
> - Roger von Oech

Uncertainty at work is a part of life in today's business world. If you don't embrace it, you can become overly timid, risk-averse, and fragile. As deep feelers and thinkers, we can all too readily spiral into fear of the unknown and fear of failure. As perfectionists, there's no clear-cut "right" or wrong," which breeds stress, self-doubt, and overwhelm.

At the same time, during ambiguity, we all like to think of ourselves as innovative and agile. Still, when our core beliefs are called into question during ambiguity, the cards are stacked against us. Our brain chemistry, social networks, and even our deprogrammed basic instinct for preserving the lower self will resist the change. Hence, dealing with ambiguity is to embrace the resistance to change, which is nothing but aversion (0-100) to change and craving (101-199) to be in the comfort zone. Unless one embraces it, one cannot think about what might be possible.

One of Steve Jobs' most prominent failures was being dismissed in 1985 from Apple, the business he founded. Steve Jobs revealed that he felt ashamed (20) and embarrassed (50) and was thinking of "moving away from Silicon Valley" at one point. He was trapped in his lowest self (0-100). At that point, he could utilize the wisdom he received during his visit to India for spiritual seeking. He reread Suzuki's Zen Mind and Beginner's Mind several times. Hence, he could connect the dots of his life with his business life situation from the perspective of inner purpose (i.e., Sage-ness). He further remarked that, after a while, this made him feel like a novice. This means he has embraced all aversion (0-100) of the past and entered into a new and fresh beginning with neutrality (250) and willingness (310) to have a new beginning. This also gave him courage (200) and released him from the complacency of success and pride (175). This transcendence in life (or self) inspired Steve Jobs to enter one of the most creative phases of his life situation. He worked at Pixar as founding and CEO at Pixar during his time away from Apple (1985-1997). He accomplished excellent achievements at Pixar that may go unnoticed because of his later accomplishments with Apple. Pixar revolutionized animation filmmaking and was later purchased by Disney in 2005. Before this, he joined back in Apple in 1997 as CEO. The essential point here is that Steve Jobs embraced his life within an ambiguous life situation, became adaptable to change, and looked into all possibilities in an antifragile way.

Greed to Quest for Growth

"He who is not content with what he has, would not be content with what he would like to have."

- Socrates.

A human being on the earth is born to express (*Sat* essence in the manifested plane) and realize its potential, thereby creating material wealth as an outer purpose (i.e., Smartness). This creative aspect also captures the evolutionary spirit's transformational essence at the life situation level. However, when this creation process has a master construct to develop, amplify, and glorify the lower self, it misses the inner purpose (i.e., Sage-ness); i.e., the transcendental aspect of evolutionary spirit at the level of life; i.e., transmutation (or repurposing), reconciliation, and manifestation of existential meaning in life.

The missing point of divergence comes when you do not feel the web of interconnection within humanity and conscious being, which is an illusion in understanding (*Chit* essence) that started two million years ago. Also, when you forget that when a human endeavor is dedicated only to the life situation, the transformation is limited, impermanent, temporary, and hence an illusion and ignorance in *Sat* essence, this also gives an impression that transformation in the physical plane alone can bring elite entertainment, which is illusion and ignorance in *Ananda*'s essence. Unless one has elite entertainment and containment, no amount of greed will satisfy one's lower self.

Hence once, Mahatma Gandhi said, *"There's enough on this planet for everyone's needs but not for one's greed."*

In summary, only when you embrace this ignorance in *Sat-Chit-Ananda*, you dissolve the attachments (aversion and craving) and shift the quality of imagination, fantasy, and visualization from with expectation to without expectation. In other words, you transcend your disposition from greed to a quest for growth. This brings the holistic purpose of transcendence and transformation. Here the sense of self is derived from the primary product (i.e., inner meaning and existential purpose in life) as well as enjoying its by-product (i.e., wealth, power, position, name, fame, and so on)

In fact, in Maslow's hierarchy of needs, the top need is self-actualization, beyond the development, amplification, and glorification of the lower self, i.e., the dissolution of the lower self. Hence in my view, it is no longer to be called a "need" but a "quest." Unless this quest sprouts, the need becomes greed and destroys the holistic purpose of life. This is one of the characteristics of the actualized self; they are motivated by eco-system-centric growth rather than self-centric or possession-centric growth. In other words, they know that possession is an impermanent life situation and that permanency is an existential ignorance. Because of this ignorance, other people cannot objectify the gap between greed and quest, making leaders, managers, and business owners crave possession of position and power instead of empowering the ecosystem. They also develop, amplify, and glorify the lower self, completely missing life's inner purpose (i.e., Sage-ness).

"No one owns money; you are just the trustee of it. Money keeps changing hands. If you succeed in life, try to return it to the society that has been kind to you,"; these words of advice given by JRD Tata when Sudha Murthy left TELCO to help her husband build Infosys always motivated and inspired her.

In 1981, Mr. Narayan Murthy, Sudha Murthy's husband, realized his big dream, and it was the beginning of Infosys, one of the biggest names in the software industry. But before deciding, he said they could not be at Infosys together. Hence, he offered her the option of joining Infosys, but she pulled back. Later, she expressed, *"It was very hard for me; it was not an easy decision because in 1968 when I joined engineering college, there was not a single girl in the university. For a person like me, who was so career conscious and so fond of technical things, it was very hard. However, Murthy being a very strong person, said either you or me, either it is black or white, or one or zero. I said, "Okay," and I made the decision, but my heart was very heavy. It took many years for me to reconcile by saying that I am not part of the Infosys team."* For her, greed makes the person forget humanity and can make one extremely unhappy. Hence, she chose to embrace self-centric growth with a quest for ecosystem growth by becoming a homemaker and helping Mr. Murthy realize his dream in all possible ways. Later, she became chairperson of Infosys Foundation, involving philanthropic activities, and also an author. The world has witnessed the growth of the Infosys ecosystem and the contented life of Sudha Murthy, bursting with elite entertainment.

The result to Process Orientation

> *"Truth is more in the process than the result"*
> – J Krishnamurthy.

Every task has a process and a result element. Focusing on the process but not the result looks very paradoxical, as you will ask what the motivation for action is if there is no focus or expectation on the result. Firstly, you need to understand that the process is closure to life, whereas the result is a life situation. The process allows transmutation (or repurposing) in all dimensions of self, i.e., existence, intelligence, and experience. Hence, focusing on the process makes the outcome more efficient and effective. Also, we have previously seen how transformation in life-situation without transcendence in life is meaningless. While transformation in life-situation (i.e., growth, success, achievement, pleasure, win, fame, etc.) represents digit-zeros of life-situation, transcendence in life represents digit-one, which makes all zeros meaningful. Hence, focusing primarily on the result is counterproductive in a meaningful life journey. When you focus on the result, you do not embrace your craving to win and loss aversion. Hence you develop pride when you win and become angry and frustrated when you lose. This orientation on the result accumulates negative Karma energy and leads to a cycle of suffering; i.e., it leads to being hurt with regret and remorse.

For example, an author cannot be happy if he expects (125) only appreciation from readers or fear (100) of the critics and criticism. In other words, the author has to get involved in the feedback process as-it-is and embrace criticism, if any, to have elite entertainment. Hence the Bhagavat Geeta (2.47) also says, *"Karmanye Vadhikaraste Ma Phaleshu Kadachana"*; i.e., you only have the right to action and response but not on the result. In other words, "giving up acting or responding is not an option but a failure is an option." This is because giving up or taking short-cut is nothing but skipping the embracing.

Also, the shift from result to process orientation brings a shift in the quality of persuasive effort. To be very specific, the persuasive effort driven by fear, desire, greed, and pride (100 – 175) is embraced and transmuted (or repurposed) to the same driven by courage, quest, curiosity, willingness (200 – 310), and enthusiasm. In other words, your action (Karma) no longer produces any residual negative Karma energy. Hence, there is joy and elite entertainment in the persuasive effort. This means there is complete involvement and devoid of any entanglement between life and life situations. Finally, the obsession is transmuted (or repurposed) into a passion. It is very important to note here that dopamine, the pleasant hormone, is released in both cases of obsession and passion. However, dopamine of obsession provides you with pleasant excitation (<200) at the surface level, and dopamine of passion provides you joy (540) at a deeper level.

A few days after Facebook went public in 2012, a good CEO buddy shared this email from Mark Zuckerberg to every Facebook employee the night before the firm went public. *"We don't develop services to generate money… We make money to build better services…"* It clearly articulates that the conception of Facebook has embraced the business outcome and is involved in making the world more open and connected.

Conformity and creativity

"I have been constantly telling people to encourage people, to question the unquestioned and not to be ashamed to bring up new ideas, new processes to get things done." - Ratan Tata.

While conformity is needed at the micro level, as it influences the formation, maintenance, and operations of social and enterprise norms and helps them to function smoothly in a standardized and predictable way, however, for transcendence, transformation, and the existential meaning of life, creativity has a primary place over conformity. For example, we need conformity to minimum ground rules before creating out-of-the-box thinking in a brainstorming session. Generally, creative impulses originate in the unconscious mind (i.e., causal body) but require conscious processing (in the astral body) to edit and integrate them into a creative service and product to be leveraged in life-situation. Creative impulses of the causal body are active only when psychic-neuro fluidity is vibrant and agile. At this stage, it gives rise to curiosity, wonder, and imagination in the causal body, i.e., space of unknown, non-manifested potentialities, which leads to out-of-the-box thinking, and a change in perspective. However, we can't touch or ignite the causal body without embracing the possible unfavorable force at that moment, including the resistance from conformists and face value within the ecosystem. Hence self-actualized people stay away from conformity if they see values beyond it.

Compliance and conformity from employees are regarded as obedient and loyal by employers and leaders of corporations. In other words, leaders have a strong desire (125) for employees' alignment to their point of view only. Crossing boundaries, even with humility and for a valid reason, is often reprimanded with anger (150). However, this is not recognized as a culture of fearfulness (100). Unless it is embraced, it can take the organization towards the quest and willingness (310) for creativity and innovation in product and service.

Ben Kohlmann, a naval officer, managed to build the culture of embracing conformists and transforming - the U.S. Navy, an organization steeped in rules, hierarchy, and compliance to conformity. For creative reasons, he took a group of unconventional recruits reprimanded for pushing boundaries and disobeying direct orders. In other words, these recruits could embrace resistance to conformity culture by their nature. He had them visit innovation centers, study books on innovation, and brainstorm approaches. For the first time, they were encouraged to be provocative and vocal about what they thought. Finally, within the next few quarters, the US Navy became the hotbed for innovation.

Once, my team had an opportunity to bid for a large transformational IT deal for one of our strategic customers. However, there was a constraint from my business unit to take up the deal only when there was conformity to the usage of our IP-based solution, which was a purely local, internal, and soft guideline. And the strategic customer was closed for the same during the sales cycle. Despite the same, we submitted the proposal to confirm the guidelines once we win the customer's heart. Finally, we won the deal, but there was little internal sponsorship because of non-conformity, even though it was local, internal, and soft. However, the winning team was fully committed with passion and a quest to deliver transformation with a conscious intent to conform to organizational guidelines as soon as possible. Finally, we did it courageously and creatively with 100% customer satisfaction. After this, the program became a most-spoken story and was in the finalist category in many internal and external awards. Also, it became an aspiring career destination for many organizational start performers. While we had to embrace many lower essences in the ecosystem due to initial non-conformity, it gave a sense of transcendence and transformation together. People who can embrace conformity are mostly field-independent as well. These people are Independent and on the other side of the conformity crowd, which is the majority crowd. They are reliant on their courage (200), neutral judgment (250), and reason (400), i.e., without depending or relying on culture and environment to form opinions and views from others. They become true to themselves rather than being how others want. While they strongly disagree with the false, they have huge space for being disagreeable; i.e., accept (350) the disagreement towards them calmly. They also become grateful to those who have helped, hindered, or become indifferent to them, as they objectify that all people create a context for transcendence in them and transformation in their life situations.

Biasness to Integrity

"Integrity is choosing courage over comfort. It's choosing what is right over fun, fast, or easy. It's choosing to practice your values rather than simply professing them."

- Brene Brown

Biasness generally comes from aversion (0-100) to unpleasantness and craving (101-199) for pleasantness within life-situation. And integrity means neutrality (250) towards life-situation irrespective of feeling-tone within the life situation. Hence, bias is part of the lower self, which has no courage (200) to embrace the aversion and craving. It forgets that all stimuli or life situations are a function of *Karma* energy, an inevitable destiny. It also forgets that all life situations are impermanent and life is not. With ignorance, illusion, and arrogance, it prefers life-situation to achieve growth and transformation at any cost with no attention toward transcendence. Hence it misses the opportunity to embrace the discomfort zone.

Integrity (250) is one of the human values most organizations have adopted as a part of their value system. This is because integrity is the mother value which automatically helps to embrace the lower essence (<200) and enables the shift to higher essence (>200), i.e., from irresponsibility to responsibility, laid-back to leading, an obsession to passion, status quo to excellence, diversity opposed to inclusion, complexity to simplicity, dullness to curiosity, hatred to mutual respect and last but not the least distrust & mistrust to trust. Research has shown that these values in employees have more influence on authentic outcomes than the employee's performance. However, while corporations have hundreds of measurements and recognition for performance, there must be a real measurement and recognition for integrity, trust, and other value systems.

Success comes and goes, but integrity endures. Integrity entails always doing the right thing, regardless of who is looking. It takes guts or courage (200) to do the right thing, regardless of the repercussions. Building an integrity reputation takes years, but it only takes a second to destroy; therefore, never allow yourself to do anything that might jeopardize your integrity. However, we live in a society where "the purpose justifies the means" has become a widely accepted way of thinking for far too many people. They often profess integrity by rationalizing biases as they do not have the courage (200) to embrace the lower essence. For example, salespeople overpromise and under deliver to meet their monthly quota; applicants exaggerate during job interviews because they are eager for work; CEOs inflate their expected profitability because they do not want to be replaced by the board of directors; entrepreneurs inflate their performance to obtain the best potential valuation from an investor; investors understate a company's worth to negotiate a lower purchase valuation; customer service professionals cover up a mistake made out of fear of losing the client; employees report "ill" because they don't have any more paid time off when they simply need to finish their Christmas shopping. The list could go on and on, and in each case, the individual doing the act of dishonesty convinced themselves that the ultimate result justified their lack of integrity. People may appear able to obtain outer purpose (i.e., Smartness) fast without embracing moral limitations; however, they are ignorant of their inner purpose (i.e., Sage-ness). Hence, they get hurt badly in their inner well-being, which leads to residual regret and remorse. In other words, smartness is only useful if sharpness is present.

As we discussed at the beginning of the book, the current state of self is full of bluntness and getting hurt in every life situation, which will flow till death as residual regret and remorse. Hence there is an urgent need for individuals dedicated only to the outer purpose (i.e., Smartness) to wake up above the courage line (>200) and adopt a technique like PEARL to invite "seer of shadow self" into the space between stimulus and response to transcend suffering and the upset human condition. Else there will be no escape from a life full of hurt, residual regret, and remorse.

Sage-Ness Is Innately Personal And Intrinsic.

All the life situations we discussed embrace challenges in the space between stimulus and response. Hence Smartness in external life-situation was manifested. However, we do not know whether the embracing has happened consciously or compulsively. Sage-ness is innately personal and intrinsic, though it gets expressed to the outer world extrinsically.

Similar challenges will always be there for you if there is a negative causal cause (ignorance and *Karma*). However, once you embrace a similar situation consciously, mastering the PEARL technique will allow you to manifest the same Smartness with Sage-ness. In other words, you will have Sage-ness while magically leveraging the power of your causal muscles and repurposing your life situations from; vulnerability to vision, from uncertainty to creativity, from arrogance to audacity, from ambiguity to adaptability, from greed to quest for growth, from result to process orientation, from conformity and creativity, from bias to integrity. This will ensure no hurt, residual regret, and remorse. In other words, you will become sharp beyond smart.

The Journey toward Smart Sage

Our society and culture in which we live, i.e., home, school, and workplace, encourage rewards and demands that the family members, students, and professionals must be oriented to adopt outer purpose (i.e., Smartness) as the primary purpose. It doesn't encourage rewards to include embracing in life-situation. In other words, it ignores the opportunity to achieve the dual purpose of transcendence of life (or self) and transformation in life-situation through embracing. Without this, life is becoming full of criticism without compassion and appreciation, compulsion without freedom, grudges without forgiveness, struggle without flow, control without inspiration, and so on. Hence the shift from a lower 78% club (<200) to a higher 22% elite club (>200) is getting constrained. Therefore, there is an opportunity as well as the potential for each one of us to be part of a 22% elite club by pursuing outer purpose (i.e., Smartness) in every life situation as "seen" in the presence of a "seer of the shadow self."

You are imbibing embracing within the PEARL space of every life situation, thereby living every life situation with playful, agile, antifragile, intelligent, and blissful, no hurt, residual regret, and remorse. When you embrace within the PEARL space of a life situation, it tunes the essence of your "self;" Sat-Chit-Ananda; by repurposing our tendencies, sensation, and perception at the level of causal body; i.e., before the potentialities become potential. Like the *Kaizen* principle, you become a bit sharper-self incrementally. The more you tune the essences (or potentialities, *Sat-Chit-Ananda*) of self-sharper, the more sweetness you get from life, as the sweetest sound comes from a musical instrument when its strings are tuned for sharpness. In summary, embracing within PEARL space in the *Kaizen* approach will lead you towards Smart-Sage with self-actualization with peak existence to expression (*Sat*), peak intelligence (*Chit*), and peak experience (*Ananda*), i.e., towards your peak-self (1000).

As Dr. David Hawkins said in the context of the conscious map (0 to 1000), *"Over the course of a lifetime, the average person's level will change approximately five points (this is not a statistical derivation, but an average discovered through). However, it is possible for an individual to have his or her level of consciousness jump (or drop) hundreds of points in a single lifetime."* Also, as you progress in your inner journey, you will influence others in your ecosystem and trigger a chain reaction, elevating the collective human condition. As Dr. David Hawkins said further, *"One person calibrated at 600 counterbalances the negativity of 10 million people below 200."*

Call to Action

Also, assess your progress in the inner journey with the help of the "NETI questionnaire" given at the end of Chapter 3 and adopt a *Kaizen* approach to increment your score. Try to cross the score of at least 80 and maintain it, which will put you roughly at higher-self with

LOC (200-400) and prevent you from hurt, residual regret, and remorse. In other words, you will become sharp beyond smart with a continued sense of flow, freedom, meaning, and fulfillment.

SMART SAGE

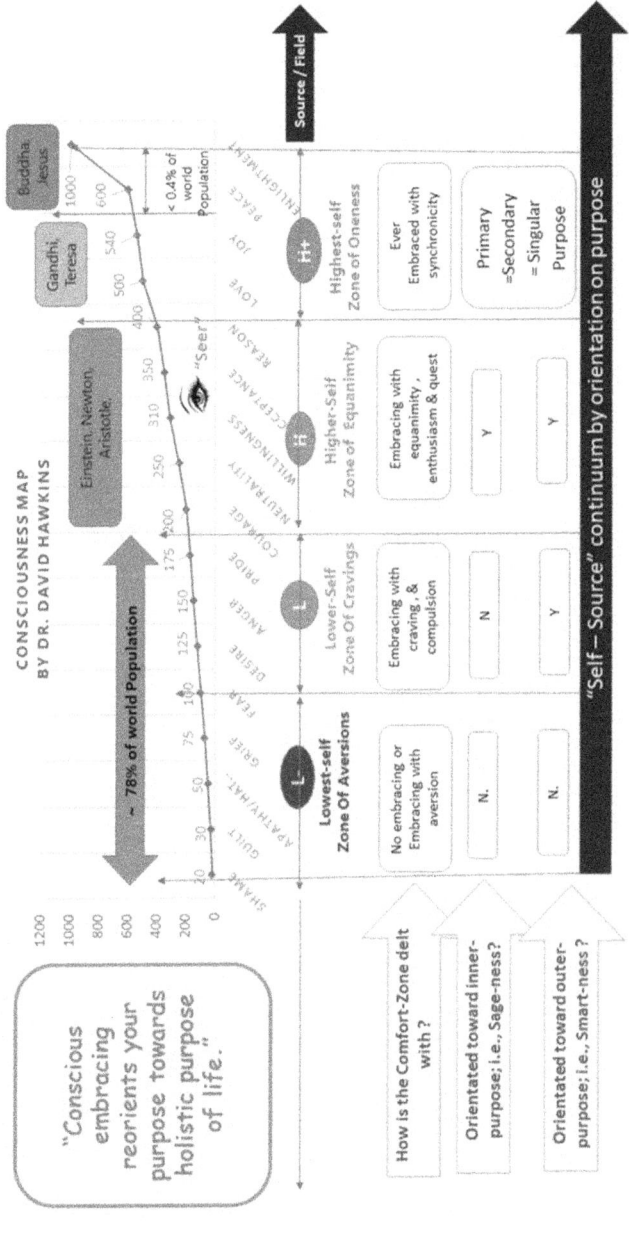

CONCLUSION

Many people don't know the true meaning of existence beyond their body and mind. Hence, they do not know what they really want from life. Some people choose to follow a religious path for the answers, some want to insure themselves a better place afterlife, some go for amassing money, fame, and material abundance, some like to control others with power, some want to do just good, some want to leave a mark in history by making a difference. Despite all these they remain unfulfilled.

Even the king of the jungle, the lion, eventually dies. At their peak, lions' rule, dominate, chase other animals, catch, devour, gulp, and leave their crumbs for hyenas. But a time comes when the old Lion can't hunt, can't kill, or defend itself. It roams and roars until it runs out of luck. It will be cornered by the hyenas, nibbled at, and eaten alive.

Our life, too, is short. Power is temporary. Physical beauty is short-lived. Smartness becomes pointless unless you have a high-resolution life of purpose and meaning. There a simple art of living to have a fulfilling life; to have Smartness and Sage-ness co-exist within us. One must accomplish Smartness in the presence of Sage-ness. Sage-ness refers to living with high-resolution intelligence, experience, and expression.

This book reveals the secret art of living in the Smart-Sage space between your every stimulus and response. It delivers the context and approaches through four parts: *Perspective,*

Potential, Problem, and Persuasion.

In PART-I (Perspective), we have covered; *what is beyond your body and mind*. The different perspective presented as the "self" is the mysticism reverberating with a vibrational-conscious-energy or level-of-Consciousness (LOC) in time and space with three fundamental essences. These fundamental essences are; existence (Sat), intelligence (Chit), and experience (Ananda). The changing self is referred to as **our shadow self,** and the changeless self is referred to as **the true self.** Here the shadow self is identified and entangled with the body-mind; whereas the true self is only involved with the body-mind; which has a disposition of intrinsic stability, love, joy, and peace.

In PART II (Potential), our "self" equates to the potentials of life, i.e., existence, intelligence, and experience, which directly influence our living and life situation. It reveals *a shift in the resolution of life and situations; once we start deriving our sense of self beyond body and mind.* This point of shift becomes apparent with the development of inner courage. With inner courage, intelligence shifts from selfishness to selflessness. Cognition becomes meta-cognition, experience shifts from a plain-pleasure trap to joyfulness, and expression moves from fight and flight to playfulness. This shift is also a paradigm shift from extrinsic to intrinsic. However, without inner courage (200), fear, desire, anger, and pride will dominate your life situation, and there is no true acceptance, willingness, enthusiasm, and love in life.

In Part III (Problem), we investigate and identify why one cannot *derive a sense of self beyond the body and mind.* We concluded that ignorance and Karma are fundamental reasons, root causes, and roadblocks for our entanglement to body and mind. In other words, these blockers are conditioning us for compulsive responses to life situations. Once there is a loss of vibrancy in the space between stimulus and response, there is a degradation in the quality of our potentialities, i.e., of intelligence, experience, and expression. Finally, this leads to a extrinsic life of disharmony, residual regret, and remorse.

In PART-IV (Persuasion), we learned that inner engineering becomes possible. We learned how to dissolve ignorance and Karma, making your response to life-situation as effective and efficient as possible to make your life and life situation harmonious. The detailed rationale and functioning of a simple, scientific, and proven tool, i.e., the PEARL technique, which can transmute (or re-purpose) your life situation from extrinsic to intrinsic and "with hell" to "with heaven". That is living and not hurting, no regret, and remorse with techniques to hack and transcend your shadow self by leveraging the power of your intrinsic causal muscles (beyond body and mind) and making your life vibrant, practical, efficient, meaningful, and fulfilled...

This book will elevate your realization of *who you truly are beyond your shadow self.*

Once you grasp this dimension, you can live a lifestyle of possession without possessiveness, pain without suffering, passion without obsession, quest without desire, being angry without anger, facing criticism without an inferiority complex, inspiring others without a superiority complex, staying present in every moment, putting full effort with effortlessness (or playfulness), working without being tired, facing challenges without being fragile, involved without entanglement, credibility with character, relationship with love and trust, wisdom with humility, confidence with clarity, freedom without friction and so on.

In summary; we have learned to master the art of becoming unshakably smarter as a professional and joyful sage; i.e., becoming Smart Sage, where smartness is the phenomenon of body-mind and sage-ness is the phenomenon beyond body-mind. We discovered that Smartness and Sage-ness could co-exist in us.

After reading this book, Sage-ness will blossom within you and complement your Smartness. With the inner power of Sage-ness, you will dissolve the associated aversion, craving, and Karma stored within to express your best possible self and experience success on every occasion (i.e., Smartness.) This implies you will have a sense of success, abundance, and blissfulness without any residual aversion, cravings, regret, and remorse.

Thank you!

ABOUT THE AUTHOR

Mr. Prashant Panigrahi, after his master's in engineering, started his career in Tata Consultancy Services (TCS) during Y2K solution days. And currently, he is a global leader in digital and cloud technologies. As a consultant, he has served many fortune 500 organisations, including General Electric, Walgreen Boots Alliance, Nationwide, Woolworth, and Alphabet. He has demonstrated consistent excellence in business by leveraging his acumen in technology, self-leadership, and six-sigma quality methodologies. In recognition of his transformational contributions, he has received several awards from CxO(s) of his employer and customers.

He has been an ardent researcher and partitioner of self-discovery and inner-wellbeing techniques for the last two decades; like Siddha Samadhi Yoga (SSY); based on teaching from Rishi Prabhakar; who was a disciple of Maharishi Mahesh Yogi (founder of Transcendental meditation movement) and guru of Sadhguru Jaggi Vasudev. He is also a practitioner of Vipassana meditation based on teachings of Buddha and a certified counsellor of the Dianetics technique, which intends to clear historical unconscious negative energy blocks called engrams.

His lifestyle promotes creating transformational business outcomes without compromising inner-wellbeing and meaning in life, which is an aspiring and inspiring dimension for many professionals in the rat race of the 21st century. Additionally, he is a system thinker and loves to connect the standalone dots to discover the meaning of life in every situation. He brilliantly blends the East's ancient experiential wisdom with the West's contemporary success principles. Hence, colleagues in his proximity call him an executive-yogi or corporate monk. He is a purpose alchemist and spends his leisure time as an "ally in service" to individuals and communities, in quest of a successful life with purpose and meaning.

www.ingramcontent.com/pod-product-compliance
Lightning Source LLC
LaVergne TN
LVHW011415080426
835512LV00005B/70